Additional Praise for
Real Estate Investing from A to Z

"You can give thousands of dollars to real estate seminar gurus, but you won't receive one-tenth of the value *Real Estate Investing from A to Z* provides. This is a book to be read, reread and never leave your desk."

Ruth Blank, CRB, CPM, CRS, GRI
Ben Blank Company (Palm Springs, California)

"As a cynic, I thought *Real Estate Investing from A to Z* would be just a rehash of what has been written time and again . . . it is a truly unique book, offering ideas and guidance for first-time investors as well as 'old pros' . . . challenges readers to analyze their needs and the needs of others in order to discover the hidden opportunities of real estate investments."

Don Rowan, Vice President
Tarbell Realtors, Inc. (Palm Desert, California)

D0985470

Real Estate Investing

from

to

The Most Comprehensive,
Practical and Readable Guide
to Investing Profitably in Real Estate

William H. Pivar

PROBUS PUBLISHING COMPANY
Cambridge, England
Chicago, Illinois

ISBN 1-55738-535-1

Printed in the United States of America

IPC

1 2 3 4 5 6 7 8 9 0

TAQ/BJS

TABLE OF CONTENTS

PREFACE   ix

Chapter 1
WHY REAL ESTATE?   1
    Advantages to Owning Real Property
    Real Estate Investments Can Buy Themselves
    Safety in Real Estate
    A Look at the Negative Side
    When to Buy and Sell
    What It Takes to Invest

Chapter 2
INVESTMENT ALTERNATIVES   15
    Single-Family Homes
    Apartments
    Commercial Property
    Industrial Property
    Farms
    Raw Land
    Lots

Chapter 3
TAXATION AND REAL ESTATE   39
Property Taxes and Interest Deductions
Depreciation for Tax Purposes
Tax Sheltering
Losses from a Sale
Tax-free Exchanges

Chapter 4
UNDERSTANDING FINANCING   45
Methods of Financing
Primary Financing
Secondary Financing
Loan Types and Terms
Finding Money

Chapter 5
CREATIVE FINANCING   65
Convincing Sellers to Finance Buyers
Methods and Techniques
Raising Cash

Chapter 6
PARTNERSHIPS, SYNDICATES AND INVESTMENT TRUSTS   83
Partnerships
Why Some Partnerships Go Sour
Advantages to Partnerships
Real Estate Investment Trusts (REITs)
Investment Clubs

Chapter 7
LOCATING PROPERTY   89

Location Value
Using Real Estate Agents
Advertising Leads
Finding the Bargains

Chapter 8
FORECLOSURES, IRS SALES, AND TAX SALES   101

Foreclosures
Buying before the Foreclosure Sale
Buying at the Foreclosure Sale
Buying after the Foreclosure Sale
When You Are in Foreclosure
Other Distressed Property Situations

Chapter 9
ANALYZING PROPERTY   119

Location
Progression and Regression
Physical Aspects
Financial History
Assessing Physical Structure
Hazardous Substances
Appraisals
Beware the Con Man
Watch Out for Your Emotions

Chapter 10
YOUR OFFER TO PURCHASE   141

Seller's Motivation
Knowing What the Seller Paid
How the Price Was Set
Timing
How Low to Go
Your Agreement

Contingency Clauses
Lemonading
Assuming Loans
Using Attorneys
Abstracts and Title Insurance
Consider All Financial Obligations
Acceptance of Offers
Auction Sales

Chapter 11
SUBDIVIDING—SMALLER CAN BE BETTER   157
The Subdivision Process
Recreational Subdivisions
Farms
Commercial Condominiums
Industrial Parks
Condominium Conversions
Current Trends in Condominium Conversions

Chapter 12
TRADING UP TO WEALTH   171
Tax Advantages
Types of Exchange
Other Advantages in Exchanging
What You Can Exchange
Problems to Watch for

Chapter 13
OPTIONING YOUR WAY TO SUCCESS   179
Consideration
Finding Option Opportunities
Negotiating the Option
Buying Other People's Options
Options to Rent

Chapter 14
SPECIAL SITUATIONS   193
Imagination and Determination Pay Off
Problem Properties Have Potential
Mobile Home Units
Factories
Land
Businesses
Student Housing
Rent-Controlled Cooperatives
Meeting Special Group Needs
Creative Conversion of Older Properties
The Value of Old Furniture
Tree and Timber Value
Moving Buildings
Gifts Can Be Profitable

Chapter 15
MANAGING YOUR PROPERTY   207
Understanding Property Management
Before You Buy
Setting Rents
Filling Vacancies
Maintaining the Rental Unit
Handling Tenant Problems
Evictions
On-Site Apartment Management
Managing to Make and Save Money
Record Keeping
Acquiring Management Skills

Chapter 16
TENANT SELECTION AND LEASES   225
Problems with Commercial Tenants
Getting Successful Businesses
Assuming Leases
Name That Building

Tenant Equity
Negotiating Acceptable Leases
Other Leasing Provisions

Chapter 17
SELLING YOUR PROPERTY   **235**
Reasons for Selling
Using Agents
Help in Choosing an Agent
Exclusive Right-to-Sell Listings
Open Listings
Determining Value
How You Wish to Sell a Property
Preparing Property for Sale

Chapter 18
WHAT'S FOR ME?   **249**
Understanding Yourself
Your Goals

EPILOGUE   **255**

INDEX   **257**

ABOUT THE AUTHOR   **267**

PREFACE

If you follow the advice of Ben Franklin, "Neither a borrower
nor lender be," you will spend your life working for wages.

—Bob Bruss

No one gets rich working for wages. You get rich *using* money — yours or someone else's. By using your money, you make your personal worth grow. By using other people's money, you will have the ability to magnify your effectiveness in your investments. This book will show you how to use not only your own savings but borrowed capital as well.

It is not enough that you learn how to purchase property with no or low downpayments. Actually, it is easy to buy with little or nothing down. This by itself is not the key to riches. The key is being able to purchase property that makes economic sense.

One of the seminar gurus of high-leverage purchasing proved to the press that everything he said was true about nothing-down properties. While he purchased several properties in a short period of time without downpayments, he ended up defaulting on the loans. The purchases just didn't make any economic sense. If a property is priced above market value and/or has a negative cash flow you can't live with, then it is a poor investment for you. There are too many good investments just waiting for you.

Anyone can buy at retail. Most people do. Some people even pay above retail. I believe that the person who came up with the phrase, "You get what you pay for," was a seller attempting to sell overpriced merchandise. The price paid is not necessarily related to value. I am going to show you ways not only to buy with other people's money, but buy at wholesale prices as well.

You would, at the very least, lose 10 percent if you paid retail for an investment property and had to immediately sell it — probably more after paying real estate fees, loan costs, closing costs, etc. If a quick sale is required, chances are you would have to discount the price by at least another 10 percent. You must therefore buy property at a discount from market value of at least 10 percent to remain even. Any less of a discount means a loss should a resale be necessary.

I will show you how to get that 10 percent discount and in many cases 20, 30 and even 40 percent discounts from market value. The easiest way to make money in real estate investments is to buy right or buy at wholesale.

The one thing this book cannot do is to get you to act. It is not easy to pull yourself out of a set of ruts and forge a new course for your life. It is far easier to let the ruts lead you where they may. It isn't even a matter of work because working for wages isn't easy. In working for wages, harder work generally results in blisters. On the other hand, smart work can equal riches.

This book can be worth millions to you. The techniques advocated have made me and many others millionaires. On the other hand, you may find this book to be worthless. Its value is in your ability to transfer the knowledge gained into practical application.

While care has been taken to provide accurate and current information, this publication should not be used as a substitute for competent legal advise. The principles and conclusions presented in this book can be effected by state and federal laws, regulations as well as court decisions. The reader is urged to consult legal counsel regarding any point of law.

Chapter 1

WHY REAL ESTATE?

Property is desirable, is a positive good in the world. Let not him who
is houseless pull down the house of another, but let him work diligently
and build one for himself, thus by example assuring that his own shall
be safe from violence when built.

—Abraham Lincoln, 1864

More millionaires have achieved their wealth through real estate than from all other endeavors combined. The progressive income tax, which takes more as you earn more, has eliminated many other paths to riches. With our current soft economy, even with both husband and wife working and earning good salaries, most families find it impossible to accumulate much wealth.

But in real estate investments are different. Profits can be realized in a number of ways:

1. Positive cash flow (excess of cash received from rents over cash expenditures).

2. Taxation benefits. You will see in Chapter 3 that real estate can still shelter income from taxation.

3. Appreciation in value:
   a. Realized upon sale
   b. Realized by borrowing on equity

4. Benefits of use.

But, as with any investment, you can lose money. Loss in real estate investment is realized in two ways:

1. Negative cash flow, where cash income is insufficient to meet required cash outlay. You will see in Chapter 3 that tax benefits in many cases will effectively overcome or significantly reduce the effect of a negative cash flow.

2. Loss realized at sale or trade.

This book will show you how to maximize your chances for the former and minimize them for the latter.

1

ADVANTAGES TO OWNING REAL PROPERTY

Taxes as an Encouragement to Real Estate Investment

Our state and federal tax laws, while harsh on earnings, actually encourage ownership of real estate. Interest and property tax payments are still deductible expenses (see Chapter 3). So, a person buying a home can afford to make a significantly higher payment for a home purchase than for a nondeductible rent payment.

Here's an example. Suppose you and your spouse could buy a property with $1,000 per month payments or rent a similar property for $750 per month. Of the $1,000 payment probably $950 will apply to interest and taxes. An adjusted gross income in excess of $32,450 for a couple filing a joint return would place any additional earnings in a 28 percent federal tax bracket. If you add the applicable state income taxes (assume a 10 percent rate), you will probably be in a 38 percent combined federal and state tax bracket. In this case you would save $361 per month through lower tax liability (38 percent of $950)—a true out-of-pocket cost of ownership of $639 per month. Since the rental payment of $750 is not deductible in this example, home ownership with monthly payments of $1,000 per month would actually result in a gross monthly payment $111 less than rent. In this case, the savings would likely be more than sufficient to cover insurance costs and additional maintenance and repair, which would normally be a landlord's responsibility. With lenders hesitant to loan on large apartment projects, the forces of supply and demand can be expected to cause rents to continue to rise. This will give the home buyer a significant future financial edge over the renter.

With rising income taxes the edge will be even greater. Actually, tax advantages apply to all real estate investments, not just your home. Interest and taxes paid are deductible expenses that reduce tax liability.

Many states have homeowner-type exemptions that reduce the property tax liability of owner occupants. One purpose of these exemptions is to encourage home ownership. Homeowner tax exemptions are generally limited to the principal residence of the taxpayer.

Inflation

Money loses value every year because of inflation. As prices for consumer goods rise, the net effect is that the value of each dollar decreases.

Inflation is categorized as either cost-push inflation or demand-pull inflation. If wages and materials costs increase, we can expect cost-push inflation to exert upward pressure on prices. Concern for our environment has led to greater development costs as well as time delays in development approvals, which have had a considerable effect on the cost of new housing. Price increases in new property will be reflected in increased prices on existing property as well.

Demand-pull inflation is the result of demand for a good or service exceeding the available supply. Because of the time it takes to build new units and the limitations on available land, an increase in the demand for housing in a particular area will result in price increases within the area. With a growing population caused by both natural increases and immigration, demand pressure on our housing stock has continued. In addition, we are seeing more singles uncoupling from their families, setting up their own housing units. The increase in number of households, not necessarily population increases, results in demand increases.

Remember: no one is making any more land. The supply and demand law of the market place dictates that even without cost-push inflation, increases in demand from qualified buyers must result in higher prices.

Investments that fail to keep pace with inflation actually result in an erosion of savings. To make matters even worse, investments generally produce taxable income so that with state and federal income tax, an investor might not only be losing purchasing power, but might have to pay up to 40 percent taxes on what is falsely labeled a gain.

To illustrate this point, suppose you earn 3 percent on a certificate of deposit while the Consumer Price Index rises 3.5 percent. The true value of your investment, even with the interest earned, will have declined. You will nevertheless be taxed on the 3 percent you earned. A combined 40 percent tax (federal and state) means you will have lost 1.2 percent of your 3 percent earnings for taxes, leaving you with 1.8 percent earnings, just about half of the rate of inflation. You can readily see why such investments are really a formula for poverty and not for riches. Real estate is considered an inflationary hedge because values have increased at even a greater rate than inflation. Unlike gold or stocks and bonds, which fluctuate in value with every newspaper headline, real estate values have in most instances been on an upward climb since World War II.

Of course, there have been market corrections during recessionary periods following rapid construction and/or price increases. However, inflation runs in cycles. When the economy gets going, the demand for money and goods drives up interest rates and prices. While inflation is currently not of great concern in many parts of the country, we can expect the economy to bounce back and future inflationary periods can be expected. These can actually be periods of great opportunity.

More and more people who desire to protect their savings are turning to real estate. Also, the United States has been discovered by foreign investors who consider our real estate prices bargains compared to values in their countries. While this foreign demand has all but evaporated because of economic problems in other countries, in the future we expect this foreign demand for our real estate to have a significant effect on real estate values.

An often overlooked advantage of inflation—at least with respect to real estate—is that when you use borrowed funds you get to pay back loans using ever cheaper dollars. By the use of borrowed funds, real estate investors are able to use inflation to their best interests. For example, a monthly house payment of $250 per month in 1970, would have been relatively high—beyond the means of a great many families. By the 1990s, such a payment would be easy to make by all but a few families. As the dollar becomes less valuable, payments become easier because you are using fewer valuable dollars to repay the expensive dollars you borrowed.

The greater part of the net worth of average homeowners is the equity in their homes. This has been caused by the greater appreciation in value that homes have had over the past two decades. Housing for a home buyer today is more than shelter. It is a long-term investment. Second homes are not looked at solely as luxuries anymore; they can be additional long-term investments. During inflationary times buyers should consider buying the finest home they can afford. As inflation continues, not only will the high payments become reasonable or low, but the homeowner will benefit by greater appreciation. Inflation does not have to rob you. You can harness it to help meet your financial goals.

If you want to be a millionaire, you can achieve your goal by going into debt and letting long-term inflation help you. If you can purchase real estate on which you owe $2 million and hold on to it for 15 years, you should be a millionaire. With only a 3 percent inflation rate (and we can expect that real estate values will increase at least that much), within 15 years your equity for average purchases should give you your million-dollar equity. And that is without even compounding the inflation or considering debt reduction. In actual practice the inflation rate applies to the increased value, not the original cost. If you make careful selections of property, you should be able to do even better than average increases. It may sound too simple to be true, but it is the formula that has turned thousands of people into millionaires. This book will show you many different ways to obtain real estate with no or low downpayments. You will find that it doesn't necessarily take money to make money in real estate.

Leverage (Other People's Money)

A major advantage of real estate is leverage, i.e., financing. Financing real estate is the easiest way to find others to help you attain financial security.

Your monthly payment will actually decrease each month for real estate investments. As inflation continues, you will be making payments with ever-cheaper dollars. The person who is most in debt therefore benefits the most in periods of great inflation. For example, if a person had $100,000 to invest and purchased a 6-unit building for $200,000, that person would get some benefit from inflation but nowhere near the benefit obtainable by buying a 24-unit apartment building for $700,000 and financing $600,000 of the purchase price (see Table 1–1.)

But what if you run into financial trouble and are unable to make your mortgage payments? Will that mean foreclosure and a deficiency judgment? A deficiency judgment is a court judgment against a borrower's property for the difference between the foreclosure sale price and the amount owed. A number of states will not allow deficiency judgments under any circumstances or restrict them to the point where they are the exception rather than the rule. If a deficiency judgment is not possible upon foreclosure, then the investor with the lowest downpayment in some ways has the lowest risk. Should real estate values significantly decline, the big losers are those owners who made significant downpayments to purchase properties. The smallest losers are those using the greatest leverage.

REAL ESTATE INVESTMENTS CAN BUY THEMSELVES

If you can buy a property where the income is sufficient to make the payments, then the property buys itself. If you could buy a $250,000 building with $20,000 down with a 20-year loan and your income from the building makes the payments, in 20 years the building will be paid for. You will have turned $20,000 into $250,000, and there is nothing magical about it. In addition, inflation should have increased the building's value at least several times, so that instead of a $250,000 building you very well might have one worth $1 million. While spendable income is nice to have, income normally will not make you rich. Appreciation in value is what makes real estate investors wealthy.

The amount of your loan payment that applies to your loan principal may seem to be a cash expense, but it is really increasing your equity in the property by reducing the loan. This is a phantom income because you don't actually see it in your pocketbook. Nevertheless, it is a positive element of ownership. This phantom income will be realized when the property is sold.

SAFETY IN REAL ESTATE

Real estate has proved to be one of the safest investments possible. While there is some element of risk to every investment, the safety of real estate investments,

Table 1–1   Percentage Return on Your Investment: The Magic of Leverage

Increase in value %	Cash %	Downpayment	
		50%	10%
10%	10%	20%	100%
20%	20%	40%	200%
30%	30%	60%	300%
40%	40%	80%	400%
50%	50%	100%	500%
60%	60%	120%	600%
70%	70%	140%	700%
80%	80%	160%	800%
90%	90%	180%	900%
100%	100%	200%	1000%

compared with business investments, is reflected in a foreclosure rate of less than one percent for residential property (see Figure 1–1.)

The level of risk in real estate varies by area and type of real estate. For example, areas where the economy is based on a single industry or firm have a greater risk for investors than an area with a more diverse economic base. The type of property also effects risk. The lowest risk real estate investments are rent-producing properties. Of rent producing properties, residential properties present the lowest risk because of the sheer number of available renters. Office buildings, factory buildings, raw land, and commercial property have a far greater element of risk than residential property. Their demand is tuned more to the economics of the time. While people need housing, businesses can delay moving or expansion, and in a period of economic contraction, they generally do.

But you can hedge your "bets." By researching a property, an area and the local economy you can gain the kind of knowledge that will allow you to evaluate the degree of risk of an investment with a fair amount of accuracy. As an investor you must learn to evaluate risk and consider alternative courses of action. Never accept extraordinary risks unless you can foresee extraordinary profits.

If absolute safety is your goal, you should stay away from real estate. Instead, consider government bonds or possibly GNMA securities. They offer absolute safety but a modest return. While you won't lose your investment, you also won't materially increase your net worth when inflation is considered. *Absolute safety* is incompatible with achieving financial independence.

Pyramiding

Your growth potential can be maximized by pyramiding your investments. This can be accomplished in a number of ways:

- Borrowing on your property (as equity increases due to inflation) to buy more property. This is known as *trading on your equity*. While real estate may be an illiquid investment, it is possible to pump money out of a real estate investment in a relatively short time. This can be accomplished by

**Figure 1–1 Elements of Risk and Safety
                    in Real Estate Investing**

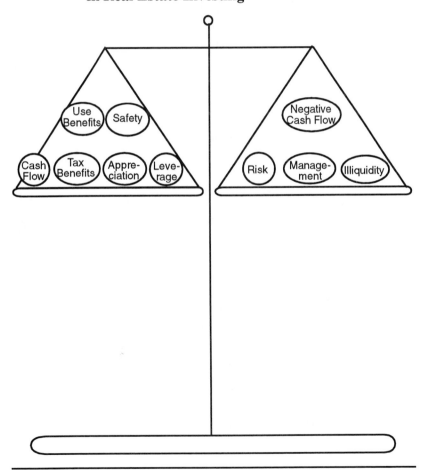

using the property as security for a loan or increasing an existing loan by refinancing.

- Selling (or, better still, trading) property to obtain larger properties.

- Reinvesting the cash generated by real estate investments into further investments. This is like compounding interest. By reinvesting your equities, they continue to grow.

Some investors start out with plans to own many properties, but after obtaining positive cash flow begin using the cash flow for their living expenses. After a while there is no spendable cash and the investment "plan" becomes just a single property. By failing to reinvest in the early years, you will fail to maximize your investment potential.

A LOOK AT THE NEGATIVE SIDE

Negative Cash Flow

Many good investments have negative cash flows, which means that your monthly cash payments exceed monthly cash receipts. Unless you can correct this imbalance, it could be difficult to hold such property for a long period of time. When you find an investment with a negative cash flow, there are two ways to correct it:

1. Increasing the income (raise rents, change use, reduce vacancies, etc.)

2. Reducing expenses (refinancing to cut expenses, more efficient spending, competitive bids, energy conservation, etc.)

If there still is a negative cash flow, keep in mind that the government probably will be paying a good part of it for you. Because your cash loss and more (depreciation) will be fully deductible expenses for most investors (see Chapter 3), the net effect will be to significantly reduce the negative cash flow and in some cases eliminate it completely.

Keep in mind that inflation works on rents just as it works on value. Therefore, if rents increase 5 percent each year, it won't take long to turn a negative cash flow into a money machine throwing off significant positive cash amounts each month.

Illiquidity

Another disadvantage of real estate is illiquidity. Depending upon the market and the type of property, it could require a significant time period to sell. Because price is related to the time available to sell, should a quick sale be required, the price would likely have to be discounted significantly. Single-family homes have greater liquidity than other real estate investments because there are greater numbers of potential buyers available.

Safety

As previously stated, real estate investments do involve risk in that changes in the area and the local and/or national economy will affect income and value. Even political changes, such as rent control or zoning changes, can have a significant affect on value.

Keep in mind that increased risks are only acceptable if you can live with the risks and if the risks are offset by increased likelihood of profit on the investment. I will show you how to analyze risk so that investment decisions can be made with a realistic risk evaluation.

If we plotted a curve based on typical investments, we would discover that low-risk investments offer relatively low profit potential while high-risk investments offer relatively high profit potential. (Investors will not accept greater risk in the absence of the possibility of greater profit.) The curve in Figure 1–2 will help you understand this concept. An investment at point A would have a relatively low risk but would also offer a relatively modest profit potential. On the other hand, a relatively high-risk investment at point B offers significantly greater profit potential. An investment at point C (below the curve) would not appear economically sound as the higher risk is not reflected in a profit commensurate with the risk. Investment D (above the curve) would offer an investor an interesting opportunity because the profit potential is greater than would be expected by the degree of risk. You will learn how you can reduce risk so that investments viewed as others to be below the risk curve can in fact be economically desirable investments.

A young person with very few assets can often afford to be a high roller, risking all in a highly speculative investment. A person approaching retirement age who needs the capital for the coming retirement years is usually more interested in capital preservation coupled with a reasonable profit than in making a killing. Risk capital, capital that will not affect a person's lifestyle, can be invested in property offering a greater appreciation potential as well as greater degree of risk.

Management

Real estate investments require management. You must know what you want to do and have a plan to do it. This is true even if you hire professional management. To maximize yield you must know what is happening and be flexible to make changes as needed. Real estate is not like blue chip stocks that you buy, put in

Figure 1–2 Risk–Profit Curve

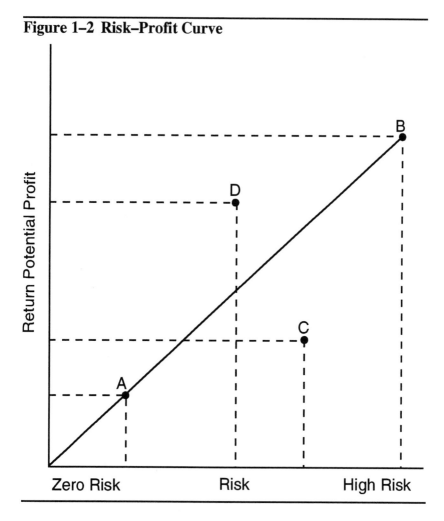

your portfolio and forget. Real estate demands your attention. Chapter 15 will cover management of your real estate investments.

WHEN TO BUY AND SELL

The best time to buy real estate is when you don't have to buy the property. In such a situation you have the bargaining power to make an offer that is economically advantageous to you but are able to walk away from if negotiations become disadvantageous. When you don't have to buy, you are likely to have your emotions under control.

The worst time to buy is when you absolutely must buy, whatever the reason. The more stringent the time requirement, the less likely you will make the most advantageous purchase. Similarly, when you fall in love with a property, you are likely to make decisions based more on emotion than your economic benefits. The best time to sell is when you don't have to sell. When you are not under any selling pressure, you are unlikely to make an agreement not in your best interests. Generally, you will not accept an offer to sell unless you have what you consider a better investment available for your money.

I have received unsolicited offers to sell properties that really were not on the market. In evaluating the decision to sell or to hold, I use a very simple technique. I ask myself, "If you didn't own this property and someone else offered it to you at the price and terms offered, would you buy it?" If I wouldn't, then I try to negotiate a sale. Otherwise, I would be bidding against myself. When you refuse a firm offer, you are saying, "No, I will pay more for it." If you wouldn't buy it at the price offered, you should sell it and buy something that you are willing to buy. Don't hold on to property without any economic basis for doing so.

You are vulnerable when you must sell. You are the kind of person you would be seeking if you were in a buying mode. It is possible to protect yourself from becoming someone else's pigeon by a basic knowledge of negotiation techniques.

We have cycles of activities in real estate. When interest rates rise, real estate activities tend to slow down. Generally, a downturn in real estate activity precedes a general economic downturn. When interest rates fall real estate activity generally increases. A real estate recovery generally precedes a general business recovery. High sales activity is generally associated with what we call a seller's market. Great demand, often exceeding supply, forcing prices up. In a buyer's market, sales activity is slow with few buyers and many sellers. Contrarians are the best investors. They like to buy when few other buyers are available. They are more likely to find highly motivated sellers whose expectations have been crushed by a lack of interested buyers. Must-sell sellers tend to get desperate in such a market. Similarly, contrarians like to sell when the market is rising and prices are going up. Actually, there are opportunities available in any market to buy or to sell.

When interest rates are high, one mistake many people make is waiting for interest rates to drop. While they wait, prices rise and interest rates still do not come down. In the last 40 years, there have only been a few years in which property values have failed to increase at a greater rate than the interest rates charged for real estate loans after tax benefits have been considered. Assume you are in the 40 percent tax bracket (total of federal and state income tax) for your top dollar of income. If you are paying 8 percent interest on a loan, it only costs you 4.8 percent. Since the interest is deductible, the government really pays the other 3.2 percent for you. With inflation, and an increasing population, an average real estate investment will likely increase in value over a 10-year period at a rate in excess of 4.8 percent each year.

Most people tend to look back as to where they have been rather than forward to where they are going. They tend to talk about deals available 2 years, 5 years, or 10 years ago that are now bargains rather than today's purchases that will become tomorrow's bargains. People who don't invest in real estate tend to say that others who did successfully invest were lucky. (They never say others were smart as this would be saying they were dumb.) But you don't have to be lucky to get rich in real estate. Luck in real estate is simply knowledge and opportunity coming together. If you gain the knowledge and look for the opportunity, people will say how lucky you are.

WHAT IT TAKES TO INVEST

You probably have heard and repeated the old maxims, "It takes money to make money" or, "Money goes to money." These slogans were probably written by real estate investors who wanted the game all to themselves. I am going to show you that having money is far from the most important attribute a real estate investor needs. There are many ways to make up for lack of cash. Personal qualities are far more important for success.

Personal qualities of successful real estate investors include:

- *Imagination:* The ability to visualize what will happen in the future and what can be done to increase desirability.

- *Resourcefulness:* The ability to solve problems. This includes the ability to structure purchases and sales in a variety of ways to meet both buyer and seller needs.

- *Persistence:* The plain gumption it takes to continue to work to find properties and to solve problems.

- *Self-Confidence:* The faith in oneself so that when an opportunity presents itself, the investor is mentally able to act.

- *Acceptance of Risk:* The ability to analyze risk, work to reduce it, and to accept it in the light of the benefits.

- *Self-Organization:* A successful investor must be organized so that he or she continues to work toward his or her goals. It takes self-discipline to work when others are engaging in leisure activities. Work by itself is not enough, it must be directed. You need a financial plan to reach a financial goal. Planning is less difficult than putting your plan into action. It is not that effective investing in real estate is difficult, it just takes courage.

- *Courage:* It is most important trait for a real estate investor.

My father was successful in both business and real estate investments. He had a saying: "You lose your money and you have lost nothing, but you lose your courage and you have lost everything." While courage is required for every investment, the greater the downside risk, the more courage is required of the investor.

One of the smartest real estate investors I know of was wiped out financially in a building project. He had even borrowed on his cars, home, and furniture in an attempt to save his investment, but all was lost. He never recovered from the loss because he also lost his courage. This man took a salaried job and was unwilling to take any risks at all. He has no faith in his own judgment anymore and asks friends their opinions on any important decision he must make. No one can give him back his courage; it must come from within. For many people an investment in other than a savings account causes great emotional stress that they are unable to overcome.

To the other extreme, a large Midwestern investor had been extremely successful. He owned over 800 fine residential units, lived on an estate with a gardener, maid, and butler and had all of the trappings we customarily associate with great wealth. His brother, a large developer, had a heart attack and he stepped in to handle his brother's projects. To keep the business going, he personally guaranteed large loans, but the business failed. When I first met this gentleman, he was $3 million in debt. Rather than go through bankruptcy, he went to his creditors and asked for their help. They agreed not to press him for the money, so he concentrated his efforts on recouping the losses. He moved to California, where he rented a two-bedroom apartment and started using many of the techniques covered in this book, especially options. Today, he has paid back the debt, lives in a beautiful home on a golf course, and drives a Mercedes. He never lost his courage and faith in his abilities.

Every 50-year-old wishes he or she had invested in real estate 20 years earlier. In fact, many of us remember our fathers or grandfathers lamenting that the days of big profits in real estate were over. They, of course, were wrong, and you are also if you think as they did. The parade hasn't passed you by. Age is not a factor in real estate investment. Some investors who retired with modest incomes have become millionaires during their retirement years. At the other extreme I know of a college freshman who started out with $2,000. He invested in a run-down rooming house and was a millionaire before he finished graduate school.

Your decision to invest in real estate should be your own, but it should be made only after careful consideration. Don't ask friends or relatives what to do if they are not investing themselves. They won't tell you to do something they are too timid to do themselves. In addition many people feel that advice not to do something is the safest advice to give. You can't win in real estate until you get into the game, and you're not in the game until you commit yourself to buy. But a word of caution: Don't jump without looking, and that means a careful examination.

Chapter 2

INVESTMENT ALTERNATIVES

The first man to fence in a piece of land saying,
"This is Mine . . . ," was the real founder of civil society.
—Jean-Jacques Rousseau, 1754

Real estate investments are divided into two categories: keepers and flippers. Keepers are property you buy for a long-term hold. You hold such property for income and/or appreciation in value and, in some cases, income tax benefits. (see Chapter 3). Flippers are properties you intend to resell as soon as possible. These are properties where you feel you can make a profit either with or without renovation, repairs, or improvements. Types of property purchased depend on the individual investor's needs and the particular market. (In Chapter 18, I will discuss determining an investor's specific needs.)

SINGLE-FAMILY HOMES

For many years the "experts" advised people not to invest in single-family homes, saying they provided a poor return on the investment. Those who failed to heed this advice prospered. When you measure income against price paid for a single-family home, it does appear to be a poor investment. However, income is not the sole criterion to use. The most important criterion is appreciation. Since World War II the appreciation of single-family homes has been phenomenal.

With construction costs continuing to escalate, with increasing demand, and with a limited supply of land, we can expect significant increases in value for the future simply based on the market forces of supply and demand. Of course, there may be a temporary leveling off and even decline in value based on changes in local and national economies, but for the long haul we can expect further appreciation in value.

While real estate is generally considered an illiquid investment not readily converted to cash, single-family homes are the most liquid of real estate investments. Generally they can be sold in a far shorter time than other real estate, and home equity can be readily used as collateral for loans. A single-family home is also the most readily rentable of real estate investments. The sheer abundance of homes is an advantage to an investor.

A major advantage offered by single-family homes is financing. You can obtain a higher loan-to-value ratio for single-family homes than for any other investment. In many instances, such as Veterans Administration (VA) financing and some low-income Federal Housing Administration (FHA) loans, owner-occupied homes can be purchased without any cash downpayment.

A disadvantage of single-family homes as investments is that rarely will the rent make the debt payments unless a very substantial downpayment is made. When the dollars going out for payments and expenses exceed the income, an owner has a negative cash flow. This makes holding the property an economic burden.

When a single-family house has a negative cash flow, this negative aspect is unlikely to continue for more than a few years because rents in most areas have been rising between 5 percent and 10 percent a year. The increase in gross income coupled with a fixed-debt service (mortgage payment) will mean that, in just a few years, what was a negative cash flow will likely turn into a significant positive cash flow.

Even if a single-family home has a negative cash flow, the negative cash flow might be effectively reduced or eliminated by the tax benefits. Depreciation (covered in Chapter 3) is a paper expense that can be used for income tax purposes. You will see that the effect of depreciation is to reduce your income tax liability.

If the buyer can live with the negative cash flow, and the appreciation and tax benefits are significant then what would otherwise appear as a poor rental investment could make a great deal of sense.

Some buyers of single-family homes are able to avoid the negative cash flow aspect of their investments by offering them for sale on a lease option basis. On a lease option with a significant portion of the rent applying to purchase, a higher payment is possible. This technique will be covered in Chapter 13.

Keep in mind that no home purchased for resale or appreciation is a bargain if you can't locate a buyer for it who will pay you more than your investment. Generally, be leery of:

- Floor plans unlikely to appeal to most buyers
- Architectural styles likely to appeal to a very limited group of buyers unless modifications are economically feasible
- Shoddy basic construction
- Likely code violations

- Work likely performed without building permits

- Rapidly declining neighborhoods.

If you are going to invest in single-family homes, it is best to stick with one area you are familiar with. It also provides for more efficient use of your management time. But the one hard-and-fast rule we have learned for real estate investing is that there are no hard-and-fast rules.

My name is Reuben G. After 30 years of service, I recently retired from the Air Force. I purchased a retirement home in a golf course community and now live off my federal retirement plus my monthly rent checks.

In my first assignment, base housing was not available so I ended up buying a very nice home for less than $14,000. I purchased it without a downpayment by assuming an FHA loan. I was transferred two years later. Unable to find a buyer quickly, my real estate broker recommended renting the house. The rent more than made the payments, and she handled the management for a modest fee.

At my new assignment, I again ran into a shortage of base housing for my family. I turned to the newspaper ads, and after several days of looking, we found a new home that suited our needs and purchased it with a no downpayment VA loan. Three years later, I was transferred again. Because we were now clearing $50 a month on the house we had rented, we decided to rent rather than sell.

Perhaps, I was lucky, but we had good property managers and good long-term tenants. Buying and keeping property became our financial plan. While we had some months where we had to dip into our savings, on a year-to-year basis we always came out financially ahead. In addition, I usually received a larger tax refund than any of my friends.

The last home I purchased for eventual rental purposes was nine years ago. My retirement home gives me eight houses. Incidentally, four of my seven rental houses are now owned free and clear. All were purchased with nothing or close to nothing down and the income from my real estate exceeds my government retirement check. I estimate my equity in my homes conservatively at over $1 million.

A side-benefit is that trips to visit my children and grandchildren and friends can be tied in with visits to my scattered rentals. My accountant says this makes most of my travel expenses tax deductible.

Your own home should be considered the start of your investment program. It is more than a shelter; it is an excellent investment. Today, buying the best home you can afford in the best area makes sense. This type of home will provide you with maximum appreciation and will increase your general quality of life.

Areas that have been hit by recession are especially attractive because homes can likely be purchased for less than reproduction costs and will likely realize a significant increase in value when the market recovers.

I'm George. In financial terms, I'm known as a bottom feeder. I buy distressed property. More specifically, I buy groups of completed homes from lenders who have taken them by foreclosure from the builder. By buying multiple homes and even complete subdivisions, I can buy homes at significant discounts from their cost to build. I generally pay no more than 60 percent of what I believe the present cost to build the homes would be. Sometimes I pay even less.

Even then, I am sensitive to location, design and decor. Salability is of prime importance to me. I turn down more projects than I buy.

Hard times have helped me because the more foreclosed property a lender is holding, the louder my money talks. I offer cash without purchase conditions. I am able to borrow funds I need on a short-term line of secured credit.

I list the houses with an agent for a quick sale. I clean the houses, if needed, and at times will put in lawns. I operate under the adage, "There is no profit until there is a sale." Therefore, I don't try to get every last dime out of a property, I price them for quick sale. Within 60 days of my purchase, I will evaluate the sales activity. If I feel sales are too slow, I will auction off the property by setting a minimum bid at my cost. It works for me. What is a problem for others I view as opportunity.

Buying Prior to Subdivision Approval

In many states buyers can make reservations on homes but can't complete the purchase until a subdivision has received final local and state approvals. Until such time as a public report is issued by the state, the buyer can back out of the purchase and receive his or her deposit back in full.

If you live in such a state, it may be practical to consider speculating in condominium reservations when the market appears to be rising. Generally, units can be reserved with only a few thousand dollars down. If the demand increases and the units sell out, reservations can be sold at a profit. The downside risk for such an investment is only the interest lost on the deposit, which must be kept by the developer in a trust account. On the other hand, the upside profit could be many times the amount of the deposit.

Some developers have discouraged speculating by requiring larger deposits and by prohibiting purchasers from assigning their purchase contracts. In other words, the purchaser must buy before he or she can resell. Nevertheless, profits can still be made in this area.

My name is Robert O. I sold my home in San Francisco in late 1977 to take a job in Southern California. I had almost $100,000 from the sale. After looking around, I put a $2,000 deposit on a new home in an Orange County subdivision. Two weeks later, when I went to see the developer about upgrading the carpet, a salesperson for the developer told me that if I wanted to make a profit he could get me $10,000 for my reservation. It seems the phase I had purchased in had sold out. There were buyers willing to pay a premium to get a home.

While I didn't sell my reservation, I discussed this with a neighbor where I was renting. My neighbor, who was an attorney, told me that investing in reservations was a no-lose situation. All I had to do was call developers to find out if final subdivision approval had been received for advertised openings (in most cases it hadn't), get there early, and put down a deposit that was really refundable at will.

I may not be the brightest guy in the world, but I don't have to be hit over the head with a two-by-four when opportunity is knocking. After some convincing and her own checking, my wife agreed that we should start putting in reservations. We went to different subdivisions on weekends and my wife went alone during the week. We never paid more than $2,500 for a deposit and often only $1,000. We placed 41 deposits in a month and a half. We wanted mid-market, three-bedroom, two-bath, two-car garage homes in desirable areas.

When I had exhausted my money, I sold my first reservation. By this time I received $17,000 net (after paying a commission to the agent). We used this $17,000 for more deposits, but we decided that from now on we would keep the cash rather than reinvest.

Most of the deposits were for homes not yet under construction or barely started. The market at the time was wild with prices being raised by developers almost on a monthly basis. We ended up selling 33 of our deposits at profits ranging from $3,000 to $35,000. Our average profit after costs was $11,500 or $380,000 total. With my original $100,000 I had a half million dollars. The whole operation took less than eight months. For those homes where the value either didn't go up or I could not find a buyer for my reservation, I received my reservation fees back in full.

In retrospect, I made money by my timing. Real estate was booming and I rode the boom period with investments that offered profit and no risk. Since that time I have looked for similar booms. From 1982 to 1987, I purchased and resold lots. I used options to keep my risk down and did nothing but make money. When the next boom comes, I intend to go with it. I don't know how but I will keep my eyes and ears open.

Vacation Homes

After their first home, the next step for many investors is a vacation home. Today a vacation home can be for investment as well as enjoyment. As stated, the fact that interest and property taxes are tax deductible helps to offset the cost of keeping a second home. Assume a couple is in the 40 percent tax bracket for the top dollar of their income (both federal and state taxes). If they have a house payment of $800, including taxes and insurance, the chances are that $750 of that payment is deductible interest and taxes. The net effect is that it actually only costs them $500 per month in cash to keep their second home, which can be partially or fully offset by appreciation.

If you live in a vacation home for 14 days a year or less, you can take depreciation on it. If you use it for more than 14 days, you are not allowed depreciation. Therefore, many owners use their vacation home only a few weekends a year and rent it at other times in order to take depreciation.

The Sunbelt is the best area for vacation homes because they can generally be rented more months of the year than in the North and are more readily sold because of the increasing demand for housing in this growing region.

I have had two vacation homes. One, a lake shore home in northern Wisconsin which I use for three months a year. I do not rent it in the off season, but the appreciation has far exceeded expenses. In addition, it gives me a great deal of pleasure. My other vacation home was a condominium in Lake Havasu, Arizona, which I rented.

My name is Sandra J. I am a school teacher in New York. My husband is an iron worker who is collecting a modest pension because of a disability. We purchased a golf course condominium in South Carolina about 10 years ago. We use it for two weeks at Christmas, a week at Easter, and in the summer. The rest of the year it is rented out by a rental office at the development. While the property cost us money for the first three years, we now get enough rent to cover our payments from weekly rentals. We paid less than $40,000 for our unit with $6,000 down and the current value is about $80,000.

We had a dual purpose in our purchase, which was to use it as a vacation home until I retire and then to use it as a permanent retirement home thereafter. I will retire next year when we will move to South Carolina. If we had waited until we had retired, we would never have been able to afford this retirement home. By buying early as a vacation home, we locked in the price of our retirement.

Condominiums

In many areas of the country condominiums, planned unit developments, and cooperatives can be purchased to provide a break-even or a positive cash flow.

Condominiums have the advantage of being relatively easy to rent with fewer problems for the owner (the grounds and exterior are handled by the association). On the negative side, condominiums generally have realized a slower rate of appreciation than other units. In a recessionary period, condo values tend to be softer than those of single-family homes. Reasons for these differences are largely based on the fact that condominiums are not the purchase of choice by many owners. While they might prefer a single-family home, a condominium is often a compromise dictated by cost.

Check the restrictive covenants before buying a condominium as an investment. Many condominiums and cooperatives have rental restrictions that could conflict with your plans. Also, obtain a copy of the last operational statement (the seller will be able to obtain this). You want to make certain current assessments are adequate to meet the association's needs. (If not, assessments will need to be raised.) You also want to find out if there have been special assessments for unusual expenses. In some associations, these special assessments seem to be normal rather than *special*.

My name is Seymour T. I am a retired accountant. Because I spent half the year renting in Florida. I decided to buy a condominium. I had a tax purpose in mind. By establishing Florida residency, I would avoid my state income tax, which was running about $5,000 per year. I felt this savings would more than pay for my condominium payments and association fees. This would give me a Florida home for free. Because of a depressed market, I purchased a modest two-bedroom, two-bath, West Coast condominium in a large development for $38,500 and got the sellers to include the furnishings. I paid $4,000 down and assumed the FHA financing. My payments were about $300 a month and association fees were $78 a month. I like the area, and I had a condominium for free because of state income tax savings.

Then my wife fell in love with a new development in our area. We put a deposit down on a very nice three-bedroom, two-and-one-half-bath single-family home. She wanted a big home so the children and grandchildren could visit. Fortunately for us the resale market was still bad. After an unsuccessful attempt to sell my condominium, I advertised it for rent by taking a small classified ad in several Canadian papers. I did this because many of the people renting in our complex were from Canada.

I asked $750 per month rent furnished. I was astounded by the number of responses I received. I rented it for six months and received a deposit by mail from one of the first callers. The seasonal rental made my payments for the year.

The first year I also rented the property for three additional months at $400 per month, so I had a good cash-on-cash return from my investment. In addition, I had the tax benefit of depreciation, which sheltered my income from federal taxes. I began checking on the availability of other units in my development. I placed purchase offers on several other units and was able to buy two furnished units. I let my tenants know of the two additional units and within a week they had found renters for me from among their Canadian friends.

I have continued to put in offers to purchase condominium units, and I now own over 30 units. My criteria is that a single seasonal tenant's rent be sufficient to make my payments for the year plus association dues. The off-season rentals, depreciation, and appreciation are my benefits. My retirement is no longer one of playing cards and lying to my neighbors, it's one of fun and activity and it has become very profitable. Because all my units are in the same development, my management has been fairly easy. While I handle the seasonal rentals, I have a rental agent who now takes care of my off-season rentals. I pay another resident of the development an hourly fee to do any required repairs and/or maintenance. Friends ask me why I don't buy apartments instead. The reasons are that I can get far better financing buying condos, and they are easier to rent than apartments. I can get more rent from condos than apartments because of all the amenities and I have no aggravation with common-area maintenance.

Many small investors are purchasing condominium units for their children in college. They can frequently purchase units for about a 10 percent downpayment and, because of present market conditions, at prices that can allow a positive cash flow. By taking in roommates, the unit can in many markets generate enough income to make the payments on the unit. For example, three roommates paying $300 each a month will give you $900 gross plus a home for your college-age son or daughter. While prices of units have dropped, rents have not. In addition, they will have depreciation on the unit and hopefully appreciation when it is sold. One woman purchased a $60,000 condominium in Santa Barbara, California, for her son while he attended college. She paid 10 percent down. While the appreciation was unusual in this area, she received $165,000 when she sold the unit five years later. That's $105,000 profit on a $6,000 cash investment.

Fixer-Uppers

Property that is move-in perfect sells first. When you sell property, you will generally maximize your net by making a property *stand tall*. However, the reverse holds true as well. Property in bad condition needing, repair, cleanup, or complete rejuvenation will often remain on the market for a long period of time. The result is that exceptional opportunities are likely to become available as to both price and terms of this type of *fixer-upper* property.

Generally, the dirtier the property is, the better the deal you can make. Property in rough shape can often be purchased at a good price and on very attractive terms. Often property like this is being foreclosed, is part of an estate, or has been foreclosed and is held by the lender.

As new costs rise, the advantages in renovating property becomes obvious. The principle of substitution is that a person will not pay more for a property than they would for one offering equal utility and desirability. If you can buy a run-down and/or older property and make it equally desirable as to both utility and desirability of other properties, then your property will have similar worth. This is true even though your initial cost plus the cost of renovation could be far less than the value of the comparable properties. For those who can visualize what can be done to increase property desirability and who have a good grasp of the expenditures required, the profit potential can be phenomenal and very often is.

Before buying these fixer-uppers, check them out carefully to see what must be done. In particular check the plumbing, electrical, and heating-cooling systems. Carefully consider what the repairs will cost. Generally, cleaning, painting, and yard work can make a big difference in value and salability. Every dollar spent on a fixer-upper can mean many dollars in profit.

Unless you have had extensive contracting experience, avoid homes that need major structural work. Corrective work is seldom within estimates. Normally, what happens is that additional problems continue to emerge as work progresses.

A buyer of fixer-upper property should also consider improvements—additions or amenities the property never had before—in addition to necessary repairs. The investor should be concerned with the principle of contribution when making improvements. Basically this means an improvement, to be economically feasible, must increase the value of the property by more than the cost of the improvement. Many buyers who purchase fixer-uppers feel that unless the property value increases by at least a two-to-one ratio (a two dollar increase in value for every dollar spent), then the improvement should not be made.

Besides repairs and improvements, buyers of fixer-uppers must consider renovation—the replacement of old amenities with new ones. Money spent in renovating kitchens and baths with new cabinets and fixtures is generally reflected by at least a two-to-one ratio in increase in value. The same holds true for new carpeting, paint, and landscaping. While you should always evaluate the effect of cost-to-sale price and plan for an adequate return, things seldom work out exactly as planned. Therefore, you must leave enough room in your estimates to deal with the unexpected.

Fixer-upper buyers not only look for bargains to buy, they also know how to get work done at the lowest cost. Some save by installing used carpeting obtained from carpet layers who redo model homes and from jobs they do for decorators. Quality used carpet can often be obtained for little more than the cost of the pad and laying the carpet.

Today there are fixer-upper operators in every price range. One successful investor buys million dollar fixer-uppers in Beverly Hills, California, and successfully turns them into $2 and $3 million homes.

Fixer-uppers don't have to be old. They can actually be new or near-new homes that need work to appeal to potential buyers.

I'm Dennis. I buy new or newer homes in prime areas in the 3,000-square-foot category. I buy homes that were foreclosed by lenders known as REOs (Real Estate Owned). I look for homes that the lender has had on the market for some time.

When the prior owner couldn't sell it and the lender hasn't been able to sell it, it's time for my offer—usually very low and for cash. I don't dicker. Right now there are a lot of opportunities for me, so if a lender won't take my offer, I move on to other opportunities.

My offers are often accepted because lenders have received a dose of reality. There are not many buyers for what they have because what they have usually has problems.

An example of a recent purchase was a custom-designed, four-year-old Spanish home. The former owner only lived in it six months and was transferred. He made payments for almost two years before he let it go. He had tried to sell it to break even by asking $695,000. The lenders had the home on the market for six months. While they originally asked $495,000, they reduced the price to $450,000. My offer, the only offer received in three years, was for $310,000. I refused a counteroffer of $390,000 and my offer was eventually accepted.

I ripped out the dark gray ceramic tile in the baths, entry hall, and kitchen and replaced it with 12" x 12" white ceramic tile. I had the maple-tone cabinetry painted white and the cabinet doors stripped and given a white tone finish. The blue carpet was ripped up and replaced with flex Berber carpeting. Pink marble was removed from the fireplace and a beehive-style stucco fireplace with Spanish tile gave the room an entirely different look. I tiled the front entrance with Spanish tile and replaced the modern front doors with massive carved doors and appropriate hardware. I upgraded lighting fixtures throughout the house. My total cash outlay was under $60,000. I priced the property at $495,000 and sold it for $485,000. After paying commission my profit was over $80,000. My total holding time: less than four months.

I want my property to offer a competitive advantage over other property in eye appeal as well as price. By pricing right I cut my holding time.

The person who wishes to buy a house, fix it up, move in, and then sell it must be willing to live a nomadic existence and have a spouse willing to go along with it. Moving can be hard on children, who must change schools and friends. Ideally, these ventures are best for individuals or couples without children. Building or renovating is not an easy life. You must be willing to sacrifice present free time and pleasures for future benefits.

Building Homes for Resale

Some developers find lots, choose plans, and build homes utilizing a general contractor. By contracting the entire job, they reduce the risk of cost overruns and are able to devote their time to marketing rather than the nuts and bolts of construction.

Instead of building for immediate resale, some developers furnish the home and use it as a model to sell from. They either know of available lots or have tied up lots with a purchase option so they can provide the buyer with a complete package. In most areas, activities like this do not require a real estate license since the developer is acting as a principal and not an agent.

When building a home for resale, don't be too innovative. Look at what is selling in your area. The further you deviate from what others are successfully selling, the greater your risk.

My name is William. After graduating college, I became involved in real estate sales. One of my close friends made a "killing" by buying a lot, contracting with a builder, and then selling the home for a profit. I decided to follow his example.

I found an inexpensive lot, a small builder who gave me a good price, and a bank that gave me an excellent construction loan. My total cash assets at the time were around $500.

Luckily, I sold the house for a profit before it was completed. I say luckily because I had made some serious mistakes. First, I had looked for the cheapest lot. In terms of resale, the cheapest lot is usually the most expensive lot. You should look for a lot in a better area because location sells. It has often been said that the three most important considerations in buying real estate are location, location and location.

Second, I picked a very contemporary plan—one of those modernistic homes with sharp angles that you see featured in the magazine sections of the Sunday newspapers but which few people build. This type of house is usually difficult to sell although everyone wants to see it. I should have chosen Colonial, Cape Cod, Spanish, or standard Ranch design.

Since then, I have continued to build one or two homes each year and sell them. But I try to stick with what buyers want. If I had one sentence of advice for would-be builders, "Don't substitute your own likes for the likes of others."

To limit risk some investors build a home, move in, and place it on the market. They live there until the home is sold. They avoid two home payments, which means they can usually afford to hold on until they can make a sale which offers them a reasonable profit. The disadvantage of this type of activity is that the investor's family is constantly being uprooted. While it can be a profitable way of life, it is not necessarily a desirable lifestyle.

Some people act as their own general contractors and hire subcontractors for all the work, while others give the entire job to a general contractor. Still others will physically build each house themselves. An advantage of building homes for yourself and living in them until they are sold is that, in most localities, contractor's licenses are not required.

APARTMENTS

Small rental units such as duplexes and fourplexes offer the advantage of your living in one unit and having the tenants help buy the property through their rents. While rentals will seldom be sufficient to make the payments, the additional cash needed for the payment will often be less than would be required for a comparable single-family home. Excellent financing is also often available for these smaller units.

Although you cannot take depreciation on your own apartment, you can depreciate the other units in the building. This will often result in a net positive cash flow when income tax liability is considered. Smaller apartments have an advantage in that, because of demand, they are usually more readily salable than larger units would be. Nevertheless, larger apartments can be excellent investments.

Some investors have found another advantage to apartments. They buy an apartment building and put one of their children in as manager who ends up with an apartment and salary. Though college costs are not deductible expenses, this method gives the student income plus free housing. (Of course the student pays taxes, but they are likely to be minimal.) Warning: If you pay your child an unjustifiable salary, it could spell trouble with the IRS. Go over any such arrangement in advance with your accountant.

Of course, there are disadvantages, and you must decide if you are willing and/or able to deal with these problems:

- In many situations the decision to do the maintenance and repairs yourself or hire it done will make the difference between a positive and negative cash flow. If you are unwilling to do menial tasks you had better be prepared to pay for the work.

- The best apartment management is by the owner who lives on the premises. If you are unwilling to give up the privacy of a single-family home, you will either have to constantly check on the property or have a resident manager.

- If you are the type of person who gets emotionally involved with problems of others, you should obtain professional management. You must be able to deal with your tenants on a professional business basis. Landlords who get involved in their tenants' problems hesitate to increase rents, allow rent arrearages to exist and are slow to evict tenants. Even when you don't live in the building, residential rentals involve interpersonal relationships. You have likely heard, "If you can't stand the heat, get out of the kitchen." Well, this applies to residential investments.

Generally you can expect the highest return from units that give you the greatest problems. Units in run-down areas or units that have collection or tenant difficulties provide higher rates of return than do quality units. However, problem apartments usually have far less appreciation than the better, more trouble-free units. As a buyer of these types of units you are substituting present income for later appreciation.

One big advantage of troubled units is that owners frequently are very motivated to sell and often will sell with low and even no downpayment.

To take advantage of these situations, you must have the time, maintenance skills, and interpersonal skills necessary to deal with the tenants.

I'm Tom C. I own apartment buildings. I look for property in older but relatively stable neighborhoods where the owners have problems. I check eviction actions to get purchase leads. I also work with several agents who are always on the alert for something for me. Out-of-town owners are usually the most motivated sellers as are people who have recently inherited the property and are having difficulty dealing with the problems.

I look for buildings that I feel I can buy with little down and where I can obtain a positive cash flow by reducing vacancy factor, raising rents, making minimum renovations, and repairing or a combination of the above. If I don't believe I can achieve a positive cash flow within 90 days, I forget the deal.

How successful am I? I currently own over 300 rental units. Not bad for a retired postman who started out 10 years ago with next to nothing.

At the present time, there are a great many opportunities in buying foreclosed apartments. The RTC (Resolution Trust Corporation), FDIC (Federal Deposit Insurance Corporation), and local lenders have bulging inventories of foreclosure properties. Many of these properties can be purchased at prices and terms where reasonable management can result in a good positive cash flow. As a point of warning, keep in mind that just because a lender has it for sale does not make a property a bargain. It must make economic sense.

COMMERCIAL PROPERTY

Commercial property can be an excellent investment. If property is already well leased, the price and downpayment required will probably be substantial. Nevertheless, the demand for these investments is great. You can expect rentals to increase with inflation, which in turn will increase the value. On the other hand, commercial property that is vacant or has problem tenants can frequently be purchased with little money down and at attractive prices and terms. These properties can be excellent investments for hard-working and imaginative people who have faith in themselves.

Compared to residential property, commercial property can be a high-risk investment. There are relatively few prospective tenants for commercial property. Because people must have a place to stay, residential vacancies do not increase at the same rate as commercial vacancies during a recessionary period. During such a period, commercial property owners might have to reduce rents significantly to keep or to obtain tenants. This could result in a negative cash flow situation for many years. Of course, the inability to locate any tenants would mean disaster. In addition, overbuilding in your local area also has a negative effect on both your ability to rent as well as in the amount of rent you can get.

The quality of current tenants, the length and other terms of the lease, the financial strength of the tenant as well as the local economy all effect the risk of commercial investments. In addition, the larger the structure, the larger the repair costs. The need for a new roof or a new boiler in a large structure could exceed the downpayment required to buy the property.

Investors love good commercial buildings with a long-term lease from a major tenant. However, if you are starting with little or no cash, these investments will usually be beyond your reach. But when commercial property has been vacant for a long period of time, owners are often willing to sell with little or no downpayment. Even when the owner wants a substantial downpayment for a vacant commercial building, it can often be purchased with little cash.

When you have limited capital to invest, consider an option to rent with the right to sublease. You would want an option to lease for one year with renewal options, such as for two periods of five years each. You would want as long a period to exercise the option as you can get. You also want the option to buy the property at an agreed price during at least the first few years of the lease. Your option should be negotiated at what you consider to be a favorable or bargain rental based on other rentals in the area.

For a small option price you now have control over a property. If you can sublease the property for more than your lease payment, you will have a positive cash flow. At worst, your downside risk is the price you paid for the option.

If you can find a good tenant and can obtain a long-term sublease (remember you have renewal options), then the value of the building will increase based on the lease. You can now try to sell the building and exercise the option to purchase when you find a buyer.

As an alternative you might be able to exercise the option to purchase without having to sell the property. Based on the lease, if it is to a tenant with financial strength, you could conceivably obtain 100 percent financing because the value of the building with the tenant should be far greater than the option price. With a strong tenant, you might even be able to obtain financing in excess of the option price. This would mean that you would have not only purchased a property without a downpayment, it would also have given you spendable cash.

When you sublease property, it is essential that any obligations under your lease be passed on to your tenant. As an example, if you are to be responsible for maintaining the heating and cooling equipment under a long-term commercial lease then you would want to pass this obligation on to your tenant. Otherwise, you could find yourself having a significant financial burden without any reimbursement from your tenant.

Clayton J. worked as an agent in a rental and property management business. He was an excellent rental agent and was able to rent property other agents considered unrentable. He left his office, lured away by the larger commissions offered in sales. Later, he returned to rentals in an unusual way. He would look for problem properties and would negotiate an option to rent them on a one-year lease with several renewal options for longer periods. The leases allowed him to sublease. The type of property he looked for usually offered limited-use possibilities and had therefore been vacant for a long period of time. He would offer really minimum rental terms that were often accepted.

Now his job was to find a tenant. The method he used was quite simple. He would go through the Yellow Pages of the local phone book for business categories he thought might be able to use the property. He would call each firm listed in those categories and make his rental pitch. He simply stayed on the phone day after day until he succeeded. In many cases, the difference between what he was obligated to pay in rent and what he received was substantial. His downside risk was never more than the option price. In just a few years he had become very wealthy. His only complaint was that he had to pay income tax on his profit.

Generally, the bigger the rental problem, the greater the profit potential in solving the problem. You should analyze a property. Ask who could use it. Then use Clayton J.'s method. Go through the Yellow Pages of a local phone book; it will give you all kinds of ideas as to possible tenants.

Office buildings generally require substantial downpayments unless they have high vacancies. Older buildings often lose their tenants to newer ones. Some owners panic when they see their vacancy factor increasing dramatically and may be receptive to offers with very low downpayments.

My name is Leroy H. and I rent space that I don't own. What I do is constantly check with the General Services Administration (the real estate arm of the federal government) as well as state, county and city agencies as to real estate rental needs.

Governmental agencies usually require large square footage but can seldom pay enough for quality buildings. I then look for vacant spaces which I feel from experience and from talking to officials will meet the government requirements. My next step is an option to lease the space at as reasonable a rental as I can negotiate with the specific right to sublease. I then try to rent the space to the government. If I am successful, I make the difference in rental that I can collect from the government. If not, I have lost the amount paid for the option plus a little time. I have learned government needs to the point where I am right at least 25 percent of the time, and this has resulted in a very nice lifestyle for my family.

With the present glut in office space, I am often able to give the government space in "A" category buildings which they could not afford just a few years ago.

INDUSTRIAL PROPERTY

Industrial property is difficult to deal in because prospective tenants are far fewer than you would find for commercial or residential property. While well-leased industrial property is highly salable, vacant industrial property requires problem solving. Many industrial buildings were built for particular uses. If you can find the right tenant for the property, you can make a good profit.

If you wish to get involved in industrial property, you should find out about past tenants who used the property. If toxic substances were released on the property, you as the owner could be held liable for cleanup costs even though you did not cause the problem.

FARMS

A home in the country with several acres sounds idyllic. It can also be a super investment. Besides the house, you have land that should increase in value. Often a home and acreage will cost little if any more than a home in the city. But don't expect to make money farming a few acres. Many people who thought they would live off the land have done so but not in the way they expected. They found that their land values had so accelerated that they achieved financial independence by selling the land, not by living on it.

The small commuter farm should only be considered by a special person. Generally, purchasers must either bring their jobs with them to the property or be willing to commute an hour or more to and from work. The idyllic existence of the "landed gentry" loses some of its luster when you have to get up at 4:00 a.m. to milk the cow, feed a few animals, and leave for work by 5:30 a.m. When you arrive home each night, the cow will need milking again, and there will be evening chores to do. Weekends are not for ball games on the TV with a bottle of your favorite brew; they are devoted to working on fences, buildings, and a thousand and one other things. Most smaller farms don't have sufficient income to support hired help. It is expensive being a gentleman farmer.

On the positive side, many people love commuter farming. With our increasingly impersonal, technical lifestyles, many people relish the manual labor and feeling of accomplishment that farms provide. The owners of small farms often live vicariously through their children, who are able to have pets, even horses. For many, the sacrifices of a small farm are worthwhile.

Also, a small farm can provide a great deal more than lifestyle. To start with, a farm has the advantages of depreciation of the improvements, equipment and even the livestock. When a homeowner goes to the hardware store and buys a bucket of paint, it is not deductible, but when the small farmer buys the same paint, it is probably a deductible expense.

While few people go into a small farm for the profit motive, it often works out as the best investment of their lives. Besides development possibilities there are thousands more city people seeking the same escape and willing to pay for it. We can expect this back-to-basics interest to continue well into the future, driving land prices higher and higher.

Large farms today are really big investments. What were once considered just family farms are in many areas worth over a million dollars for agricultural use, not for development. Economical farm size varies depending upon the area and crops. For example, 40 acres in an orchard could be very profitable, but it might take several thousand acres in grazing land to make an equal profit in cattle.

Although large farms are frequently profitable, the profits tend to fluctuate. One year's profit can be followed by a huge loss. Real farming investments should only be made by people able to farm themselves or who have large disposable incomes to cover loss years. While there are many professional farm management firms providing complete service, they are expensive. With the high cost of farm management, a purchaser who is not going to personally farm the land should not expect the income to make the payments. Though there are federal loans to buy farmland, generally farm purchases require substantial downpayments. The only exception is marginal farmland or land that is completely raw and has never been under cultivation.

RAW LAND

A significant risk of holding raw land is its illiquidity. It takes time to sell and during recessionary periods, the only way you might be able to sell it is at a giveaway price. Because of the risks involved, raw land purchases should only be a part of a person's overall investment program and even then it should be purchased with risk capital. While raw land has often had fantastic appreciation, it is still a crap shoot.

Many investors like raw land because it offers excellent appreciation potential plus the advantage of no management problems. If there are no tenants and no structures, there are few things that can go wrong.

The investor should realize that investing in raw land is a long-term investment that involves a negative cash flow without any advantages of depreciation. Even if property is fully paid for, taxes still must be paid. No depreciation benefits are possible because only improvements can be depreciated for tax purposes (see Chapter 3). Your income should be sufficient to make your payments. Since most of the payments are applied to interest which is deductible, the higher your income the less it really costs you to buy raw land. Owners customarily finance the buyers on raw land sales. In many areas 10 percent down is common. Sellers will often carry the balance at interest rates far less than market rate.

Raw land sales have attracted many sharp operators who want to sell you small parcels at prices far greater than the land is worth. There have been many fraud convictions for this type of sale. I have advised buyers to contact their sellers to renegotiate their purchases when after several years they still owed more than the land was worth. Actually, they can negotiate from a position of some strength as the alternative to the seller could be to have the property back.

Don't buy land that is part of a heavily advertised development. The television and glossy mail order presentations are usually made by firms that buy wholesale and sell at many times retail value in order to cover high promotional and sales costs. Often land purchased from these dealers would have to appreciate 500 to 1,000 percent in value for you to just break even. While these land dealers offer great terms, terms are meaningless when the value isn't there.

The best time to buy raw land is when new construction is slow. When there is a low demand and many sellers, the negative cash flow element of holding raw land increases the likelihood of an advantageous purchase as to both price and terms.

While raw land in many cases has increased in value several thousand percent in short periods of time, it is more speculative than other investments. Tremendous profit is possible from raw land during growth periods, but if you must sell during a slow economic period, you will likely have to take a severe reduction in price. Raw land is the least liquid of real estate investments often taking several years to sell, and it is almost impossible to borrow on. Therefore, it should be only a part of any investment plan.

One danger to recognize in buying any land is that zoning can be changed. A change in zoning can mean a change in value. A change from residential zoning to commercial zoning could result in a substantial increase in value; conversely, a change from commercial to residential zoning would have serious adverse effects on the value of the land.

Some investors have found ways to get income from land until it is ready for development.

My name is Steve K. I achieved financial success because of recreational vehicles. I purchased a travel trailer in 1966 for our family vacations. I discovered that the restrictions in my subdivision would not allow me to keep the trailer in my driveway. I contacted the dealer who sold me the trailer. He suggested I find a friend who has a big yard, or arrange with one of the local ranchers to leave my trailer on their property. I have a degree in business administration, and my situation seemed to be just like the case analysis method problems we had used at school. Here was a problem that could also be an opportunity.

I checked with the county and found out that a storage yard required industrial-type zoning. I also obtained county zoning information. By checking tax records, I began contacting owners of land. I found 10 acres on a good road about three miles from the city. The owner wanted $5,000 per acre for the parcel. While electricity was available, it did not have municipal water or sewer and it would be many years before it did have them. I obtained a 60-day option to buy the property at the full price of $50,000 with 5 percent down ($2,500), and the balance at 6 percent interest with payments amortized over 30 years, but all due and payable in 10 years. (This means a balloon payment.) I paid $100 for this option.

My next step was to advertise in our local papers, including the free throwaway papers. My ad indicated secure storage for motor homes, trailers, boats, construction equipment, etc., at $15 per month. Before I carried out my plan, I wanted to see if I had correctly perceived the need. I spent about $400 on ads. From the ads I received 28 deposits (one month's rent.)

I then exercised my option to buy. I put up storage yard signs and put cyclone fencing with barbwire around a section of land large enough to hold about 100 units. I put the fencing up so it could be relocated for expansion. I put up security lights (on a timer) and let two Dobermans run loose when the yard was locked. The yard was open from 7:30 a.m. to 9:30 a.m. and from 4:00 p.m. to 6:00 p.m. For opening at any other time we charged a $5 fee.

At first my wife handled the yard. Within three months we had to increase the size of the yard. Within six months, our income from our storage yard far exceeded my salary, so I quit my job to devote full time to my storage yard. I eventually had well over 1,000 tenant units, from small trailers to bulldozers at rates ranging from $15 to $50 per month.

My total cash investment for my yard was less than $6,000. (I financed the fencing.) It provided great income for more than 20 years. In the back of my mind was always the thought that the land price would eventually be so great that I would be better off selling. Well, it recently hit that point. I recently sold my 10 acres of highly desirable industrial land for $4.5 million. Actually, I didn't really sell it. We worked out a delayed exchange for new apartment units in order to defer taxes on the sale. (Editor's note: This will be covered in Chapter 12.)

A young person buying raw land might prefer buying larger tracts of land at lower prices. These larger parcels seldom fall significantly in value but can appreciate enormously.

People buying for retirement should be concerned with the quality of the land. They should buy smaller parcels of higher priced land within 30 miles of large residential centers (in excess of one-half million people) or within 5 miles of cities in the 50,000 population category. I recommend the parcel purchased be in the direction where greatest growth is forecast even though it will likely cost more than property in other areas.

And there are other possibilities.

My name is Oscar W. I purchased 40 acres about 20 miles outside a city where I lived. I paid $1,000 per acre for the parcel of marginal pasture land with large rocks and clumps of trees. I purchased the parcel with $4,000 down and monthly payments of $271.92 including interest at 7.75 percent. My idea was to retire at 62 (10 years after I purchased the parcel). I hoped to sell half the acreage then and have enough cash to pay off the other half, as well as cash for a downpayment to build a house.

It didn't work out the way I had it planned. I was able to retire at 58 and buy a Florida condominium. Six years after I purchased the property, I was able to sell my 40 acres to a developer for $550,000. My investment gave me the pride of ownership of the land, and a feeling of security and finally almost as much money from this one investment as I had earned in a working career of almost 40 years.

LOTS

Because of the costs of large parcels, some investors buy improved lots. While lots generally offer a lower profit potential than raw land, the profit can nevertheless be substantial. Bargain prices are possible on residential lots in periods of low building activity. In addition, the seller usually finances the buyer with a low downpayment. An advantage of improved lots over raw land is that lots are usually more readily salable than raw land.

The easiest residential lots to sell are the best lots in terms of location. Builders realize that a bargain price on a lot will often be regretted when it is time to sell.

Some positive features of good residential lots include:

- Trees.

- View.

- Size and shape. Larger lots and rectangular shaped lots are generally easier to sell than smaller, irregular shaped lots

- Slope. In many areas, a sloping lot is desirable because it allows for an open lower level or basement and is suited for an upper level deck. In some cases, a garage can be incorporated into the lower level.

During times when housing is undergoing a rapid appreciation in value, you may find that prices of new homes significantly exceed the cost of a lot plus the cost of construction. This is the time of opportunity. Buy lots. What generally happens is that builders seek to build as many units as they can to take advantage of the marketplace. The result is that the increased demand will cause lot prices to soar.

The opposite of the above is when resale prices of newer homes fall below the cost to build the home plus the value of the lot. If you see this happening, it's time to unload your lots quickly.

Some young people can't afford the downpayment or the payments on a house. They might, however, be able to purchase a lot. Lots can usually be purchased with low downpayments and at below-market interest rates.

Frequently, lot ownership can lead to home ownership. The lot, when paid for, will often give the buyer sufficient equity to qualify for a loan to build a house or provide the trading material to trade for a house. In addition, a lot purchase allows the buyer to tie down the price of a major portion of the total house costs.

As you can see, real estate investment covers a wide range of opportunities. You may have discovered that you are already a real estate investor but didn't realize it. Your investment choice should be based on your own needs as well as investments you feel comfortable with. Real estate can provide for your future: let it be the foundation. Remember, "under all is the land."

Analyzing Types of Investments

	Advantages	Disadvantages
Single-Family Homes	Easily financed. Most liquid of all real estate. High loan-to-value ratio (leverage). Appreciation possibilities. Readily rentable. Tax benefits of interest and property tax deductions. Readily refinanced to gain cash.	Can seldom be rented for enough to meet debt service. Risk of loss if sale is necessary. Management duties (if rented).
Apartments	Appreciation. Income. Depreciation. Tax shelter. Many prospective tenants.	Lower loan-to-value ratio (greater down payment). Management requirements. Risk of negative cash flow and/or loss on sale.
Commercial Property	Appreciation. Income. Depreciation. Tax shelter.	Illiquid. Risk of negative cash flow and/or loss on sale. Lower loan-to-value ratio and greater difficulty in financing and refinancing. Value and vacancies effected by local and national economy.
Industrial Property	Appreciation. Income. Depreciation. Tax shelter.	Can be vacant for years (limited number of prospective tenants). Can take a long time to sell. Risk of negative cash flow and/or loss on sale. Very low loan-to-value ratio. Value and vacancies effected by local and national economy. Possible liability for hazardous substances.
Farms	Lifestyle (if used as home). Appreciation. Income. Depreciation. Tax shelter. Special farm loans are available.	Strong risk of negative cash flow. Expensive management if not managed by owner which means a great deal of time. Risk of loss on sale.
Raw Land	Appreciation. Owner financing frequently available.	Always a negative cash flow investment. Illiquid. Risk of loss on sale. Difficulty to borrow on equity. Generally a long-term investment.
Lots	Appreciation. Owner financing frequently available.	Always a negative cash flow. While residential lots are more readily sold than other types of lots, they are still relatively illiquid.

Chapter 3

TAXATION AND REAL ESTATE

The spirit of property doubles a man's strength.

—Voltaire, 1764

With our progressive income tax, the more money you make, the more taxes you pay. As your regular income increases, the increases are taxed at increasingly higher tax rates. Because the federal tax brackets have not really been indexed for inflation, a cost-of-living increase means your take-home pay is actually lower in terms of purchasing power. As wages go up, higher percentages are taken for taxes.

It has become extremely difficult to accumulate substantial savings from a salary alone. Even when you are able to save, our tax laws tax the interest you earn as ordinary income, raising you still further up in the federal and state tax brackets. Our tax laws really have the net effect of penalizing people who are able to increase their earnings or who are able by thrift to save and earn interest on their savings.

Tax evasion is a federal crime, but tax avoidance is not only legal, it is just good common sense. It is still possible for an investor to work within the tax laws and pay little if any income taxes and yet have significant spendable income.

PROPERTY TAXES AND INTEREST DEDUCTIONS

Real estate makes tax sense. To start with, property taxes are a tax-deductible expense. (They are a deduction for all real estate.) Interest paid on home purchase loans for a principal residence and one second home is deductible providing the loan balance does not exceed the cost of the residence plus improvements and provided the indebtedness on the principal residence (plus secondary residence) does not exceed $1 million. (For debts incurred before October 13, 1987, there is no interest limit.) Interest on home equity loans up to

$100,000 is also deductible as long as all combined home loans don't exceed the fair market value of the home(s).

Because interest is a tax-deductible expense, Uncle Sam effectively reduces the rate of interest a tax payer must pay below the stated rate.

True Interest Costs

Based on an assumed 40% combined income tax bracket (federal and state)

Stated Rate	Net Cost to Taxpayer
12%	7.2%
11%	6.6%
10%	6.0%
9%	5.4%
8%	4.8%
7%	4.2%
6%	3.6%
5%	3.0%

Because of the deductibility of interest, a person can refinance real estate and obtain cash that is not taxed as income and have the interest paid a deductible expense. All interest for business and investment properties is deductible without limit.

Deferring Taxes (Two-Year Rule)

Gains from the sale of real estate are now taxed at the same rates as other income. However, it is possible for homeowners to defer taxes from the sale of their residence by buying another residence costing the same as or more than the sale price within two years of the sale. (The two years for purchase can be before or after the sale.) The homeowner keeps his or her old cost basis for tax purposes increased by the amount they paid over the sale price of their previous residence. For example:

Cost of Home #1	$ 28,000
Improvements to Home #1	$ 6,000
Sold for	$ 52,000
Cost of Home #2	$ 58,000
Sold for	$ 84,000
Cost of Home #3	$ 88,000
Improvements to Home #3	$ 24,000
Sold for	$192,000

If the homeowner purchased each home within two years of the sale of the prior residence, there would be no tax. Assume, however, that the homeowner is not going to buy another home after the sale of home 3. To determine the seller's cost basis we start with:

Cost of Home #1	$ 28,000
Improvements to Home #1	6,000
Added to proceeds of Home #1	
(to buy Home #2)	6,000
Added to proceeds of Home #2	
(to buy Home #3)	4,000
Improvements to Home #3	24,000
Adjusted cost basis of Home #3	$ 68,000

Taxable gain is the sales price less the adjusted cost basis:

Sale price	$192,000
Adjusted cost basis	- 68,000
Taxable gain	$112,000

$125,000 Exclusion

If in the case above the homeowners were 55 years of age or older and had lived in their residence (home 3) for three of the prior five years they would pay no taxes because there is a one-time 55 year or older exemption of $125,000.

If either spouse had taken this exemption in the past (previous marriage), then neither spouse is entitled to take it again. In cases of second marriages of persons over 55 years of age, the parties should determine if either has previously taken the exemption. If one spouse has and if the other spouse has significant appreciation in his or her residence, he or she would find it advantageous to sell the home prior to the marriage. In this way the exemption will not be lost.

If two persons are contemplating marriage and both are over 55 and each owns property that has appreciated and neither has taken the $125,000 exemption, both parties should sell prior to a marriage because it will effectively double their $125,000 tax benefit. If the parties were going to be in the 40 percent tax bracket (federal and state) after marriage, the sales prior to marriage would mean a real savings equivalent to $50,000 in cash (40 percent of $125,000).

I was told of a case where a couple did not realize the tax consequences of their marriage until after they were married. The couple divorced, sold their property, and thus regained their eligibility for the $125,000 exclusion. I don't know how the IRS views this procedure.

Installment Sales

Because income tax is progressive in nature, the tax rate increases with income. It is possible for some taxpayers to keep their income taxes at a lower rate by spreading the profit from a sale over a number of years. This benefit is available for total obligations under $5 million. Dealers cannot defer income by use of installment sales. Dealers are persons in the business of buying and selling property. In answer to a question posed to a CPA as to when a person is a dealer, the CPA replied, "When the IRS says you are one."

Depreciation for Tax Purposes

Many investors look for depreciation because depreciation is treated as an expense for tax purposes. While only a paper expense, since an owner pays nothing out, the expense offsets or shelters other income from taxation. Unfortunately, some investors buy a tax shelter rather than first analyzing it as an investment. Anyone can get a tax break because he lost money on a venture, and it doesn't take much intelligence to lose an entire investment. Don't buy a tax shelter; buy the total investment. Your first consideration should be: Is it a good investment? Look at the investment from the standpoint of appreciation and income. Depreciation is the frosting on the cake.

As stated, depreciation is a paper expense only. The IRS realizes assets such as an apartment building will not last forever. They therefore allow an owner to deduct an amount as depreciation that allows the owner to recoup the investment. Each year the investor deducts the amount of depreciation taken from the cost basis of the property. *Cost basis* is an owner's cost plus improvement made, less the depreciation that the owner has taken.

Only improvements can be depreciated. Land is never depreciated. Only property held for business and investment purposes can be depreciated. Therefore a homeowner cannot depreciate his or her own home. It is possible, however, to depreciate portions of a home used for business purposes providing the homeowner has no other office.

Residential property is depreciated over 27 1/2 years while nonresidential property is depreciated over 31 1/2 years. A straight-line method of depreciation is used for tax purposes, which means that an equal amount is depreciated each year until the asset has been fully depreciated. For a residential property you would depreciate $1/_{27.5}$ per year ($27\frac{1}{2}$ year life) or 3.636% per year, ($^{100\%}/_{27.5}$ = 3.636%). Therefore, if a depreciable improvement cost $100,000, the owner would show $3,636 each year as a depreciation expense until the asset was fully depreciated. Prior to the 1986 Tax Reform Act, a shorter depreciation life was possible as were accelerated depreciation methods that allowed greater depreciation after purchase of an asset in its early years.

To gain the greatest depreciation, an owner will want to apportion as much of the purchase price as possible to improvements and as little as possible to the land. Remember, land cannot be depreciated. One way to go is to use the same proportion of land to value as the tax assessor does. For example, if the tax assessor has shown 95 percent of the value attributable to improvement and only 5 percent to the land, you can use this apportionment even though it might not necessarily reflect a proper apportionment. The IRS will generally accept the value apportionment of a tax assessor. While tax assessors tend to place less value on the land than appraisers would, this is not always the case. Should you feel the tax assessment proportions are not realistic, you should have a fee appraisal made and then base the value of your depreciable improvements on your cost and the proportion of value the appraiser placed on the improvements. (Keep in mind that you depreciate from your cost, not from an appraised value.)

TAX SHELTERING

Assume a property has a cash flow of $5,000. This means that the cash income exceeds cash expenditures by $5,000 for the year. In other words, the investor has $5,000 spendable cash in his or her pocket. If the property also had depreciation of $10,000 in that year, it would mean that the property actually suffered a paper loss of $5,000. Not only would the $5,000 in spendable income not be taxed, but the $5,000 loss could offset $5,000 of additional income. The depreciation "shelters" this income from taxation. Real estate is the only real tax shelter left for the average investor.

The 1986 Tax Reform Act has limited this tax shelter. Real estate losses are considered passive losses. Passive losses can still be used to offset passive income (from other real estate) without limit. In other words, if you show a loss on one property of $100,000, it will offset $100,000 in what otherwise would be taxable income from another property. The 1986 Tax Reform Act also limited a taxpayer's ability to shelter active income (income from wages and other activities) with passive losses.

Investors with an adjusted gross income of less than $100,000 can use passive real estate losses to shelter up to $25,000 of income from other sources. For taxpayers having between $100,000 and $150,000 of adjusted gross income, this shelter has been phased out. For each two dollars adjusted gross income over $100,000, the $25,000 limit is reduced by one dollar. Therefore, an investor whose adjusted gross income was $120,000 would be limited to a $15,000 tax shelter. This investor could still use real estate losses to offset $15,000 of active income as well as unlimited gains from other passive real estate investments.

Another limitation imposed by the 1986 Tax Reform Act is that investors who do not actively manage their property cannot use their passive losses to shelter any active income. This means that investors who purchased limited partnership shares or similar investment can no longer use these paper losses from depreciation as a shelter against other income.

If a person has a tax shelter, such as a limited partnership (syndicate) interest that cannot be used as a tax shelter, there is one way it can still benefit her. If she buys a second limited partnership interest that has a taxable income, then the loss from the first limited partnership can be used to shelter the income from the second limited partnership.

LOSSES FROM A SALE

For income and investment property a loss from a sale (capital loss) can be used to offset a gain from another sale. (You suffer a loss when your adjusted cost basis is greater than the sale price.)

If you are going to take a loss on a sale, you want the loss to be worthwhile. You want to be able to fully use it. You should consider selling property that has appreciated in value in the same year as you take your loss. In this way your loss will shelter a gain. If you don't have a gain, then you are able to use your loss to shelter $3,000 of other income from taxation. You can carry your excess loss forward and shelter $3,000 each year in subsequent years until your loss is used up. (This only applies to income and investment property.)

While gains from the sale of your residence would be taxable, losses from the sale of your residence will not be recognized. Some taxpayers will change the character of their personal residence to income property so they can depreciate it and lower their adjusted cost basis to avoid the loss. By renting your home you might be able to change the character of the home to income property in order to utilize a sale loss, but please see an accountant or tax attorney before you do anything.

TAX-FREE EXCHANGES

Tax-free exchanges allow the taxpayer to get the equity out of his or her property and into another property without paying any tax on the appreciation in value of the property. Tax-free exchanges are covered in detail in Chapter 12.

Chapter 4

UNDERSTANDING FINANCING

> The best investment on earth is earth.
> —Louis Glickman, 1957

It is unusual for a buyer of real estate to pay cash for a purchase. Besides the fact that the amount of cash required is very large, a cash purchase normally is not generally good business. The average sale is generally financed either by an individual, in the case of the seller financing the buyer, or by a lending institution. Lending institutions use money supplied by savers who are satisfied with a comparatively low rate of return coupled with safety. By using financing to buy real estate, you use other people's money (OPM) to make money for yourself.

METHODS OF FINANCING

The three primary instruments of financing are mortgages, trust deeds and land contracts.

Mortgages

A mortgage is a two-party instrument in which the mortgagor (borrower) gives a promissory note and a mortgage to a mortgagee (lender).

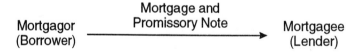

Mortgagor (Borrower) ⟶ Mortgage and Promissory Note ⟶ Mortgagee (Lender)

While the mortgagee is customarily a lending institution such as a savings and loan association, sometimes the seller finances the buyer. When this happens, the seller is the mortgagee and takes a mortgage as security for the balance of the purchase price.

A mortgage is recorded with the county recorder. Once recorded, it gives notice of the mortgagee's interest in the mortgaged property. When the mortgagor pays off the mortgage, the mortgagee gives the mortgagor a satisfaction of the mortgage, which is also recorded. Once the satisfaction of mortgage is on record, the mortgagee's interest in the mortgaged property is terminated.

Should the mortgagor default on the payments or fail to pay the taxes or insurance, the mortgagee can foreclose on the mortgage. In some states, the mortgagor is given a period of redemption in which to pay off the loan after the foreclosure sale.

When a mortgage is foreclosed, the property is sold at auction. If the sale brings less than the amount owing to the mortgagee, in some states it is possible to get a deficiency judgment against the mortgagor for the balance. However, in many states deficiency judgments are either not possible or are very difficult to obtain. I recommend that you check with an attorney in your state to determine your state's laws regarding deficiency judgments so you understand your liability in the event of foreclosure.

Trust Deeds

In order to avoid the lengthy redemption period allowed for a mortgagor in default, many states have gone to trust deeds. A trust deed is a three-party instrument by which a borrower (trustor) makes payments on a note to a lender (beneficiary). In order to provide the beneficiary with greater security, the trustor actually gives title (a trust deed) to a third person (trustee) to hold.

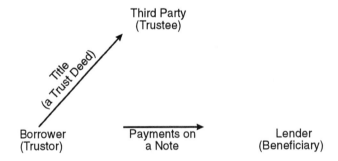

Like the mortgage, the trust deed is recorded to show the interest of the beneficiary. When the trustor has paid the beneficiary in full, the beneficiary orders the trustee to return the title to the trustor. This is done with a deed of reconveyance from the trustee to the trustor. Once the deed of reconveyance is recorded, the interest of the beneficiary is terminated. In the event the trustor defaults, foreclosure is relatively quick. After a short notice period, usually several months, the trustee has a sale and the trustor's interest is lost. Generally, no redemption period is allowed after the sale.

Land Contracts

A land contract (contract of sale or contract for deed) is a two-party instrument in which the vendor (seller) retains title and the vendee (buyer) is merely given possession. The vendee does not receive a deed until the vendor has been paid.

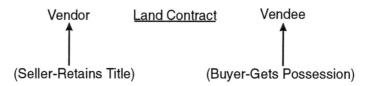

Land contracts are normally used in situations in which the seller is financing a buyer who is buying with a relatively low downpayment. Since, under a land contract, the seller retains the best possible security, the title, foreclosure is generally relatively quick and simple. However, foreclosure under a land contract in some states can be as time consuming as for a mortgage. While most states have legislation to protect the vendee, land contracts can still be dangerous. The vendor might be unable to deliver clear title after the vendee has paid for the property. It is now possible for the vendee under a land contract to obtain title insurance for protection. I recommend such insurance very strongly. The vendee should also insist that the land contract be recorded.

The priority of mortgages, trust deeds, and land contracts is determined by the time and date of recording. A mortgage that is recorded later than another one on the same property is a second mortgage, which makes it a secondary lien. (A lien is a claim or charge against property. A creditor can enforce a lien by foreclosing or forcing the sale of the debtor's property to pay off the claim.) The problem with a secondary (junior) lien such as a second mortgage is that, should a prior lien be foreclosed, the junior lien is wiped out. In order to protect their interests, holders of junior liens can generally step in and make the payments on the foreclosing lien, thus stopping foreclosure. They can then foreclose on their junior liens. In this way they end up owning the property with a prior lien on it. If a junior lienholder waits for the foreclosure sale of a prior lien, he or she then has to bid cash to protect his or her interests.

PRIMARY FINANCING

Primary financing refers to first mortgages and trust deeds. These loans are usually made by institutional lenders, such as banks, savings and loan institutions, and insurance companies. Banks generally prefer short-term, high-interest loans. They therefore like construction loans, which seldom exceed two years and bear a high interest rate. They will also finance personal property such as furniture involved in a sale. Banks will make home purchase loans although they will often resell these loans to other institutions.

Banks prefer home equity loans, which are second mortgages (or trust deeds) and are at a higher rate of interest than purchase loans. Many banks will preapprove you for a home equity loan up to a stated amount. This really serves much like a line of credit because it becomes a quick source of cash. By having preapproval for a home equity loan, you will have the ability to act quickly if an advantageous opportunity arises.

Insurance companies prefer larger loans for commercial or large residential projects. They often insist on an equity participation (participation loan). They are generally not much help to small investors.

Savings and loans, since deregulation, can make both first mortgages (primary financing) and second mortgages (secondary financing). Savings and loan institutions can make relatively large (loan-to-value ratio) loans. Savings and loans will often agree to a lower downpayment if you agree to pay for private mortgage insurance (PMI).

What savings and loans can do and will do, however, are not the same. Because of past abuses, regulators have scared many savings and loans to the point where they now turn down loans that historically would have been considered desirable.

Mortgage bankers are private money lenders who generally use their own money to originate loans. They sell the loans (on the secondary mortgage market) to insurance companies, pension plans, trusts, etc. Mortgage bankers have been growing in importance as a source of real estate financing.

SECONDARY FINANCING

Secondary financing refers to second mortgages and trust deeds. In the case of purchase money loans, the loans are carried by the seller. Otherwise, they are made by institutional and noninstitutional lenders. Noninstitutional lenders include private individuals, mortgage brokers, union pension funds, and trusts. Because secondary financing involves a greater risk than first mortgages, the interest rate for these loans is higher. As a general rule, the greater the risk, the higher the interest rate the lender will demand. In some states usury laws limit the interest an unlicensed lender can charge to a rate lower than lenders are willing to accept. In these states the sources for hard money loans through private lenders has dried up.

Mortgage loan brokers are active in the secondary financing market, although they can arrange primary financing. They advertise to the public that it's easy to borrow on a home. They also advertise for investors by emphasizing a high rate of return. The mortgage loan brokers charge commissions and fees for putting borrowers and lenders together. They are really expensive loan middlemen.

Good-Guy/Bad-Guy Lenders

Conventional lenders will often resell loans they make to Fannie Mae (Federal National Mortgage Association—FNMA) or Freddie Mac (Federal Home Loan Mortgage Corporation—FHLMC). These organizations buy FHA, VA and conventional loans that conform to their guidelines (conforming loans).

Bob Bruss, the syndicated real estate columnist, has come up with a practical classification of lenders as good guys and bad guys.

Good-guy lenders are lenders who keep the loan. Because of this, the loan does not need to conform to loan standards of Fannie Mae and Freddie Mac. He considers these loans standards unreasonable at times in that they act to constrain what could otherwise be healthy real estate market. Good-guy lenders are more flexible and are not likely to turn down a loan because the borrower's credit history reveals a late payment three years previously.

Bad-guy lenders are lenders who intend to sell the mortgages they make on the secondary mortgage market. These lenders are at the mercy of Fannie Mae and Freddie Mac. If Fannie Mae or Freddie Mac reject a loan they originate, then they are stuck with it. In some cases they have to agree to buy back loans that default in order to sell them. Because of this, bad-guy lenders want every "I" dotted and "T" crossed. If they have any doubts at all, they reject the loan.

Some lenders are bad guys on their fixed-rate mortgages but good guys on their adjustable rate mortgages, which are less risky for them. When shopping for a loan, ask if they are going to keep the loan or if they intend to resell it.

Think twice about advancing significant loan application costs to a lender who is a bad guy unless you are certain you will pass the qualifications with flying colors. Incidentally, if you are self-employed, look for a good guy. Bad guys are tough on self-employed borrowers.

Assuming Loans

When you purchase a property that has an existing loan against it, you can either refinance it, which means that the old loan is paid off and a new loan placed against the property, or you can "assume" or "take subject to" the existing loan. A loan can be assumed if it does not include a prohibition on assumption (a due-on-sale clause). When you assume a loan, you agree to be liable for it. Depending on the state, you may be liable for a deficiency judgment should you assume a loan that is later foreclosed and the foreclosure sale yields less than is still owing on the loan.

A take subject to loan is different. You recognize that there is a loan against the property and that if you wish to keep the property you will have to make the payments on the loan. However, if you don't make the payments and the property is foreclosed, no deficiency judgment is possible against you because you never agreed to be obligated for the existing loan.

Due-on-Sale Clauses

Due-on-sale clauses (or alienation clauses) provide that upon transfer the entire loan balance is due and payable. Basically, they accelerate payment to the lender. Loans with due-on-sale clauses cannot be assumed or purchased subject to the loan.

Due-on-sale clauses are not enforceable for every transfer. They cannot be enforced when the transfer is to a spouse or children (divorce) or to an heir (death). There is no acceleration when the transfer is to a surviving joint tenant or when title is given to a living trust.

Many methods have been devised to avoid the acceleration of the due-on-sale clause, most of which involve keeping it a secret from the lender. If a lender doesn't know of a sale, he cannot enforce the due-on-sale clause. While some buyers take the position that the worst that can happen if the lender learns of the sale is the loan will have to be repaid, this can still present a real danger in that it could be discovered at a time of tight money where alternative financing is both costly and difficult to obtain. Another danger of secret agreements is the possibility that creditors of the seller will be able to foreclose the property. No matter how appealing avoidance of the due-on-sale clause may appear, an unrecorded interest presents too great a danger to the buyer.

One interesting method of avoiding a due-on-sale provision involved a commercial building where the owners were a corporation. The corporation assets consisted of just one large building. Instead of selling the building, which would have triggered the due-on-sale clause, the corporations sold the corporate stock. The corporate entity thus retained ownership, but the effect was the same as if a sale had taken place.

Lenders will sometimes agree to allow a change in manner of ownership (from individual ownership to a partnership or corporation) if the security for the loan is strong. The interest in the partnership or corporation can then be transferred and the due-on-sale provision of the loan can be avoided.

If a low-interest loan contains a due-on-sale clause and you think you have a method to avoid the clause, see an attorney. Understand the risks and pitfalls before you commit yourself. If you are going to use one of the alternative methods of getting around a due-on-sale clause, you want to be in a position where you can cover the risk of having to pay off the loan.

Bargaining with the Lender

When asked if a loan has a due-on-sale clause, lenders will almost automatically answer in the affirmative when the loan interest rate is below prevailing rates. Therefore, you should ask to see a copy of the note and mortgage. I have been told of a number of instances where lenders claim that a loan must be paid in full where it is later discovered the loan did not have a due-on-sale clause. Loans without due-on-sale clauses would generally be loans originated at least 20 years ago or loans made by private lenders.

If the current interest rate is the same or lower than the loan to be assumed, lenders will frequently agree to allow a loan assumption or a novation, which really is a substitution of parties to the existing loan. The reason you might want to assume a loan at the same or even higher interest rate than you could obtain with a new loan is loan costs. The costs associated with obtaining a new loan might raise the effective rate of the new loan above the rate of the loan to be assumed. In addition, assumption is much quicker than refinancing.

If a lender, after knowing of a prior loan assumption, failed to enforce the due-on-sale clause, the lender could have jeopardized his rights. Failure to enforce a due-on-sale provision could result in a court determination that the lenders had waived their rights to a later enforcement of the due-on-sale clause, even upon a later loan assumption. While you may not want to chance a lawsuit because of both time and expense, you could use the prior waiver as a bargaining tool with a lender. For example, you could agree to a slightly higher interest rate while asking that the loan be increased.

Some lenders with an inventory of many foreclosed properties will not enforce a due-on-sale provision even when they learn of a sale. The one thing they don't want is another foreclosure. Nevertheless, they may indicate they will foreclose. If you can cover the loan you might want to call their bluff, if it is one, by telling them to go ahead and foreclose and they will just have one more problem property. While I have seen this bluff work with a large loan where the owner's equity was relatively small, it is less likely to work if the owner has significant equity. If you are going to bluff, you had better be prepared to pay off the loan if the lender calls your bluff.

If a below-market-interest-rate loan is assumable, you can also bargain with the lender. You can point out that you could assume the loan and obtain secondary financing, or as an alternative the lender could refinance the property with a new higher interest rate loan at a greater amount. The lender, by advancing additional money will thus clear its books of a low-yield loan.

For example, assume there is an existing $100,000 loan at 7 percent interest. You might offer to increase the rate to 9 percent if the lender agrees to increase the loan to $150,000. Point out that this really means the lender effectively receives 13 percent interest on the $50,000 that the lender advances:

2% increase on $100,000 or 4% on $50,000 plus 9% on $50,000
= 13% for the additional $50,000 advance.

If a loan is not assumable, you should strive for a new "blended rate" loan—a rate of interest higher than the rate on the current loan, but nevertheless lower than the market rate of interest. If the seller has little equity in the property and the alternative could well be the lender ending up owning the property, the lender might be persuaded to accept less than market interest on a new loan. Again, in a depressed market, a lender does not want to own more real estate. The same is true for problem properties.

You may run into a loan officer who absolutely refuses to even consider allowing a loan assumption. I suggest an end run if this happens. Send a certified letter to the president of the lending institution pointing out that you tried to help the institution and prevent them from having to accept ownership and management of a property with serious problems, but their loan officer refused to work with you on a loan assumption. From the experience of those who have used this technique lately, you have a very good chance of receiving a call from a loan officer who is willing to work something out with you.

LOAN TYPES AND TERMS

Amortized and Unamortized Loans

Amortized loans pay off total interest and principal in equal payments over the full term of the loan. Unamortized and partially amortized loans have balloon payments. They have a series of equal payments followed by a last, usually significantly (balloon) larger payment. Customarily such a loan will include a statement like "all due and payable in __ years."

As a buyer you should be aware of the fact that if a loan has a balloon payment, it means that you will have to make a very large payment—much more than the regular monthly payment—when the loan comes due. If you are unable to obtain refinancing or otherwise cannot make the balloon payment, you could be foreclosed. Usually you can expect to obtain refinancing because of your increased equity. However, it is wise to arrange new financing well in advance. Often, by agreeing to increase the interest rate before the balloon payment is due, you can persuade the person holding the loan to extend it. But it depends on the market. Lenders tend to be very cooperative in a depressed real estate market, less so in a hot market.

Seller financing and some adjustable rate loans are often structured with very low payments but negative loan amortization. When there is negative amortization, the amount you owe increases rather than decreases with each payment. Your payments, while low, are not sufficient to pay the interest that is accruing. Before you get yourself into a negative amortization situation, realize that the day of reckoning will come. Eventually, you will have to refinance. The amount of your payment will be significantly more than if you had gone with an amortized loan in the first place.

A *straight loan*, or *term loan*, is a loan with payments of interest only. Because the loan is not amortized, the payments are lower than for a loan that repays the principal as well as the interest. Straight loans are due in full at a set date. Because the entire principal must be paid at a specified date, the owner must generally refinance the property. Payments on an amortized loan are only a few percentage points higher than the payments on a straight loan. Because of this, you would only want a straight loan when you absolutely must keep payments as low as possible.

Prepayment Penalties

Loans frequently have prepayment penalties. Lenders feel that the agreement is for a long-term loan and that by wanting to pay the loan off early, the borrower is breaching the agreement. They feel that the penalty is justified because it takes time and money to put the money out again to earn interest. Lenders frequently require six months' interest on the loan balance for prepayment.

Lenders will ask for this prepayment penalty even when you wish to prepay a loan that is at a rate of interest below the current market rate. You can very often talk a lender into waiving the prepayment penalty by indicating that you don't have to prepay but will only do so if the penalty is waived. If the lender believes that you are selling the property and it will be refinanced, then the lender will refuse to waive it.

If a loan allows payments of a set dollar amount "or more" per month, there can be no prepayment penalty. The borrower has the right to prepay.

While normally only found in personal property loans, some states allow some real estate loans (generally nonresidential) to have lock-in clauses. These clauses are vicious because while they allow the borrower to prepay a loan, they lock her into paying all interest as if the loan had gone to maturity. Even with a lock-in clause, lenders are frequently willing to negotiate a prepayment penalty much lower than they are entitled to.

Hard Money Loan

A hard money loan is a loan in which the lender actually supplies cash. The lender either puts up money for the borrower to buy property or gives an owner money based on the security of the property. Hard money loans bear a high market rate of interest.

Purchase Money Loan (Soft Money Loan)

A purchase money loan is a loan in which the seller finances the buyer. The seller really carries the loan, or paper. Suppose an owner sells a property to a buyer taking a downpayment. If the balance of the purchase price were a mortgage given by the purchaser to the seller, then the seller is financing the purchaser.

Sellers will frequently carry the paper on loans at a lower interest rate than would be required for a hard money loan. One reason is that individual sellers cannot usually get a higher rate of interest on a long-term investment. If a seller is only getting 3.5 percent at a savings and loan association, he or she might be willing to carry paper at 6 percent even though the going mortgage rate is 8 percent. Another reason is that the part of the purchase price carried by the seller is usually mostly profit. Sellers are often so interested in the dollars they will receive as profit that they fail to realize that the interest can be a material part of their profit.

15-Year Loan versus 30-Year Loan

Because of lower lender risk, lenders are willing to give 15-year loans at from .125 percent to about .5 percent lower interest rates than they are asking for 30-year loans.

While a longer amortization period means a lower loan payment, a longer amortization period also means significantly more money spent on interest. If you can afford a slightly higher payment, consider the following facts:

- The monthly payment to amortize $100,000 for 30 years at 8 percent interest is $733.77.

- The monthly payment to amortize $100,000 for 15 years at 8 percent is $955.66 or $221.89 more per month. However, let us see the effect of that $221.89 per month:

  $733.77 \times 12 = \$8,805.24$ in annual payments $\times 30 = \$264,157.20$ total payments on an 8 percent, 30-year loan. If we deduct the $100,000 principal payment, we can see that we are paying $164,157.20 in interest.

- On a 15-year loan the payment of $955.66 \times 12 = \$11,467.92$ per year $\times$ 15 = $172,018.80. When we deduct the principal we can readily see that at 8 percent interest a $100,000, 15-year loan has total interest of only

$72,018.80. A 30-year loan for the same amount and interest rate totals more than twice the amount of interest at $164,157.20. If the 15-year loan were at a lower rate (which is usually the case), the difference in interest paid would be even greater.

Table 4–1 clearly shows you the advantage of paying off a loan with the shortest amortization period possible.

On loans that allow the borrower to pay more than the loan payment, a borrower can save considerable interest by making an additional payment each year. The borrower must make certain it is a payment on the principal or a lender could regard it simply as an early payment.

Wrap-Around Loan

A wrap-around loan is seller financing where a new loan is written to cover the existing loans plus the seller's equity. This kind of loan enables a seller to keep the benefits of a below-market-rate assumable loan.

The same net effect of a wrap-around loan can be obtained by use of a land contract (contract for deed). The land contract would be written at a higher rate of interest than the seller is paying on the existing loan(s). The seller then takes advantage of the interest differential.

Adjustable Rate Mortgage (ARM)

An adjustable rate mortgage has an interest rate that can be raised or lowered during the term of the loan. The interest is usually tied to a cost-of-funds rate, a Treasury rate, or a prime rate. When the interest rate increases, the payments increase.

It is very difficult for a borrower to compare adjustable rate mortgages offered by different lenders because they tend to differ in a number of key areas such as:

- Loan costs (points, appraisal fees, fixed fees, etc.)

- Initial or teaser interest rate

Table 4–1 $100,000 Amortized Loan at 8%

Length of Loan	Monthly Payment
10 Years	$1,082.46
15 Years	955.66
20 Years	836.45
30 Years	733.77
35 Years	710.27
40 Years	695.32

- Period of time that the initial rate is guaranteed for
- Total cap on increases in interest
- Cap on annual increases
- Negative amortization (allowed or not allowed)
- Assumability of the loan (APR loans are often assumable).

An adjustable rate loan has some advantages. The *initial interest rate*, or teaser rate, is usually below market. Often this rate is guaranteed for one year. This allows buyers to qualify for a loan when they could not qualify at the going market rate. The lower loan cost will allow you to work to raise a property's income so that you will have the income to make the payments when they increase. This is particularly important on property having a high vacancy rate or requiring work to bring it up to its income potential.

The danger of an adjustable rate loan is that you don't know what your expenses will be. You must ask yourself if you can make the payments if the interest rates rise to the loan ceiling. If not, you should consider a fixed-rate loan.

During tight money periods, lenders will often insist on adjustable rate loans. The opportunity to raise the interest rate reduces the lender's risk. When there is competition between lenders to get their money out, lenders will offer long-term fixed-rate loans as well as adjustable rate mortgages. They will, of course, use a low teaser rate to persuade borrowers to take the ARM loan.

Investors who only expect to hold a property for a few years like adjustable rate loans as opposed to fixed-rate loans. The reason is that they can take advantage of a low initial interest rate. The adjustable rate loan also has lower initial loan costs and fees and might also allow prepayment without penalty. In addition, the loan is likely to be assumable. However, if the investor intends to hold the property for more than around three years, a fixed-rate loan might be preferable.

Rollover Loan (Short-Term Fixed-Rate)

A rollover loan is a short-term fixed-rate loan often for 5 to 7 years. The payments are usually based on a long-term (20 to 30 year) amortization schedule. When the loan is due, the borrower has the option of paying the loan off or refinancing a new rollover loan at the current interest rate. Rollover loans reduce lender risk in that they are not tied to what might become a below-market interest rate for a long period of time.

In order to induce borrowers to accept these short-term loans, lenders offer a lower interest rate (up to .5 percent) and/or eliminate or reduce loan costs.

When you expect to have a short holding period, these short-term loans make sense.

Government Loans

Government loans are government-insured by the FHA or guaranteed by the VA. FHA loans are only for housing, including homes, apartments, mobile homes, and even mobile parks. VA loans are for homes, farms, or businesses. The federal Farmers Home Administration also offers loans. Since government loans are generally made at rates of interest lower than those charged by institutional lenders, they should be considered.

Many different types of federal loans are available. Some programs are limited by insufficient funds, but often available loans are without takers. The following is only a partial listing of the special loans available: home improvement, single-family homes, farm labor housing, rental housing, housing for the elderly, housing for the military personnel, low-income housing, mobile homes, mobile home parks, housing sites, nursing homes, hospitals, medical office buildings, farms, industrial development, and recreational enterprises. I strongly recommend that you become familiar with available FHA and Farmers Home Administration programs. For information on FHA loans, write:

> U. S. Department of Housing and
> Urban Development
> Washington, DC 20250

For information on Farmers Home Administration loans, write:

> U. S. Department of Agriculture
> Farmers Home Administration
> Washington, DC 20250

FHA Loans. Title I FHA loans are for home improvement and Title II loans are for home purchase (one to four residential units). FHA loans have a maximum amount that varies by the area of the country. FHA loans originated prior to December 15, 1989, are assumable. Loans made since then are only assumable by owner-occupants who qualify for the loan.

Because of the low downpayment requirements, you should consider an FHA loan if you are buying a home for your primary residence. FHA loans are made by conventional lenders.

VA Loans. These veteran loans are for home, farm, or business. Currently, the VA does not require any downpayment for loans up to $184,000 although lenders may require downpayments. VA loans, which are guaranteed, are also made by conventional lenders. For housing loans the veteran must intend to occupy the premises. Loans originally made prior to March 1, 1988, are assumable by anyone. Loans made after this date are only assumable if the buyer qualifies for the loan. Because of the no or low downpayment requirements, VA loans should be considered by eligible veterans for the purchase of one to four units.

State Loans. Many states have loan programs, such as special loans for veterans, first-time buyers and/or low-income families. These loans are limited to home purchases for owner occupancy. The loans usually have either a very low or no downpayment and/or a below-market interest rate. If you qualify for such a loan, you should of course apply. One problem is that these loan funds are very limited and every applicant will not be successful.

Participation Loans

Participation loans create a limited partnership between the buyer and the lender. The lender receives an equity position in the property for giving the loan. When the loan plus interest is paid off, the lender still has an ownership interest.

Insurance companies often demand a significant equity position when making large commercial loans. They are successful because of their economic clout. Some private lenders do the same thing. Where a borrower would otherwise have difficulty in obtaining financing, the insurance company will put up the money if they receive a sweetener. The sweetener is ownership up to 50 percent.

This concept is turned around by some investors. In cases where they are seeking 100 percent financing on properties they have lined up, they offer the lender an equity position as a limited partner for a lower interest rate. Investors who use this approach don't look at it as giving away part of an investment. They take a positive approach: they are getting equity in a property that will pay for itself without any downpayment.

Sharing Appreciation Mortgage (SAM)

A SAM is a type of participation loan. The lender typically puts up all or part of the downpayment, allowing the buyer the chance to own a home. The home is sold or offered to the buyer (for refinancing) after a set period of time. The appreciation in value during the holding period is then split between lender and home buyer.

For equity sharing to pay off, there must be appreciation. An investor could find himself or herself with the equivalent of a zero interest loan should the property fail to appreciate. With sales costs, the investor could lose money. This is the danger of setting time limits for selling property. Another danger to the investor is by the owner-occupant. The occupant likely has possession with little or no money down, and since the occupant is a co-owner, a simple eviction might not be possible. There have been horror stories about the occupant retaining possession for over a year without making any payments while the owner sought to foreclose the co-owner's interests. To avoid this problem, equity-sharing agreements should clearly indicate that the co-owner takes possession as a tenant, not as an owner.

Equity-sharing percentages of ownership are agreed upon by the parties. The advantage to the buyer-occupant is:

- Little or no downpayment

- Tax and interest deduction

- A share of the appreciation

The investor gets:

- Appreciation (share)

- Depreciation

- Taxes and interest deduction (if share in payments)

The best equity sharing is between family members where one member advances the downpayment. Equity sharing allows the relative to have a secure loan and an opportunity to share in appreciation.

The typical equity-sharing agreement includes:

- Title ownership with both parties

- Percentage of ownership

- Buyout agreement

- Profit split on refinance or sale

- Arbitration of disputes

- Payments for capital improvements and extraordinary repairs (cost splitting)

- Rental agreement

FINDING MONEY

Besides contacting local lenders and mortgage bankers, there are other sources of funds.

Advertising for Financing

One way to reduce your borrowing cost as well as obtain financing is to advertise for it. Many newspapers have classified sections for loans. The following is an example:

$46,000 Needed
Will pay 12½% on well secured second mortgage.

To make the loan attractive, you could offer prospective lenders a due-on-sale clause as well as a balloon payment in 5 to 7 years.

My name is Pat L. I frequently buy property with 100 percent financing and, in some cases, I actually borrow more than my purchase price. This means I am a cash-out buyer.

What I do is look for motivated sellers of income property where I can envision a positive cash flow and/or sales profit by raising rents, improving the property, or changing the use of the property.

I will put in a purchase offer that requires the seller to carry financing. My offers normally call for 80 percent to 90 percent total financing in new loans, loan assumptions, and/or seller financing.

I strive for below-market financing. For example, assume I can get 6 percent financing of 80 percent on a $100,000 purchase price when the market interest is around 9 percent. (It is quite easy with motivated sellers—all you need do is ask.)

Then, I would advertise as follows:

12% Interest
I will pay 12% interest on a $20,000 mortgage
on a quality property for a 10-year loan.

If I am able to locate a lender, my total loan cost is 7.2 percent, which is still a below-market interest rate.

$$80\% \text{ at } .06 \ (6\%) = 4.8\%$$
$$20\% \text{ at } .12 \ (12\%) = \underline{2.4\%}$$
$$7.2\% \text{ interest}$$

The lenders for the second mortgage make an above-market mortgage rate from a borrower who consistently has met his or her commitments, and I get 100 percent financing. I have found that it pays to advertise.

(Author's note: Make certain that the second mortgage does not violate state usury limitations on private loans.)

If you have a mortgage you are collecting on, you can offer to sell the mortgage without having to sell it at a discount (less than face value) by agreeing to guarantee payments. You could guarantee the payments by giving other property or mortgages to a trustee who would sell the property should the mortgage default, or use the income to pay the defaulting mortgagor's payments.

Because of the personal liability, you should only agree to this on well secured loans with a history of prompt payment. Such a loan could be advertised as:

10% Guaranteed yield
Well secured and seasoned second mortgage (guaranteed
by _____) being sold at the face value of
$ _____. Call _____at _____.

Real estate licensees who wish to guarantee mortgages should check with an attorney because some states place regulations on licensees who guarantee loans.

Money Finders

If you are unable to find mortgage money, there are professionals who will do so for a fee. Their fees vary with the market, although 10 percent is not unusual for hard-to-obtain loans. Inquiries to bankers, commercial brokers, and industrial brokers should reveal if any money finders are active in your area.

Avoid anyone who wants an advance fee. Chances are you will never hear from that person again unless it is for another advance. There are quite a few shady operators who claim to be able to find money. Beware of the deal that is too good to be true. The loan through an offshore bank at a below-market interest rate with a hint that it is either Arab oil money or Columbian drug money being laundered is very likely neither. The money-finder agreement may require a hefty fee upon loan commitment. The borrower will receive formal papers (usually by Federal Express) that the loan has been approved and the fee must be paid. Of course, no loan will ever be made and the lender's office is just a mail drop.

Evaluating Alternatives

As in buying anything else, you should shop the available loans. Differences in interest rates, points, and loan terms can be significant. Look for the loan that best meets your needs.

In evaluating various loan possibilities consider:

- Interest rate
- Loan period
- Fixed rate or adjustable (terms of adjustable)
- Balloon payment or amortized
- Possibility of negative amortization
- Prepayment penalty

- Loan costs (appraisal fees, fixed fees, points, etc.)

Points are charged by lenders when they feel the rate of interest is insufficient. For example, suppose a lender could make a good, safe, long-term investment at 8.5 percent interest and you want a loan at 8 percent. The lender would be foolish to give you a loan at a lower rate of interest than was available elsewhere. By obtaining points, the lender makes up for this differential. As a rule of thumb, 8 points are considered equal to a 1 percent interest differential. To give you the loan at a .5 percent interest advantage, the lender will ask for four points. This will give the lender the equivalent of an 8.5 percent return.

The most important thing is to look at the end result of the purchase, not at the interest rate.

Refinancing

While real estate is an illiquid investment, it is possible to pump money out of an investment by refinancing a property. What you are doing is milking your inflation cow by taking out your swollen equity. As a property increases in value with appreciation, further refinancing is possible.

One Los Angeles investor I know has refinanced the same property four times in a little over 12 years. Each time he refinances, he takes more cash out. He uses the cash to "pyramid" by acquiring more properties. He then refinances the new properties as soon as he is able to take out significant cash. He started on his career by refinancing his home to obtain the downpayment on a fourplex and has continued ever since.

This process of borrowing on one property to invest in another offering a rate of return greater than must be paid to borrow the money is known as *trading on your equity*. It is an important tool for pyramiding yourself into more and more properties.

The investor I have told you about never sells, just refinances to increase his holdings. He is not really concerned that refinancing often turns a positive cash flow into a break-even situation, as long as he can still make the payments.

You should consider refinancing when interest rates drop. As a general rule, it makes sense to refinance if your savings in interest within three years will make up for prepayment penalties and new loan costs.

Arbitrage

Arbitrage is the term given to making money on the interest differential when you buy at one interest rate and sell at a higher rate.

About 30 years ago many people had great difficulty in obtaining home loans. At the time, lenders only considered part of the wages of married women when they were of childbearing age. Single men and single women also had a difficult time obtaining financing, as did minorities.

One couple had excellent credit and purchased a great number of homes, primarily by loan assumptions. They resold the home with the identical down-payments they had paid, but asking a 10 percent increase in price plus a 2 percent interest differential. They found many trustworthy buyers who had been unable to obtain financing on their own and were eager for this chance to own homes.

On each $10,000 of their purchase price, the couple would obtain $1,000 in profit plus the interest on it. If they were obtaining 9 percent interest on a 20-year loan, the total payments for $1,000 profit would amount to $2,160. The 2 percent interest differential on each $10,000 of the land contract over a 20-year loan period amounts to $3,086. Therefore, for each $10,000 in loans the couple agreed to be obligated on, they would receive a total of $5,246 in interest and profit over the period of the loan. The best part was that they had none of their own money left in the transaction. Using this simple formula, the couple purchased and resold more than 50 homes. They had only one foreclosure, which they actually resold at a profit. The interest differential on well over one million dollars in loans became their own retirement annuity.

For you as a seller, it can be far more advantageous to sell on land contract or with a wrap-around loan than to have the buyer assume a low-interest loan and give you a second mortgage for the balance. Of course, if you are a buyer, you will want to assume the existing loan and give the seller a second mortgage for the balance of the purchase price.

Usury Laws

Real estate investors must be aware of their state usury laws. Generally, individuals are precluded from charging more than a maximum rate of interest. Loans above that rate are regarded as usurious. Depending on state law, usurious interest may be uncollectible or will be set at a legal rate. There may also be severe penalties for usurious interest collected.

Seller financing is generally exempt from usury restrictions, but check with an attorney if you are unsure as to your state usury laws.

Evaluating Conventional Loans

Straight Loan	Because the total amount is due on due date and the payments are not much less than the payment on an amortized loan, this loan should only be used for short-term borrowing with a full understanding that if financing is not available on the due date, the property could be lost.
Amortized Loan	
15-Year Loan	If a borrower can make payments of 20-25% higher than those on a 30-year loan, the 15-year loan makes economic sense. While the same effect could be obtained by a borrower making additional payments, they seldom do so. This loan is a simple way to cut interest to less than half the costs on a 30-year loan. In addition, the interest rate is lower than for similar 30-year loans.
30-Year Loan	This is a loan of choice for most homebuyers who are usually obligating themselves to a maximum loan. Lower payments and locked in interest add to its desirability.
Adjustable Rate Mortgage	Because of a lower qualifying interest rate, these loans allow people to buy who otherwise could not become homeowners. The generally lower loan origination costs and an absence of a prepayment penalty make these loans particularly attractive to buyers who expect to resell in just a few years. On the negative side, buyers could find themselves unable to make the payments if the rate would increase to the cap.
Rollover Loan	These loans offer significantly lower interest rates which makes the loan qualifying easier than for amortized loans. They offer a danger in that the new loan (usually in 5-7 years) will be at a significantly higher market rate. They are best suited for borrowers who expect to resell in around 8 years or less.

Chapter 5

CREATIVE FINANCING

> When men have yielded without serious resistance to the
> tyranny of . . . dictators, it is because they have lacked property.
>
> —Walter Lippman
> *The Method of Freedom*

Creative financing is simply financing other than conventional financing. Some buyers can't qualify for conventional financing. The most common reason is the downpayment. But whatever the reason, if you can't qualify for conventional financing, creative financing is the way to go.

CONVINCING SELLERS TO FINANCE BUYERS

Most creative financing involves the seller financing the buyer. The buyer is often able to assume existing loans and give the seller a second mortgage for her equity. If a seller has no real need for cash, she might be persuaded to sell without any downpayment at all if she has faith in the buyer. Just because a seller asks for cash doesn't mean that she won't sell and carry the paper. If she intends simply to invest the sale proceeds in a savings account or bonds, she can frequently be induced to carry the paper by the offer of higher interest. After all, she knows the security value of the property.

If you ask a real estate agent if a seller will "carry back" financing, you might get a negative response even when the agent isn't certain. Some agents worry that carry-back financing won't leave them enough cash for their commissions. Your best bet, therefore, is to ask for seller financing even when agents have indicated the owner wants cash. It is easy for an owner to set forth his wish list when listing the property, but it becomes hard to throw out an offer when it is the only one the owner has seen.

The more difficult a property is to sell (because of market conditions or type of property), the easier it becomes to obtain seller financing. Thus, you are more likely to obtain seller financing in buying raw land than in any other type of real estate because it is the least liquid of all real estate and is a negative cash flow investment. (It costs an owner taxes even when the land is paid for.)

Owners are more likely to finance profit dollars than equity dollars reflecting actual cash invested. If an owner has owned a property for a number of years, you can assume you are asking the owner to finance profit dollars. In selling an owner on creative financing, you should be selling the idea for its benefits not simply as a way for them to sell the property. Benefits include:

1. Taxes. By taking the payments over a long period of time the seller is likely to be able to take his or her profit in a lower tax bracket. This is especially important to a seller who is retiring and whose income will be decreasing in the future.

2. Annuity value. Carrying the buyer will often give the owner a greater monthly return than if he or she purchased an insurance annuity package with the proceeds. In addition, the balance due is payable to the heirs upon the deaths of the sellers, while in an annuity returns are only for a lifetime.

3. Interest rates. Interest rates on seller carry-back financing are usually significantly higher than the owner can get from investing the sales proceeds in a certificate of deposit, government bonds or a money market account. With present CD rates low, this is a very strong argument for seller financing.

4. The owners are receiving more cash back at the sale than they originally invested as their downpayment. (This will likely be true if the owners have owned for a significant period.)

5. They are receiving profit well secured by their real estate.

METHODS AND TECHNIQUES

Assuming Loans

Even if you have the cash to meet the seller's downpayment requirement or to pay off the seller's equity in full, try to conserve your cash. Liquidity offers you protection in an emergency as well as allowing you to take advantage of additional investment opportunities that come along.

As a buyer, you want to assume or take subject to assumable favorable loans. An astute seller will want to sell on a land contract or with a wrap-around loan in order to take advantage of the lower interest rate rather than pass on the benefits to the purchaser. Keep in mind that while conventional lenders can be unyielding as to interest rates and terms, rates and terms are usually negotiable when the seller is carrying the loan.

Balloon Payment

In order to induce a seller to carry a loan, you might have to agree to refinance the loan and to pay the seller off within a relatively short period of time, say, five to seven years. It can be difficult to get an average seller to carry the paper for any longer than this, although when yields on certificates of deposit are signficantly lower than the interest rate you are proposing, owners are often very willing to carry paper for long periods of time.

Let the Seller Borrow

If an owner indicates that she must have a stated amount of money, one solution is to have her borrow that amount on the security of the property with an assumable loan. Adjustable-rate loans are often assumable. You can then assume the new loan or purchase the property on a land contract or a wrap-around loan.

The Real Estate Commission

If a property is listed through a real estate broker and the owner is asking a low downpayment, such as 10 percent, it is obvious that the seller is really only asking for enough cash to pay the real estate commission. If a broker is involved, ask him to accept a commission in the form of a personal note or second mortgage. While some will not agree, many sophisticated brokers will go along with such an arrangement. Your offer to purchase might then state that you are offering a particular price and that you will pay the commission. The seller and the broker together can end up financing you for the entire purchase price.

Many investors who have real estate licenses earn commissions on their own purchases. In this way, they reduce their cash requirements for the purchases.

If you have a real estate license and want to share in the commission, just keep in mind "full disclosure." If the information is of the type a seller would want to know, then disclose it.

Free Rent

When a seller has not yet purchased another property or does not have firm plans, a low downpayment offer can be sweetened in an unusual manner. Offer the owner rent-free use of the premises for a stated period of time, such as three or six months after the closing. Such a provision will make you appear in a better light and will increase the chance of a low downpayment offer being accepted.

Giving a Life Tenancy

Offers should be tailored to the seller's needs. The following case explains how one buyer did just that.

My name is Russell L., and I'm 50 years old. I work for a large manufacturer as a purchasing agent. Sending my two children through college had decimated what I had thought were sizable savings. I still had $14,000 in cash plus my home equity, which was only around $30,000. I could see a retirement of eating tube steak (hot dogs) and beans. Though my employer had a retirement plan, it was anything but generous. When I was ready to retire, I would probably have to sell my home and move into an apartment, the thought of which I hated.

Out of necessity, I actively sought a way to protect my future. I had 15 years to do it. I decided my best bet would be to buy a modest apartment building. It would provide a hedge against inflation, and if it would break even now, in 15 years it should provide a significant cash return to supplement my company retirement plan plus social security.

I began reading everything our county library system had available on real estate investing. I also visited several dozen apartments that were for rent in order to get a feel for rental value. I attended meetings of a local apartment owners' association. I also talked to brokers who were having open houses for rentals. I pumped them for sales information, taking all my preparation very seriously.

I then began a search for a building to buy. A few agents were not interested in working with me when they found I had rather meager capital to invest, but several agents did show me smaller units.

On the third Saturday of my weekend hunts, an agent who had shown me several units asked if I could do him a favor. He had a 24-unit apartment building that had been on the market for six months without an offer. He wanted me to look at it because he wanted to show the owner he was working on the property.

The apartment complex consisted of three, two-story brick structures each with eight units. The owners wanted $800,000 cash. The property had not sold because of a tight money situation. The price actually was reasonable for the area based on comparable sales. It was about eight times the gross income. After going through several units, I realized the price was really a bargain. Tenants paid all their own utilities, and the apartments, which were all two-bedroom units, were renting at least $100 less than comparable units. After reading all those investment books, my mind was racing to figure out how I could take advantage of this bargain.

When the agent and I returned to the real estate office, I told him I was interested in the 24 units and would get back to him. I am sure he thought I was crazy because with $14,000 in cash, I was just $786,000 short of the owner's asking price. I arrived home around 3 p.m. And from then until

2 a.m. on Sunday morning I worked at the kitchen table figuring out how I could present an offer that would interest the owners. Some of my ideas were far out, but I finally came up with what I thought would make sense to the seller:

1. Purchaser to give sellers a rent-free life tenancy in their present unit (to end upon the death of the last survivor).

2. Purchaser to pay all closing costs, including escrow fees, title insurance, etc.

3. Purchase price to be $750,000. Price to be paid as follows:
   a. $100,000 at closing. This sum to be obtained from a $100,000 first mortgage to be placed on the property by the purchaser.
   b. Seller to assume owners' obligation to pay the agent's commission in the amount of $45,000.
   c. Seller to take back a second mortgage on the amount of $605,000 with payments of $4,439.31 per month based on a 30-year amortization and 8 percent interest. The entire loan balance shall be due in full 10 years from the date of closing.

I contacted the real estate agent on Sunday morning and met with him and his broker. I told them that if they would agree to carry their commission on a note, I would make my offer. After some discussion, it was agreed that I would pay them $5,000 in cash and the balance of the commission on a $40,000 note secured by a third mortgage. The agreement was to be an 8 percent note amortized over 5 years. The broker indicated that normally he wouldn't carry paper but because the listing was close to expiration, he would.

Well, my offer was accepted. The broker indicated that the owners liked the rent-free life tenancy and felt the 10-year payoff really would meet their needs and their children's needs. That's how I purchased a prime building with less than 1.5 percent as a downpayment. By raising rents, I immediately achieved a positive cash flow.

My payments are:

$100,000 1st mortgage 10% (25 years)	$ 908.71
$605,000 2nd mortgage 8% (30 years)	$ 4,439.31
$40,000 3rd mortgage 8% (5 years)	$ 811.06
Monthly payments	*$ 6,159.08*
Estimated Maintenance	$ 1,000.00
Taxes and Insurance	$ 1,600.00
Utilities (common areas)	$ 100.00
Total Monthly Outgo	*$ 8,859.08*

My monthly income is:

23 Units (based on new rents)	$10,345.00
less estimated 5% vacancy factor	- 517.25
Effective gross income	$ 9,827.75

While I have to spend my Saturdays at the apartment building making repairs, cleaning, etc., I have an additional $1,000 each month to spend or save.

If rents go up just 3 percent per year, I should have an additional $1,600 plus per month in income within 5 years. I will also have paid off the agents in 5 years so I will have another $800 in my pocket.

While I love the sellers dearly for giving me this opportunity, eventually their apartment will be available for me to rent. Right now, I think it would rent for at least $600.

I don't envision having a problem refinancing the loans in ten years. With just moderate inflation in rents, the cash flow should justify a loan in excess of what I will require.

Right now my intentions are to take an early retirement in five years. While I won't get much from my company plan, my cash flow from the apartments should more than meet my needs.

Sweat Equity

Some owners will accept "sweat equity" downpayments. Often purchasers of new homes are credited by the builder for tasks such as painting. It reduces the cash downpayment required.

One of my former students buys "fixer-uppers." He purchased a house with no downpayment from a seller who did not need the cash. The seller nevertheless wanted additional security. The seller agreed to the no-downpayment sale providing the buyer painted the exterior of the house and put in a sprinkler system and lawn. The escrow did not close until the work was completed. With the labor and money the buyer invested in repairs, the seller felt secure with no downpayment. The chances of the seller defaulting were greatly reduced. In addition, the improvements and repairs increased the value of the security.

Borrowing Based on the Lease

Suppose you have an option to buy a lot for $100,000, a contractor who will put up a building for $400,000 and you have found a national tenant who has signed a long-term net lease for the premises to be built for $60,000 per year. Because of this lease, the property is really worth more than the $500,000 it would take to buy the lot and build the building. A lender might set a value of $800,000 on the property and agree to give you permanent financing of $550,000, which would mean a loan for $50,000 more than your total cost. (They are really loaning on the lease.)

Payments in Advance

To make a relatively low downpayment appear more substantial to an owner, consider adjusting your purchase offer to reflect that part of your downpayment that is really the first year's payment in advance. This is to your advantage for a number of reasons:

1. Interest is a tax-deductible expense, but a downpayment is not. Most of the monthly payments would be interest, so most of the first year's advance payments would be a tax-deductible expense. If you are in the 40 percent tax bracket (both federal and state combined), the government pays almost 40 percent of your advance payment.

2. Since you have made one year's payments in advance, you have no payments for one year.

This technique is likely to be acceptable to a seller only if she owns the property free and clear or has existing loans that are being assumed. If the seller must make monthly payments, she would be unlikely to accept this arrangement.

Graduated Interest

Owners can often be induced to carry back loans with a low-down buyer by using greed as a tool. For example, if an offer provides 8 percent interest the first year, 9 percent interest the second year, 10 percent interest the third year, 11 percent the fourth year up to a limit such as 15 percent, such an offer will often excite a seller. What you gain in such a purchase is a short-term, high-leveraged loan. It is short-term because it would not be economical for you to keep such a loan very long. By waving the prospect of an almost obscene interest rate in front of them, owners can be induced to finance you with little or no downpayment. Be certain such an arrangement does not violate your state usury laws. (In most states, seller financing is exempt from usury.)

Graduated Payments

A seller can be induced to give you low initial payments on a property by offering a graduated payment schedule with payments increasing each year. The payment for the first year may result in negative amortization (the interest actually exceeds the payments, resulting in the loan principal increasing). Such an arrangement will allow you to make repairs and renovations and could give you a positive initial cash flow that otherwise might have been impossible.

Insured Mortgage

Mortgage insurance really doesn't insure that a mortgage will be paid. In reality, it is a declining policy of term life insurance. The cost of mortgage insurance is based on your age, so the offer of an insured mortgage is best for younger buyers who would pay a lower premium. Your estate would benefit by having a property free and clear in the event of your death. The seller benefits from your death because the loan would be immediately paid off. The lender would not be faced with collecting payments from a widow who might be financially pressed, or worse yet, having to foreclose on the family of the deceased buyer.

Unsecured Notes

An unsecured personal note can be used as part of a downpayment. Including the note with the downpayment serves to magnify the downpayment in the eyes of the seller. For example, assume a seller wants $10,000 downpayment for a property but will carry the balance. Your purchase offer could read:

> Purchaser shall make a downpayment of $10,000 upon closing in the following manner, $5,000 cash upon closing, $5,000 in the form of a promissory note bearing interest at the rate of 9 percent. Said note shall be due in full one year from date of closing.

The $5,000 note is really a deferred downpayment, but to show it as such would result in stating that the downpayment was only $5,000.

In the case above, the note does not call for payments so the property's cash flow is not negatively effected. If the seller objects to the unsecured note, then you can add the $5,000 to the amount of financing to be carried back by the seller and provide for a partial balloon payment of $5,000 in one year.

Price versus Terms

An owner can be induced to sell on a low or no downpayment by an offer to pay the full purchase price or even more. Often the seller doesn't really expect to get that much. You should couple the offer with a reduced interest rate.

While bargains in price are seldom available in a seller's market, a purchaser can nevertheless often obtain favorable terms equivalent to a bargain price. For example, assume the going mortgage rate is 8 percent. If savings and loan institutions are paying depositors 3.5 percent, an owner might be persuaded to carry the paper on the transaction at 6 percent interest if the full asking price is paid. If the loan is $100,000 at 6 percent, the monthly payment on a 20-year amortized loan will bé $716.44. This amount at a 8 percent rate would only make the payment on an $86,000 loan. In this case, by getting a favorable interest rate, the purchaser has obtained an advantage equivalent to a $14,000 reduction in price. There is more than one way to get a bargain. (While you can buy amortization booklets at most bookstores, many title insurance companies will supply you with a free book of tables. This is an important tool for a real estate investor.)

Actually, there is some disadvantage for the buyer in raising the price and cutting the interest. Since interest is a deductible expense while payment on the principal is not, you do lose tax deductions by this method. A seller should check with a CPA before accepting a below-market interest rate. If the rate set is too low, the IRS may impute a higher interest rate and tax the seller as if it had been received.

> My name is Carol P. In the mid-1960s I purchased a home in a new subdivision in Utah. The developer had a number of unsold homes. He turned down my original offer of $2,000 below his listed price. He told me that he had lived in the area all his life and if he gave me a bargain, other purchasers in the development would be unhappy. He said that someone at the savings and loan would talk about his cutting his prices and soon everyone would know.
>
> I therefore presented a new offer for the full price contingent upon the seller agreeing to finish the basement and pour a patio slab at a price that was acceptable to me. I signed a separate agreement for this work at a price of $10. This really amounted to more than the $2,000 price reduction I had originally asked for, but the seller was pleased.

Using Mortgages

If you are holding a mortgage or trust deed on property you sold, you can use that existing loan in three ways to buy other property:

1. Offer the mortgage or trust deed as the downpayment (or part of the downpayment) on another property.

2. Sell the mortgage or trust deed and use the cash for purchase purposes. This might involve having to accept less than face value (discounting the loan).

3. Borrow from a lender using your mortgage or trust deed as security.

The first alternative is the best approach because you receive full credit for your paper. When using existing mortgages you hold to buy property, you effectively convert them to a cash equivalent without suffering a discount. Chances are you would receive less than the face amount if you tried to sell the mortgages. Cash can be added as a sweetener. In other words, a package of cash and a mortgage can be used to buy property and/or pay commissions. A sweetener increases the chance of acceptance.

Manufacturing Mortgages

Some sellers want a substantial downpayment more as a matter of security than necessity. In such cases it is possible to supply additional security by manufacturing paper. While it might be difficult or very expensive to borrow on your equity, you can use this equity as downpayment material for acquiring more property. The seller not only has the security of the property you have purchased, but also the additional security of the property mortgaged for the downpayment.

By putting a mortgage on your own property to use as a downpayment, you can in effect obtain 100 percent financing. The property you buy can now be used to create another mortgage for a downpayment on yet another property. An endless chain becomes possible limited only by your sales ability and the available properties.

If you own undeveloped land, creating mortgages on such land is one of a very few ways you can use your equity. Most lenders will not loan on such property. If you don't have other property, you may still be able to use property of others to buy property for yourself. If you have relatives or close friends who would help you if they had the cash, you might be able to borrow their paper. I know of a father who put a lien on his home which his son used as a downpayment on a house. The son pays the lien on his father's home as well as the lien on his own. You should realize that you are asking a great deal when you ask to use someone else's property to buy property. There has to be a great deal of trust or love before a person is willing to do this.

One investor has pyramided herself to great wealth. She used her paper equity in property by giving second mortgages as downpayments. As values increase, she gives second mortgages on her most recent acquisitions as well as additional mortgages on other property. She claims she has had as many as five outstanding mortgages on one property. To understand this concept, suppose you owe $80,000 on a house worth $100,000. You give a $10,000 second mortgage on that property as a downpayment on another property. If the value of the original property rises to $120,000, you can then take another mortgage to use as a downpayment on a third property since you have a $30,000 equity. You would now owe $90,000 on a property worth $120,000.

Even though it is possible to borrow on your property to get cash, you are better off giving the loan directly as a downpayment. Not only can you significantly reduce the interest rates, but you can save the substantial loan costs and commission necessary to arrange a cash loan.

Mortgages not only can be used as your downpayment, they can also be used for fees to real estate brokers. You should structure your offer so you will pay the real estate commission. You should have the broker agree in writing that if the offer is accepted, he or she will accept your mortgage in total or part payment of the commission.

Separating the Land from the Building

William Zeckendorf, a renown real estate investor of the 1950s and 1960s, was one of the first investors to separate land from buildings as a technique to maximize his leverage and his sale price. He went even further in some cases and created a separate master lease from the building. For example, the land would be separate from the building and the building owner would pay a ground rent to the owner of the land. The building owner would lease the entire structure to an operator under a master lease. The master leaseholder would then lease the space to the users. Mr. Zeckendorf found he could borrow on and sell the land separately, the building subject to the ground lease and the master lease.

By separating the land from the building, you should be able to create very interesting investment opportunities. You should be able to reduce the sales price by the land value, and the seller will usually like the idea and security of retaining title to the land. Owners who otherwise would not consider a low or no downpayment find this type of offer very tempting. As part of the purchase agreement you should try to negotiate an option to buy the land for cash within a stated period of time (as long a period as possible). The seller may require that the building be paid off when the option is exercised. This would mean that you would have to refinance the property to include land and building. If values increase, you will be able to refinance and buy the land and end up in the same position as if you had purchased the land and building together.

While you might cringe at the thought of buying the improvements without the land and having only an option to buy the land, this is really no worse than having to make a balloon payment five to seven years after purchase. With this usual method of seller financing, you must refinance to pay the balloon payment. When buying the building without the land but with an option to buy the land, you are actually better off because you don't really have to refinance. If you fail to exercise the option, you still have the building and a lease. If you fail to obtain financing to pay a balloon payment, you would probably be foreclosed.

My name is Ronald D. I am an investor who strives to understand sellers' needs and to prepare offers to purchase that sellers will find difficult to reject. In other words, my offers to purchase really look good. As an example, let me explain a recent purchase I made.

An owner owned a commercial property free and clear and wished to sell it for $1 million. The building, which had four tenants with relatively short-term leases, was generating $75,000 income after expenses. Assuming the building was purchased at $1 million with $200,000 down, there would still be a negative cash flow with 10 percent interest.

Because the building was in a very desirable area and had good strong local tenants, I was still interested, even though the owner appeared tight on price and terms.

I decided on an end run, an offer that would catch the owner off-guard but would nevertheless make a lot of sense.

I offered to buy the building alone for $400,000 with 25 percent down ($100,000). I would lease the land for 20 years on a triple net lease at $30,000 per year (triple net means I pay taxes, insurance, and all other costs.) At the end of the 20-year lease the owner would get the building back and own the land and building again. The owner was getting $400,000 for a building he would get back plus a 20-year annuity of $30,000 each year. It sounded pretty darned good.

What I received for my $100,000 downpayment was a $75,000 cash flow from which I needed to pay debt service on the $300,000 due plus the ground rent:

Income	$75,000
Debt Service	- 35,000
General Rent	- 30,000
Spendable Income	$10,000

For the first year I would have a 10 percent cash on cash invested cash flow, but I didn't buy the property for just a 10 percent return. (Even though it would be tax-sheltered income because of depreciation.)

The gross rent was $100,000 and expenses were figured at $25,000. If the rent and expenses would each increase just 5 percent each year, at the end of 5 years my gross rent would be $127,627 and my expenses would be $31,907 leaving $95,720 for land rent and debt service cost of $65,000. This would mean a 30 percent cash return on cash invested.

At the end of 10 years, I would have a spendable cash flow of $57,165 and by the end of the 20th year my annual cash flow would be $133,994.

Now, 5 percent per year for increases in rent and expenses is a relatively conservative figure, but you can see what happens with the magic of compounding. (Each year it is 5 percent increase from a higher number.)

I added a twist to my offer: I paid $5,000 additional for an option to buy the land any time during the lease for $1,200,000 (in addition to the

$400,000 I paid for the building). Anyway, my offer was accepted and if history is any indication of the future, I will be exercising my option in the 20th year and my purchase price will be a bargain.

I have been separating land from structures for some time now. It makes for offers they can't refuse and gives me positive cash flows right from the start.

Moving a Mortgage

Many people, especially retirees on pensions, like mortgages. After they have been receiving steady payments to supplement their income, they often don't want the loans paid off. Chances are they will not like having to invest the money in certificates of deposit or Treasury Notes, as the interest will be significantly less than you are paying them.

If because of a sale or refinance, you will be paying off a loan on which you have been faithfully making payments, consider asking the mortgage holders if they would like to transfer the mortgage to another property you own or are buying.

The mortgage holder continues to get the payments to supplement their pensions and/or social security and you get additional financing at a relatively low cost.

Don't offer to increase the interest rate as an inducement, as the mortgage holder will likely think the security is less than the other property. You should convey to the mortgage holder that you are giving them first opportunity at the mortgage so they can keep their payments.

I have learned from experience that younger working mortgage holders are far less likely to agree transferring a mortgage than are retirees.

Subordination

When you look through ads for lots, you will often see the words "owner will subordinate." In a subordination, the seller not only finances the buyer, but agrees that his or her lien will be secondary or subordinate to another loan. To illustrate, assume that an owner agrees to sell you a lot for $100,000 with $10,000 down and to subordinate a mortgage for $90,000. You could now go to a conventional lender and ask to borrow to build a $200,000 structure. As far as the lender is concerned, you would be asking for a two-thirds loan because the lot, to the lender's way of thinking, is free and clear. The lender, by giving a $200,000 loan, would have both the land and building as security under a first mortgage. You have really used the lot seller's equity to finance your loan, even though you have not paid for the lot.

Why would a seller agree to such a deal? If the lender foreclosed, the lot seller would either lose his or her equity or be forced to step in and make the borrower's payments and foreclose on his or her second liens, however, some sellers are very motivated. If they are having difficulty making tax payments, they may be willing to subordinate. When there are few sales being made, a seller who has faith in a buyer might agree to subordinate. A buyer with a good reputation in the community or a buyer who has previously purchased property from sellers who subordinated their loans without problems could influence a seller to subordinate.

Often sellers who subordinate are owners of a large number of lots. They want to see some of the lots developed, so as to increase the desirability and value of their other lots. In order to obtain development, they take a calculated risk by subordinating. As an example, several high-priced homes built in a new subdivision will increase the value and desirability of the other lots. Many speculative builders look for subordination opportunities to keep from having their capital tied up in land. Also, by agreeing to subordinate, a seller will often be able to obtain a premium price.

If a seller agrees to subordinate for a particular loan, such as a short-term construction loan, then when the construction loan is repaid the seller's loan becomes a primary loan. It would be foolish for a seller to agree to just subordinate without reference to a particular loan, since in such a case the subordinated loan would always be the last in terms of priority.

A no-cash purchase is possible when there is a large private first mortgage against a property. As an example, assume theirs is a first mortgage of $100,000 on a property you are considering buying for $200,000. If you can obtain a new $150,000 loan on the property you could approach the holder of the first mortgage with the following offer, $50,000 cash plus a $50,000 new second mortgage for the balance (with a $150,000 first). This would give you a $150,000 first mortgage and a $50,000 second mortgage. The first mortgage holder would have sacrificed some security in that he or she would now carry a second loan, but offsetting that is the fact that the loan would have been cut in half.

This is really a subordination, but don't use this word as it is often associated with fraud. It is strongly recommended that the second mortgage holder know in advance the amount of the first mortgage and its terms.

The above approach is possible even if the first mortgage contains a due-on-sale clause. You could point out that if the mortgage holder says no, there will be no sale. It's $50,000 cash and a $50,000 second mortgage as opposed to having the money tied up for a long period. A sweetener to the offer, if required, would be to agree to pay off the second in from five to seven years (balloon payment).

The word *subordination* is now a dirty word to many people. Unethical purchasers inserted the word in seller financing purchases. They were then able to borrow on the seller's equity by refinancing the first mortgage. They thus became "cash-out" buyers who then walked away and defaulted on the loans.

An example of the above was a California purchaser who agreed to sell a home for $550,000. The home had a $200,000 trust deed against it. The buyers gave the sellers $50,000 cash and gave a $300,000 second "subordinate" trust deed which was due in full in six months. The sellers thought they had a good deal but what the buyers did was to refinance the first trust deed. They obtained a $350,000 loan. This not only reimbursed them for their $50,000 cash investment, it left them with $100,000 cash. Of course they defaulted on all of the loans and the sellers had to bid in at the foreclosure sale to save their remaining equity.

Be on the alert as sellers if a buyer uses the word subordination. You may be viewed by others as targets.

RAISING CASH

If you are buying an apartment building in which the tenants have made large security deposits or prepaid the last month's rent, you should realize that these deposits are turned over to the buyer at the closing of the transaction. They may reduce the amount of cash you need to complete the transaction. (In states where tenant deposits must be kept in trust accounts, buyers cannot utilize these deposits as part of the purchase funds required.)

Most rents are due on the first of the month. An excellent time to schedule a closing is on the second of the month. In this way, as buyer, you will be credited with practically the entire month's rent receipts. This amount will reduce your cash requirements as of the closing date. The net effect of taking over security deposits and the prorating of rents could reduce your cash needs considerably when you are buying with a very low downpayment.

If you don't have enough ready cash to complete a transaction, you should consider the following possibilities:

1. Insurance policies. It you have a whole life insurance policy, you can borrow up to your loan value. The loan value is usually shown on a table on the policy.

    An advantage of borrowing on your insurance is that loans are at a very low rate of interest. I borrowed on my GI policy to finance my honeymoon. I borrowed on it again to buy real estate. Since I am paying five percent interest, I cannot imagine paying it back.

2. Personal property. You can borrow on your personal property such as furniture. This is a high-interest loan.

3. Family loans. Relatives are an excellent source of money.
    I recommend that family loans be in writing and bear interest. All payments should be by check. Avoid any possibility of a misunderstanding about the obligations and repayments. If you would rather not take money directly from relatives, you can borrow their credit instead. By having relatives cosign for you, you may be able to qualify for a loan.

4. A line of credit. Approach the bank where you do business as to a line of credit. A line of credit allows you to borrow on your signature only up to the line of credit limit. The effect of having a line of credit provides you instant cash for deposits with offers, as well as money for short-term loans until other financing can be arranged.
    If you have a strong financial partner, you could arrange for a significant line of credit requiring both signatures. You really don't always need a partner's investment; his or her credit will often do.

5. Credit cards. You have probably received letters from banks offering you cash credit lines on their credit cards. Apply for those where there are no fees. Having the option of immediate credit card money gives you the ability to rapidly respond to opportunities. You can use your credit card as a type of swing loan until more permanent financing can be arranged. While the interest rate for credit card borrowing is high, the cost for a short borrowing period will likely be acceptable. In many cases, interest will be less than an interim bank loan because of the absence of loan costs.

6. Redevelopment Funds. Redevelopment grants and loans are available within designated areas of many communities. Loans are usually at below-market interest, and generally grants require the owner to expend his or her own funds as well, such as in matching grants. These funds are primarily available for exterior renovation, but they could be given to demolish and rebuild. Check your local redevelopment agencies. The availability of these funds could significantly increase the desirability of many investment opportunities.

Your ability to buy real estate depends directly on your credit. If you fail to meet obligations, you cannot expect others to trust you in dealings involving many thousands of dollars. In business, we measure a person by his or her past actions. You must therefore be zealous in protecting your credit, for in business your credit is your honor.

Some Basic Financing Choices

1. New loans
   Conforming loans
   Nonconforming loans

2. Assuming an existing loan

3. Taking subject to a loan

4. Sharing appreciation

5. Borrowing all or part of downpayment

6. Seller financing

7. Using mortgages to buy

8. Manufacturing mortgages

9. Moving a mortgage

10. Subordination

11. Options

Chapter 6

PARTNERSHIPS, SYNDICATES AND INVESTMENT TRUSTS

The natural tendency of every society in which
property enjoys tolerable security is to increase in wealth.
—T. B. Macaulay, 1835
Edinburgh Review

PARTNERSHIPS

An often-quoted definition of a partnership is "two people getting together for a business or investment, one of which has the money and the other the experience, after which whose positions become reversed." This cynical definition has unfortunately been true in too many cases. Many partnerships don't work out.

WHY SOME PARTNERSHIPS GO SOUR

Whatever the reason, most partnerships are relatively short-lived, even when the business or investment is profitable. It also seems that the more partners there are, the more partnership problems there are. Don't form a partnership for a fixer-upper property. It will more often than not end in a disastrous relationship between parties. A partnership like a marriage requires total dedication if it is going to succeed.

Four friends asked me for advice on a real estate investment I told them of the problems of partnerships, but they said I didn't understand. They were very close friends, almost family. They would not have any problems in that area but just wanted an opinion on a six-unit building in which they were interested.

The four friends purchased the building, which was well located but in bad shape. They were going to fix it up, get better tenants and sell it. Well, only two partners showed up to start work on the weekend after the purchase. One of the other two partners had a family affair he "had" to attend and the other one had to work at his job. The second weekend it was the same. It turned out that two partners carried the burden of work while the other two helped only on rare occasions. One of these men was completely incapable of performing the simplest mechanical task.

During the renovating period, the property had a negative cash flow because the units were vacant for the renovation. In addition to the payments on the loans, materials had to be purchased. One of the partners who performed the largest share of the work refused to contribute additional money for the payments. He argued that if everyone had worked as he had, the job would have been done; he would not pay for their laziness. The other three had to make the payments to avoid foreclosure. The building was put on the market for sale "as is" before the work was completed and while it was vacant. The four former friends sold the property and luckily got their money back, but they now won't have anything to do with each other.

Partnerships don't have to end this way. I have a partner in some of my investments. We get along great and have for years. While we are good business friends, socially we move in different circles. We have agreed to a division of responsibility and we stick to it. Our teamwork has been fun as well as profitable; our different backgrounds complement each other.

Partnership agreements need not be in writing to be enforceable; nevertheless, I recommend putting them in writing. It is not so much a matter of trust as business. To avoid misunderstandings, write down rights and duties. Having it in writing can help a partnership to work.

ADVANTAGES TO PARTNERSHIPS

A big advantage a partnership offers to an investor is courage. Many people will not move to invest alone but will invest with a partner. Another person who agrees that an investment is good reinforces a person's convictions. Without the psychological crutch of a partner, many investors would not have made their first real estate investment. Another advantage of a partnership is that it can provide greater capital, thus allowing the investors to buy higher-quality investments. Occasionally, you will see a "partner wanted" ad. Though the investment may be excellent, don't jump at it. Don't enter a partnership with a stranger.

Financial Partners

Many successful investors take financial partners who put up the money in exchange for interest and/or equity in the purchase.

The problem with partners is that many people will indicate an interest, but most will hesitate to actually commit to the deal when it is before them.

Nevertheless, partners can be used in many ways. For example, parties could agree to the following:

- Partner puts up entire purchase price (or downpayment) secured by a mortgage providing for a fair rate of return.

- Partner has an equity position as a limited partner. Partner receives his or her percentage of the operating and/or sale profit.

The above arrangement is similar to the participation loans insurance companies made to developers during the 1970s and 1980s. The lender put up the money for the loan, which was secured by a first mortgage. As a sweetener to make the large loan, the lender was given an equity position as a limited partner, often up to 50 percent. When the loan was paid off, the insurance company was still part owner in the property (usually office buildings or shopping centers).

If you have locked in a deal such as land, construction costs and a prime tenant but are still unable to obtain financing, you should consider a venture capital firm. They really are just another financial partner. The firm will either agree or decline to supply capital after evaluating your project. In addition to interest, they will want an equity position if they supply the money. You should be able to find the venture capital firms active in your area by checking with local redevelopment agencies and industrial development agencies.

Limited Partnerships/Syndicates

So far we have been primarily discussing general partnerships. Another type of partnership—a limited partnership—is quite different. A limited partner is an inactive partner who contributes only money to an investment. While in a general partnership a partner has unlimited personal liability for the partnership debts, in a limited partnership the limited partner's liability is limited to his or her investment. If the partnership fails, the limited partner is not personally liable to unpaid creditors.

Because a limited partner cannot utilize any tax loss from an investment, investments should be made based upon income and/or likely appreciation. On the plus side, the limited partner has none of the landlord's hassles. They are taken care of for him or her by a general partner.

A school teacher became quite well off because of limited partnerships. This young man was a native of a developing area and had an excellent knowledge of the real estate and agriculture in the area. With a wife and three small children, he didn't have money to invest. He saw what he considered to be "steals" go by because he couldn't put together even a modest downpayment.

The young man heard of a ranch for sale and thought it was a terrific opportunity. He went to see the owner, who agreed verbally to give him a 10-day option to buy the property. This option was not legally enforceable because it was not in writing and no consideration was given for it. Nevertheless, this young man felt that it would be honored.

He contacted quite a few of his friends and acquaintances, including his doctor, dentist, and attorney, and had a meeting at his home. With maps of the area, he explained why it was a good investment. He told them about the depreciation possibilities on the citrus trees (at the time depreciation was allowed to pass through to syndicate investors) and why he felt that a quick resale for profit was possible if desired. The terms were $400,000 with a $50,000 downpayment. The young man told his audience he wanted five investors as limited partners. Each would put up $15,000, which would give them some money for payments. The groves could be leased to another grower, but the property would still have a negative cash flow and the investors would each have to plan on coming up with at least another $5,000 every year. For acting as the general partner he asked for one-sixth of the investment to be paid out of profits after a sale. His share was not to be computed until all monies invested by the limited partners were repaid. He found his five investors that night, and within a few months the property was resold for $600,000.

The teacher found other properties, and his partners rolled over their profits into his new ventures. Several of those who failed to get into the first venture now wanted in. Friends of investors became interested as well.

Once you have demonstrated success, investors tend to find you. While this young teacher succeeded without a cash investment, limited partners are more willing to invest if the general partner has a cash position in the investment. Investors prefer the general partner to have a very positive interest in the success of the group.

This young man has quit his job teaching and spends all of his time on his partnership business and is still riding a wave of success. His latest partnerships have been to buy distressed property at bargain prices.

Not all limited partnerships are successful. In striving for great profits, limited partnerships are usually highly leveraged. That is, they are financed as much as possible. Sometimes an unexpected vacancy rate can make the difference between success and failure. Many people have lost their life savings when limited partnerships failed because of high office and commercial vacancy rates as well as reduced rents.

If you are interested in setting up a limited partnership for real estate investments, have an attorney draw up the papers. An attorney can also advise you as to any state regulations governing small syndicates. A syndicate is simply a real estate partnership in which the investors have limited liability.

Buying shares in new syndications is generally not a good investment. Syndicators add on costs and profits so that property usually must appreciate a minimum of 20 percent before the value of the property equals the purchase price of the shares. Instead of buying wholesale, investors in real estate syndicates generally pay above retail prices.

Before you buy a syndicate interest, check with the general partner, with other purchasers, evaluate financial statements and the contract with the general partner, and, most important, evaluate the assets. The track record of the general partner is very important. Find out what else he or she has done in the past. Get the names of previous investors, and call them to verify profits and the relationship. Ask if they know of other investments the general partner has been involved in. The general partner might neglect to tell you of investments that didn't work out well.

If you are interested in a major syndicate, check with a stock broker who has access to the National Partnership Exchange (NAPEX). This computerized system has about 25,000 members and allows you to find what the asking and bid prices are for 1,400 listed partnership interests. For information on NAPEX, you can call 1-800-356-2739.

REAL ESTATE INVESTMENT TRUSTS (REITs)

REITs are organized under federal law. There must be at least 100 members and at least 90 percent of the income must be distributed to the investor each year. The shares in the trust are freely transferable and for tax purposes are treated as a partnership rather than a corporation. A corporation is subject to double taxation in that the profit is taxed to the corporation and the remainder is again taxed to the individual stockholders if it is paid out as dividends. In a partnership, profit is simply taxed once to the partners. In a REIT, only the earnings retained by the trust are taxed to the trust.

In the past, there has been fraud in some REITs and syndicates. Property has been purchased from the organizers at exorbitant prices. In other cases property has been purchased and sold to generate brokerage fees for the organizers, not because of market or investor profit considerations. I would recommend that you check before you invest and that you stick with experienced organizers.

Many of the organizers of REITs started out working with small groups of their friends. Many have long records of success. With partnerships, syndicates, and trusts you really don't have to have money to make money in real estate. You just have to be able to find people who do have money and who trust your judgment.

INVESTMENT CLUBS

Many stock market investors first got involved in the market as a member of an investment club. Each member put up a set amount of money each week. Members were given assignments to research stocks and report on them. They also had brokers talk at their meetings. The group decided what to buy and what to sell and usually developed a diverse portfolio.

I know of a real estate investment club similar to the stock clubs of the past. The eight members all work in the same area. They meet once a week for lunch plus one Saturday morning a month to visit properties. The group has now purchased and resold several lots and made over 100 percent profit in their first year on their cash investment ($5,000 each).

This particular group has incorporated for liability protection and intends to dissolve the corporation in another two years. The group will have accomplished its purpose, which was to educate its members in real estate investments. Acting as a group also gave the members the courage to make financial decisions. Profit on each individual's $5,000 investment will just be an additional benefit. Land is probably the best investment for clubs since it does not involve the problems of renovation and division of physical work.

Chapter 7

LOCATING PROPERTY

If you want to make money in real estate,
find out where the people are going and get there first.
—Will Rogers

Anyone can find property to buy. The papers are full of ads and the streets are full of for sale signs. What is difficult is finding property that makes economic sense at a price significantly below market value.

LOCATION VALUE

The old axiom, "The three most important factors for real estate investment are location, location and location," is still true. The best location offers the greatest liquidity (shortest sale time) and the greatest appreciation during periods of growth. It is also easiest to obtain loans for well located property, and lenders are more willing to lend to their maximum loan-to-value ratio for such properties. And the downside of such property is less severe. During periods of economic recession, well located real estate will suffer a much lower percentage of decline in value than less desirable locations.

The best location, therefore, offers a real estate investor the least risk even though the initial cost will be higher than a similar property in a less desirable location. For example, two college professors who came to the same California college in 1971. One purchased a 2,000-square-foot, eight-year-old home in a prestigious subdivision for $40,000. The other professor wanted a brand new home. He purchased a 2,200-square-foot home on a large lot in a small subdivision with many smaller homes. He felt he had a great bargain at $40,000 because he definitely got more house for the money. Today, the home in the better subdivision has a value in excess of $300,000 or about a 700 percent increase in value. The larger home is still a better structure but has a value of $120,000 at most. The walled subdivision it's in sits in a high crime area. Now who has the bargain?

Stick to Your Own Backyard

Avoid investments outside your geographical area unless there is a strong reason
for the investment. The following case illustrates the danger of such investing:

> My name is Peter S. I have been a successful California businessman and
> real estate investor. I was in a horrible auto accident and the result was a
> lawsuit that looked as if it could wipe out everything I had been working
> 30 years for. While I knew I was not at fault, there were no witnesses. The
> injured party's account of the accident was far different from mine. I had
> allowed my insurance coverage to lapse due to carelessness aided by a
> change in address.
>
> While I knew I was doing wrong, I borrowed on several of my
> properties and used my savings to buy property in another state under my
> wife's maiden name. I purchased two commercial parcels and one large
> tract of raw land. Even though I spent about 10 days researching the
> properties, which I had thought were good values, every one of them
> turned out to be losers.
>
> The raw land was in a community where a hostile attitude was growing
> toward uncontrolled growth. The result was that within a year growth
> control legislation cut the value of my land by one-half. My two commer-
> cial buildings were located in an area which experienced extra ordinary
> growth. The result was overbuilding and a high vacancy factor. Because
> of competition, when the leases expired, I had to significantly reduce rents
> to keep my tenants.
>
> I was finally able to settle the lawsuit for $150,000. My attorney costs
> were almost $60,000, and I ended up losing over a half million dollars on
> my out-of-state real estate ventures. Having sold them, I am now investing
> money in my own backyard. It was a painful lesson for me.

Property advertised outside its normal market area should generally be
avoided. It is either overpriced or has a problem, which is why it hasn't sold to
a local buyer. You should avoid property outside the United States because of
high risk. Political turmoil, outright government appropriation of your property,
and other factors make it impossible to monitor your investment. The less
familiar you are with the country, the more this is true.

USING REAL ESTATE AGENTS

The easiest way to find property is through real estate professionals—the real
estate brokers and salespeople active in your area. They know what is available
and frequently what isn't available but could be. A knowledgeable real estate

agent can also give you a good perspective on price and current market conditions. In a few hours an agent can often present many properties for consideration. What could have taken months might be accomplished in a few days. Most active brokers belong to multiple listing services (MLS), so they have access not just to their own office listings but also to the listings of many other offices.

In order to get the maximum benefit of a real estate agent's time and expertise, tell him how much cash or other assets you have available for a downpayment and for monthly payments. You may find some unimaginative real estate agents who are not interested in working with you if you can't make a substantial downpayment. This type of agent usually lacks the ability to structure purchases with little or no downpayment.

In selecting real estate agents, look for success. A successful agent is usually better informed about available property. Actually, you want more than just a successful agent, you want an agent who is successful in the type of property that you are interested in. He or she will have the skills necessary to match your needs with appropriate property in a professional manner. If you feel an agent is not really interested in working for you, don't hesitate to contact other agents. Many successful investors have developed a close working relationship with just one or two real estate agents they trust and respect. An agent who fully understands your needs and is willing to expend his or her effort to meet those needs in an expeditious manner is a valuable asset.

You must keep in mind that, though the real estate agent may try to find property that meets your needs, in a normal sale transaction the agent represents the seller and not you, the buyer. Some agents will therefore try to sell you property unsuitable for your purposes. To some agents, earning a commission takes priority over serving customer needs.

Why a Third Person Can Make a Difference

A third person often has a greater chance of getting your offer accepted than you would have in dealing directly with the owner. Owners tend to be calmer and more objective when they are dealing through an agent. They are less likely to let emotions affect their judgment.

Some time back, C. P. found a condominium she liked. She felt that the owner, who was selling it directly, was asking an unrealistically high price. She made an offer that was a little over 20 percent less than the asking price. The owner became indignant and refused to talk to her. Six months later she discovered the condominium was listed with a real estate broker at an even higher price, apparently to cover the commission. She contacted the broker and presented the identical offer that had been refused months earlier. This time the broker was able to discuss her offer with the owner calmly and it was accepted.

Hiring Your Own Agent

If you are going to use a real estate agent and you have faith in the agent's ability, consider signing a buyer's listing with the agent. These buyer listings may provide that if the agent introduces you to property that you purchase, you will pay the agent a commission (typically around 3 percent, which is approximately the selling agent's share of a co-brokerage sale). The agreement states that if the property is listed in a multiple listing service so the selling agent will be sharing in the sales commission, then the buyer does not pay any commission. The net effect of this agreement is that you as a buyer only pay a commission when your agent locates a property that you buy where no commission is paid. This would usually be a for-sale-by-owner or foreclosure. Buyer agencies make many more properties available to you when dealing with an agent. Ordinarily, if the agent couldn't see a commission, she wouldn't show you a property. This changes with a buyer listing. There are now a number of agents who act exclusively as buyer agents. Buyer agencies make sense, especially for less experienced investors.

Working without an Agent

While real estate agents can lead you to many distress properties, some of the best deals will be found by searching on your own. Real estate salespeople are unaware of many situations because of the lack of funds available for commissions. This is often the case in sheriff's sales as well as foreclosure and tax sales, where the total property indebtedness might exceed the property value. In these cases, purchases must be at the sale or arranged with the foreclosing lienholder or high bidder after the sale.

Owners Who Don't Use Agents

Often owners try to sell without an agent because they feel they can save a commission. Occasionally, an unsophisticated owner does not have a good idea of values and will ask a bargain price. Usually, however, if the property has been on the market for any period of time, the owner has been contacted by many real estate agents and will have a good idea of values.

Sometimes an owner will place an unrealistically high value on property. The price may be based on what the owner believes some other house sold for or on what a real estate agent said the property could bring. Unfortunately, some real estate agents will try to "buy a listing" by appealing to an owner's greed and promising a sale at an unrealistic price. When an owner is given this sort of misinformation, it becomes difficult to purchase the property at a fair price.

Beware of the sophisticated seller looking for an unsophisticated buyer. These owners may attempt either to hide something detrimental about the property or to obtain a price much higher than the market will justify. They may use deceiving ads. I have come across some shrewd operators who posed as "bumpkins" in order to trick a buyer. Be on your guard when dealing directly with owners.

ADVERTISING LEADS

You should get in the habit of reading classified ads for both property for sale and lease. Even though you should concentrate on sale ads, when an owner sounds desperate to lease (because of rental concessions offered), he or she is also likely to be motivated to sell.

While you will quickly find out that appearances on paper are often far different from the physical property, you are more likely to find property represented as it actually is in for-sale-by-owner ads.

Look for ads that indicate a seller is under pressure to sell such as divorce, relocation, pending foreclosure, etc. By making up a list of questions based on the ad, when you call you will be able to find out if it is worth taking the time to physically inspect it. Keep in mind at all times that the more motivated an owner is to sell, the greater likelihood of a purchase that makes economic sense.

Whenever you see a neighborhood bulletin board, such as those frequently found at supermarkets and laundromats, take a few minutes to scan the ads. You will find real estate listed for sale that frequently is not advertised in newspapers. This will give you the opportunity to contact owners before they have been bombarded with calls from agents.

Advertising for Property

Besides looking for the ads of others, you can effectively advertise for property to buy. You will be amazed at the variety of responses you will receive from your own ads.

Exhibits 7-1, 7-2, and 7-3 are examples of classified ads successfully used by real estate investors who buy and resell single family homes.

Some investors use a direct mail approach with flyers similar to the above ads. They mail to owners likely to be highly motivated, such as owners in foreclosure, divorce, owners delinquent in taxes, and even owners who have tenant problems evidenced by evictions. A great many leads are available from legal notices.

Figure 7–1

Sell Me Your Home

$ for Cash $

Highest Prices - Fast Close

Call Tom Jones

at 328-7133

Figure 7–2

I pay cash

for your real estate equity even if

you are delinquent or in foreclosure.

Call me for my evaluation. No fees - No Cost.

Tom Jones   328-7133

Figure 7–3

I will buy your home

Cash in 7 days

Tom Jones   328-7133

Some buyers prefer post cards over letters. An advantage of using post cards is that they must be read. Owners in default are often besieged by creditors and might otherwise assume your letter is just another collection letter.

FINDING THE BARGAINS

Don't dismiss property from consideration because the asking price is too high. Keep in mind that the majority of real estate sales are made at prices lower than the asking price. The only way you can find out if an owner will accept your offer is to make it.

As a prospective purchaser you should bear in mind that when an owner has owned a property for a long period of time, even offers that slash the owner's asking price usually provide the owner with a profit. If the seller has held his or her property more than 10 years chances are that, with inflation, the asking price is considerably more than the owner paid for the property. Properties that have been vacant for long periods and on which owners have been making large mortgage payments are ideal candidates for a low offer. To purchase this type of property, you should have the means to make the payments and faith in your ability to find a buyer or a qualified tenant. Out-of-the-area owners are also often more receptive to low offers than area owners would be.

Don't be concerned that a property is dirty or needs maintenance. This helps you as an informed buyer, since many other buyers would be turned off by such conditions. When there is little competition to buy, a bargain is more likely. A house that needs painting and yard work might be available for $80,000, even though it would be worth $100,000 or more when properly maintained. You can buy a lot of paint and lawn seed for $20,000.

The longer a property has been on the market without an offer, the greater the chance that you can obtain a bargain in price or terms. If an owner has recently placed his or her property on the market, very low offers are likely to be rejected. But when a property has been for sale for a long period without buyer interest, any offer is likely to receive serious consideration. Ask your real estate agent which listings have been on the market for an unusually long time.

In a rising market, new homes can actually be a bargain. Builders often set prices based on their costs rather than the market. When a project has exceptional sales activity, it generally indicates that the prices were set too low based on market demand.

I know of a successful investor who does nothing but buy new homes and condominiums that he resells, usually at a profit. His criterion for buying is the public acceptance of a project. When sales are greater than expected for a subdivision, he will wait until they are almost sold out and then buy several units. When a desirable project is completed, the resales are usually significantly higher than the original sale price.

He has another formula for really large projects being developed in phases. If the first-phase sales are exceptionally good, he will buy several units before they are sold out. When a developer has exceptional sales on the first phase of a project, the developer can be expected to raise prices significantly for later phases of the project.

There will be some bargains available regardless of the real estate market. Personal problems, such as divorce, death and legal or business problems, can create situations in which the seller wants a quick sale. Such situations can result in bargain purchases.

My name is Irwin L. Many years ago my wife and I were relocating to Milwaukee. We stopped at a for-sale-by-owner home and my wife fell in love with their beautiful home. When we asked the price, we were told $50,000, which was beyond our means. I told the owner we were sorry, but it was much more than we could afford. The owner asked me what we could afford and how much cash did we have right now to work with. Since we had just sold our old home, we had over $10,000 cash. The owner said that if we would pay $10,000 and assume his $21,000 loan he would sell the house to us for $31,000, providing we could close within a week. We agreed and purchased our present home for at least 40 percent less than market value. After our purchase, the seller was indicted for a felony and was believed to have left the country.

Expired Listings

While MLS listing books are not to be given to individuals, there is a good chance an agent will give you his or her old listing books if you have given the agent business. Calling owners whose listings have expired can be an excellent source of advantageous purchase opportunities. From the listings information you will find owners who have no- or low-dollar mortgages and owners who have assumable loans. (From the material in Chapter 5 you will see how these situations allow for no- or low-downpayment purchases.)

Concentrate on recently expired listings. Call the owners and let them know you are an individual buyer, not a real estate agent. Ask if the home is still available and if you will have to deal through an agent. (The home may have been listed with an agent again.) Owners will at times accept offers directly from buyers that would have been rejected if an agent had brought in the offer.

It is amazing how competition can lower a price. In negotiating directly with owners, never let them feel your offer is arbitrary. You must have reasons such as competing property available. When a person feels their property is in competition with another property, they want to be the winner. You also want the seller to like you as a person.

Evictions

Owners of single-family homes who have to evict tenants for nonpayment of rent are usually very motivated to sell. Often they rented their homes, hoping for a trouble-free income only to discover they are living a nightmare. Evictions, therefore, often can lead you to unusually attractive opportunities.

My name is John N. and I am a 37-year-old jack-of-all-trades. I found my niche in buying fixer-upper property, making necessary repairs and selling it for a profit.

While working on one of my properties, I met the property owner next door. He was very upset because he had just evicted a tenant who not only didn't pay rent, but had also left the premises in a shambles. The owner, who lived out of the area, asked what I would charge to make required repairs to his property. Instead of offering to do the work, I purchased the property on the spot.

Since that time the bulk of my purchases have been made by using public records. My wife checks eviction notices filed in the county court house. She looks for owners living outside the area who are evicting tenants for nonpayment of rent. From the addresses we determine if we are interested. (I want property in desirable areas because it usually means quick and profitable resale). We then call the owners and ask if they are interested in selling their property. Usually they are unsure, so we tell them we will call back the next day after they have talked it over with their spouses. The second telephone call often results in a positive response; in fact, after talking it over, they are often eager to sell. After I inquire about loan details, I tell the owners I will prepare an offer.

Often I buy property before the tenant has vacated. By going to the door and being polite, I usually can get to see the interior of the property. If I am unable to get inside, I ask questions of the neighbors. If I have not seen the interior of the property, my offers reflect a worst-case scenario. Of course, if the property has been vacated, I arrange with the owner to enter the property.

I present my offer, which is usually highly leveraged, in person. What I like about buying from evictions is that I am not in a competitive environment with other buyers. I have reached the owners first and they are mine to negotiate with.

Divorce Records

While divorce agreements might mean that one spouse gets the real estate, today the real estate is more likely to be sold and divided because the couple's real estate equity is likely to be their only significant asset and will therefore usually be split between them.

In a divorce, the spouses are often very eager to get their cash and get on with their lives. The owner motivation can be such that I have included divorce property under the category of distressed property. Letters, similar to the ads shown in Figures 7–1, 7–2, and 7–3, are an effective way to find possible sellers. Your mailing list is readily available from court house records and/or legal newspapers.

Probate

Information on property in probate can be obtained from legal newspapers, as well as by checking the filings in probate court. This is public information.

Heirs often can't use, don't want, or want the money more than they want estate property. This is especially true when heirs live outside the area where the estate property is located or the number of heirs requires a division of the property.

In looking to buy probate property, you might be in competition with real estate agents who will be seeking to list such property for sale.

Notices of Abatement and Code Violations

Owners who are not sophisticated investors tend to get agitated when confronted with problems. Owners who have received notices to abate a public nuisance (such as noxious weeds or acts of tenants) as well as of code or fire violations are usually a bit disgusted. The timing could be right for a sale. The owner is likely highly motivated if he or she responds positively, so advantageous price and terms might be possible.

The notices are matters of public record and information can be obtained from the applicable department at your county court house or city hall.

Before you put in an offer on such a property, be certain you have a fairly accurate knowledge as to the costs of corrective action. You might also want to find out if time extensions as to completion of the work are possible.

Friends

Let friends and acquaintances know what you are looking for. Many sales are made because a friend knows someone who is considering selling his or her property. In this manner, many sales are made without property ever being officially on the market.

Lenders

Small loan companies, real estate loan brokers, and mortgage bankers will often provide information, if asked, about homeowners who are delinquent in payments. These lenders are generally not as restricted as banks, which are precluded by law from giving out this type of confidential information.

While not always the case, loan delinquencies often seem to go hand-in-hand with failure to properly maintain the exterior of a property. Many investors look for neglected property even though there is no for sale sign. They, then, contact the owners who they find are quite often in financial distress and motivated to sell.

Earning Finder's Fees

In many states you can legally accept a finder's fee for introducing a person to a property even though you are not a licensed real estate salesperson or broker.

In you search for property, you will likely come across other investors and learn what they are looking for. You will likely have to pass up great opportunities because they aren't right for you.

You don't have to waste these opportunities. There are just so many properties one person can effectively handle. Obtain a written finder's fee agreement from another investor or from the agent involved before disclosing particulars about a property or investor. If the investor buys it, you get a fee.

Chapter 8

FORECLOSURES, IRS SALES, AND TAX SALES

> The moment the idea is admitted into society
> that property is not as sacred as the laws of God . . .
> anarchy and tyranny commence.
>
> —John Adams

In foreclosures, IRS sales, and tax sales there is generally no place for an agent. While there are some agents who, for a fee, will locate sales for you, they are the exception. If there is no sales listing, most agents don't even want to know of these sales. You are going to have to find them for yourself, but I can help.

FORECLOSURES

Why is there such great interest in foreclosure property? Why do we see foreclosure seminars with standing room only? The reason is very simple: Foreclosure provides an opportunity to buy at wholesale rather than retail. A resale at market price will yield a profit.

But don't look at foreclosure buyers as vultures. The simple truth is that *someone* is going to make a profit from a foreclosure. Foreclosures are caused by a number of reasons. They might result from personal problems having to do with alcohol, divorce, or employment difficulties. On the other hand, some are the result of simply spending beyond one's income.

There actually are three separate types of "foreclosure" purchases:

1. Buying from an owner prior to a foreclosure sale
2. Buying a property at a foreclosure sale
3. Buying from a lender after foreclosure.

Foreclosure publication notices required by your state laws might be in special legal newspapers or in newspapers of general circulation. In larger metropolitan areas there are frequently legal papers published strictly to meet the statutory publication requirements of foreclosures and other notices. See if your community or county is served by such a paper. If so, you will want to subscribe if you are going to be dealing in foreclosures.

Many people don't even know of the existence of these legal papers. Therefore, default and foreclosure notices published in such papers are likely to mean fewer preforeclosure buyers as well as fewer bidders than if the notices had been published in a general newspaper.

In some areas foreclosure notices are posted in public places, usually on a bulletin board at a county court house. You will also find foreclosure opportunities as well as other distress property by advertising that you buy property (see Figures 7–1, 7–2, and 7–3).

In some areas, private newsletters provide information on distressed property (property in foreclosure). These newsletters can save you a great deal of time if you are interested in buying at the foreclosure sale or from the lender after the sale. However, you will want the information as soon as possible if you want to buy from the owner prior to the sale. Because of the newsletter delay, you are better off scanning the legal notices in your local and legal newspapers.

BUYING BEFORE FORECLOSURE SALE

An advantage of buying a home from an owner before a foreclosure sale is that you are able to avoid a competitive auction.

Contact the owner in foreclosure with a phone call emphasizing that you are looking for properties in a particular area and that you buy homes fast for cash without real estate fees. *Do not* mention foreclosure during these contacts. Don't claim to be a foreclosure consultant. You are dealing for yourself as a potential buyer. Don't claim to be anything else.

If you get a positive response from an owner, you want a property profile from a title insurance company to check the indebtedness against the property. Although you should also ask the owner, because they expect it, don't take the owner's word for what they owe. They forget, they don't actually know, they lie—or a combination of the above.

Never buy from an owner before you have checked out the owner's equity situation. Jumping too fast to buy a property could land you in the fire. It is far better to miss an opportunity because you didn't act fast enough than to be burned. You won't run out of opportunities.

The customer service department of a local title insurance company can give you information on ownership, liens, and encumbrances at no cost. You will need the assessor's parcel number or the legal description. They will give you a property profile. This is not a policy of insurance. If they make an error, you have no recourse unless you actually purchase a title policy. Ask the title company to search the files for IRS liens, bankruptcy filings, tax liens, and judgment liens. These may be in separate files, and they might otherwise not check for them unless asked.

A cooperative title company expects you to give them your business. You can expect future cooperation if you do. Because a property profile is a no-cost service, don't give the title company long lists of properties. Don't ask for a property profile until you talk with the owner or have otherwise decided you will pursue a property. If you ask too much from a title company, you will overwork their courtesy.

When a property is not overencumbered, a purchase before foreclosure should be considered. As the time for the foreclosure sale approaches, owner's expectations tend to decline.

As a point of beginning for purchase negotiations, ask the owner to name a "walking-away price," a price to be received in cash over and above all encumbrances.

When an owner is in default, you should consider a package offering such as:

1. A small amount of cash

2. A note

3. Several months free rent and a rental agreement thereafter (if desired by the owner).

Some buyers offer the owner a sharing agreement. In addition to the above, they agree to give the seller a percentage of the net profit realized if the property is resold within a stated period of time.

Don't give the seller an option to buy back a property without checking with an attorney. In many states, a transaction such as this is regarded as a mortgage, not as a sale. The seller could still have redemption rights, and your anticipated sale profit could place you in the position of charging a usurious rate of interest, which could result in severe penalties.

In making any purchase offer prior to foreclosure you must find out if existing mortgages or trust deeds are assumable. If they are not, then new financing will be required. Make certain you can obtain such financing before you make your offer. Loans that include a due-on-sale clause (alienation clause) cannot be assumed (see Chapter 4).

If you intend to reinstate an assumable loan you also must make certain that it can be reinstated. In many states, the reinstatement period ends a specified number of days after publication of the sale notice or during a specified period prior to the foreclosure sale.

If you are working to arrange financing to purchase a property from an owner where a foreclosure sale is imminent, consider contacting the lender for a postponement of the sale. Most conventional lenders don't want to go through with foreclosure because they know they will have security problems with the foreclosed property, as well as expenses to prepare the property for sale. In addition, the lender will not be earning interest on the investment during the period of holding the property. For these reasons, lenders will often agree to one postponement if you can show you will be able to buy the property and either refinance or cure the current default.

Of course, if the seller owes too much, you should be looking beyond—to the foreclosure sale or after it. You should be honest with the owner. Don't let her believe you are interested when you know you cannot buy before the foreclosure sale.

At times, a preforeclosure sale purchase is possible even though the property has more against it in liens than it is worth.

My name is Al D. I buy medium-priced homes prior to foreclosure. I recently purchased a home in my neighborhood that I felt had a resale value from $140,000 to $150,000. (I limit my purchases to a geographical area that I know well and am comfortable with.)

I found out about the foreclosure action from a legal newspaper I subscribe to. I called the owner and asked if they would consider selling their home. The owner indicated he couldn't sell; in fact, a local real estate firm even refused to take a listing. Questioning revealed the source of the problem. To verify the information I had received, I called a title company I have used in the past for a property profile. The property profile on this house indicated an $80,000 VA mortgage that was foreclosing and a $92,000 recorded judgment from a local medical center.

I went to see the owners with this proposition: If I could get their personal judgment taken care of with no further obligation on their part and if I would give them four months of free rent in their home, would they deed me their home? They agreed.

I next contacted the medical center and set up a meeting with their collection officer. I carried with me a cashier's check for $20,000. I told them they had a choice: Sell me their claim for $20,000 or hold on to a worthless claim that would likely be eventually discharged in bankruptcy. The only asset of the debtor was the house, which was being taken away from them.

My offer was accepted. Judgment-lien creditors seldom bid at foreclosure sales and usually are realistic. I have also found that second-trust-deed holders who were former owners and financed the buyer also seldom bid because they often don't have the money to do so. If they are not prepared to bid, they stand to lose everything. Therefore, even a deeply discounted offer makes economic sense.

In this case, the $80,000 mortgage was assumable so I did not need to seek new financing. I had a happy seller because I removed what to him was an oppressive burden (the medical judgment), and I gave them four months free occupancy.

I have been very successful in getting junior lienholders to discount their liens. Instead of profiting on the misfortunes of others, I honestly feel what I do is mutually beneficial to all parties.

Keep in mind that most foreclosures don't reach the point of sale. Generally, foreclosure actions end in reinstatement. Some states allow a homeowner in default the right of rescission from any contract to sell their equity. Other states offer a rescission and/or criminal penalties for taking unconscionable advantage of an owner in default. If your state offers a rescission period, don't pay consideration or accept the deed while the owner can still rescind. If your state provides a penalty for taking unconscionable advantage of an owner in default, it is strongly suggested that the owner be represented by an attorney. You don't want even a hint of impropriety.

Another approach is to buy the interest of the foreclosing lienholder. When a property is in foreclosure and the foreclosing lienholder is a private party who holds the first mortgage, you should consider contacting her and offering to buy the mortgage. Besides a cash offer you could offer to exchange mortgages you hold on other properties that have a history of prompt payment. (Generally, an individual foreclosing is a prior owner who wants payments not aggravation.)

If you offer cash for the loan, consider asking the owner to discount it. By buying at less than face value, you can end up getting an exceptional return on your money should the buyer redeem the property in foreclosure. If the property is not redeemed, you end up with a purchase at less than the amount of the first mortgage. You can also make a quick profit of the amount of discount you were able to obtain should the price be bid up at the foreclosure sale. Ten percent and 20 percent discounts are common when purchasing first mortgages held by private parties in foreclosure.

When a property that interests you is in foreclosure, keep track of it. If a purchase is not feasible prior to the foreclosure, then consider the foreclosure sale. If you will not be able to cash out the foreclosing lienholder, contact the foreclosing lienholder prior to the sale and try to arrange a purchase agreement contingent on the lienholder being the successful bidder. You want to arrange a purchase prior to the lender having to incur management and/or fix-up costs as well as additional interest expense.

BUYING AT THE FORECLOSURE SALE

In addition to won't-sell owners, we have can't-sell owners where total indebtedness against the property exceeds its value. Because the foreclosure of a priority lien wipes out junior liens, such a property could be advantageously purchased at the foreclosure sale while it could not be economically purchased prior to the sale.

Foreclosure sales notices specify where the foreclosure sale will take place. If you are unsure, contact the attorney (or other party) handling the sale. Often it is on the court house steps and a crier announces the sale. In other areas, it is just inside the courthouse doors. In some areas of the country it is the county recorder's office. You have to be alert because unless you know what is happening, the foreclosure sale could be over before you realize it has even begun.

Before a foreclosure sale, call the person who advertised the sale to make certain the sale is still on. The property may have been redeemed, the owner could have declared bankruptcy, which serves to delay foreclosure, or the sale could have been postponed for some other reason.

One reason there generally are few bidders at foreclosure sales is that bidders other than the foreclosing lienholder must bid cash (depending upon the state), which they must have with them or be able to obtain quickly. By arranging a line of credit with your bank, you can bid at foreclosure sales using your credit line to obtain cashier's checks.

Another reason that there are few bidders at many foreclosure sales is that most people are afraid of what they don't understand. Foreclosures are an unknown to most people, even most real estate professionals. Not understanding a foreclosure makes it something to be avoided.

While most conventional lenders would prefer to have a loan paid off than to foreclose on the property, some finance companies and merchants look at foreclosures as a separate profit center of their business. They don't want the owner to redeem at the sale, nor do they want other bidders to buy at the sale. For example, some carpet dealers reportedly make as much or more on their real estate foreclosures as they make in selling carpet. These dealers advertise no money down if you own your own home. They are not concerned if carpet buyers are unemployed or have poor credit, as long as they have sufficient equity in their home. To encourage borrowing, carpet dealers often advertise before Christmas that the dealer will give a gift to the family and no payments for periods as long as six months. The salespeople secure their sales by taking a mortgage on buyers' homes. If the payments are not made, dealers will foreclose and resell properties through their own property sales organization.

These types of lenders often go to great lengths to avoid competing bidders at their foreclosure sales. Quite a few San Diego County foreclosure sales are scheduled in Borrego Springs, California, at about 8 a.m. Borrego Springs is a remote desert town about two hours from any significant population center. Even then, when competing bidders show up, the sale is often ordered to be postponed. In California, and in many other states, the lender is allowed to postpone the sale. Statutes generally limit the number of postponements to no more than two. This tactic is used by some of these lenders to tire out the competition. If you hang in there, you can prevail.

Never bid at a foreclosure sale without personally ascertaining the position of the foreclosing lienholder. There could be prior recorded liens, in which case as buyer, you would take title with those obligations intact. The purchaser at a foreclosure sale only takes the priority of the foreclosing lender. While junior loans (recorded at a later date) are wiped out, the purchaser takes title subject to prior liens. Keep in mind, property tax liens and liens for special assessments are generally priority liens.

Most bidders at foreclosure sales have not seen the interior or the property. Often buyers discover a total disaster area when they finally open the doors. Because of this possibility, a great many investors assume that they will need new floor and window coverings, paint, cabinet repair and refinishing as well as 10 days work from a general handyman. In expecting a worst-case scenario, bidders aren't in shock when they see what they have purchased.

If you have contacted the owner to see if purchase if possible prior to the foreclosure sale, you are likely to be the only bidder who has seen the property's interior. Knowing the condition of the interior will allow you to bid from a position of knowledge rather than total ignorance. Some prospective bidders will approach an owner in foreclosure and explain that a sale price in excess of the liens against a property will go to the owner—and be allowed to inspect the property in order to bid intelligently.

In cases where you are unable to obtain permission to enter a property in foreclosure, consider knocking on a few neighborhood doors in the immediate area. Explain that you will be bidding on the property and ask the neighbors if they had been in the house and when, as well as the general condition at the time of their visit. Also, ask if the owners have mentioned any problems with the house. By questioning a neighbor, a foreclosure buyer I know discovered that an owner had just removed and sold the built-in appliances as well as the central air conditioning unit.

While a house might be in excellent shape a week before foreclosure, this may not be the condition you'll find the house in after the sale. Though rare, some owners will actually trash the interior of the house when they finally realize that they have lost their home. Because of this possibility, some foreclosure buyers drive by the house early on the day of foreclosure in order to detect any outward signs of damage.

Notify your insurance agent that you might require coverage before you bid at a foreclosure sale. Let the agent know that you will be calling for a binder if you are the successful bidder. You don't want to be in the position of having taken title and then suffering a loss for which you were not insured.

Title insurance is not always obtainable on foreclosed property since the title insurer cannot ascertain if the sale was properly conducted. Therefore, it is important to have checked the records for liens and/or obtain a property profile from a title company. Bear in mind that if a policy of title insurance is not issued, the title insurer has no liability even though you may have relied on incomplete or false information they supplied.

You should also make certain the sale met all statutory notice requirements. You can do this by questioning the person conducting the sale. If there is an IRS lien, ask the person conducting the sale if they have a copy of the IRS notification. The IRS must be notified at least 30 days in advance.

Before you bid at foreclosure sales, attend a few sales to familiarize yourself with the procedures in your state. In some states, you need to qualify yourself for bidding at a foreclosure sale by showing your cash or cashier's checks. Certified checks are generally unacceptable because it is possible to stop payment on them. Even though you must have all cash (or cashier's checks) in some states, in others you only need have a percentage of the sale price, such as 10 percent in cash or cashier's checks. You will then have a period of time (such as 30 days) to pay the balance.

If you are bidding at a foreclosure sale you will want to have a cashier's check for the amount of the foreclosing lien or required percentage as well as additional cashier's checks in $1,000 increments (or larger) up to the amount you have preset as your maximum bidding limit.

By use of a line of credit you can obtain these cashier's checks and, if you are not the successful bidder, you can return them to the bank so that you will be charged minimum interest. While cash can be brought to a foreclosure sale, don't do it. It serves no purpose other than to subject you to a risk of loss and even bodily harm. Use cashier's checks. In a foreclosure sale, cash has no emotional effect. It is the highest bidder, not the show of greenbacks that decides who is the buyer.

If you attend a number of foreclosure sales, chances are other bidders who might be *regulars* will approach you. You could be offered cash not to bid, a bidding partnership (where several of you will bid as one and then either draw straws to see who gets the property or agree to share in the profits), or a rotation agreement whereby you will take turns in buying property where there are no other bidders. Don't make any agreements that restrict bidding. These actions known as "bid chilling" are felonies punishable by a fines and/or imprisonment. It could be ignorance of the law on the part of the offeror or an offer with criminal intent. It might even be a government sting operation.

If there are a number of other bidders, a tactic used by some bidders is to qualify at a price far more than a property's value. The purpose is to intimidate other bidders and keep them from competing. Normally, you should qualify for the maximum for which you have cash or cashier's checks.

Many foreclosure bidders will not bid more than 75 percent of what they believe the quick turnaround value to be. In this way, they are protected against unexpected problems.

It isn't just dollars that determines the successful bidder. Understanding bidding tactics can mean purchases at lower prices. Some of these tactics are discussed under Auctions (see Chapter 10).

One of my friends was recently at a foreclosure sale where an unusual and unethical tactic was used. Two men were talking before the sale (within hearing of most of the other bidders) about the problems with the interior of the home and what it would take to put it in a salable condition. This was a pure scare tactic. My friend had been invited into the house by the owner on the day prior to the sale and the house was in generally good condition. What these men were trying to do was to cast doubts in the minds of their competition as to how high they should bid and even if they should bid at all.

If you buy a property with a recorded IRS income tax lien against it at a foreclosure sale, the IRS has a 120-day redemption period after the foreclosure sale. They only need to pay you your high bid plus 6 percent interest. Therefore, don't spend money on property until IRS rights have expired. If the IRS was not properly notified of the sale, then the IRS lien will remain in tact against the property after the foreclosure sale. You could find yourself owning a property with a lien against it that exceeds the property's value.

Similarly, some states give the foreclosed owner a redemption right for a period of time after the foreclosure sale. These periods are as long as one year. You should check with a real estate attorney as to redemption rights in your state. You wouldn't want to have invested a considerable sum in improving a property and then have the former owner redeem the property.

If there is an SBA (Small Business Administration) lien against a property, be aware that the SBA has a one-year redemption period after a foreclosure sale, even though the foreclosure was a prior lien. Even though the chance of SBA redemption is probably slight, consider this possibility before expending considerable funds on the property.

In some states, you can get quick possession after foreclosure sale by an ejectment action. In other states, the former owners have a redemption right after foreclosure sale and are entitled to remain in possession. However, you are entitled to a fair rental. If the foreclosed property is tenant occupied, go to the tenants after the sale and either give them legal notice to vacate or ask them to sign a new lease. Generally, the foreclosure of a prior recorded lien wipes out tenant's rights under a later lease. If you can't work it out, see an attorney.

BUYING AFTER THE FORECLOSURE SALE

When the lender is the successful bidder at the foreclosure sale, the property becomes known as an REO (Real Estate Owned) by the lender. This is your third opportunity to buy foreclosure property.

Actually, the best time to buy REO property is before it becomes a REO. One tactic is to send an offer by registered mail or special messenger to the president of a foreclosing lender prior to the foreclosure sale. The offer, which has an acceptance period that expires 24 hours after the sale, includes a check for at least $5,000 made out to the closing agent. If the lender is the successful bidder, the lender is now in the position of being able to immediately flip the property without the problems associated with taking it over. By only giving 24 hours after the sale and giving a sizable deposit, the lender must take the offer seriously and make a quick decision.

When you buy after foreclosure from a lender, the property is usually vacated. If it isn't, your offer to buy can be contingent upon property being vacated. However, a lender would be more responsive to an offer where you save them the problem of evicting tenants or holdover owners. Some lenders are reluctant to provide information on their REO property. If you can't get it from a loan officer, send a registered letter to the president of the institution. Some employees act as if they will be without a job if the bank gets rid of their inventory of foreclosed real estate.

Though some lenders just want to get their money out of foreclosures, others will try for a profit and mark up the property. Therefore, don't take what a lender says as to fixed dollar amount or as to "all-cash sale" as gospel. The best approach is "listen, then ignore." The lender must dispose of property so you are helping the lender. Make your own offer. Don't let the lender make it for you. If a property is in bad condition, don't be afraid to offer less than the amount the lender bid at the foreclosure sale. Whenever you make an offer on a lender-owned property that is in bad condition, consider taking some Polaroid photographs depicting the problems. Attach these photos to the offer. Chances are the officers of the lending institution have never seen the property, so such a graphic display can be valuable in inducing a lender to rid themselves of an obvious problem.

If a lender refuses an offer, ask the lender about other REO property. For that matter, if the lender accepts your offer, you are in a position to build up a working relationship with that lender. Many lenders offer properties immediately upon foreclosure to one or more investors who have proven to be people of their word. They, thus, are able to quickly rid themselves of what they regard as problems. Often bids are turned down by lower-level employees who are given little flexibility. Should a lender turn down an offer made shortly after the foreclosure sale that is at or over the sale amount, send a registered letter (as well as a copy of your offer). to the president of the lending institution. asking why the institution turns down offers that allow it to dispose of foreclosed properties. without a loss. By going to the top you have a chance to reverse this refusal.

You should of course ask the lender to finance your purchase. If you didn't need seller-financing, you would have bid at the foreclosure sale. Lenders often say they must have all cash, but what they say and what they will accept can be vastly different. When lenders finance the sale of their foreclosures, they are generally not as particular as to the credit of the buyer as they would be if they were making a cash loan.

Lenders often trade loans to sell REO property. Two lenders might be financing each other's REO sales. The reason they do this is so they are not financing their own sales. It helps to keep their reserve requirements down and is less likely to be viewed negatively by bank regulators.

There are additional ways to persuade lenders to finance buyers of their foreclosure inventory.

I'm Robert R. I am just getting into foreclosures (a little over two years). I attended a foreclosure seminar, but I felt uncomfortable about approaching owners in foreclosure and didn't have the cash to bid at foreclosure sales. Therefore, I contacted lenders prior to foreclosure sales with purchase offers.

My first offer was to buy a home being foreclosed by an $81,000-plus first mortgage. There were also several judgments against the owner that would be wiped out by the sale. My offer was for the full amount of the foreclosure, $81,326, in cash. The offer was contingent upon the foreclosing lender being the successful bidder and the lender giving me a $90,000 home loan on my personal residence. (I had sufficient equity to justify such a loan.)

After the foreclosure sale (the lender was the only bidder), the lender contacted me. After an appraisal of my home, they made a new loan to me, a person with a good credit rating, and they had disposed of their foreclosure property for cash. This is the type of transaction that looks good on the lenders books.

My next step was an offer to another lender to buy a similar home in foreclosure. My offer was again for cash but conditioned on the lender making a loan on the first home, which was free of encumbrances. Well, I have been working this back and forth between lenders. I have found two lenders who will work with me. I solve their problems and I make money. I have enough cash to pay off the home equity loan on my residence if I want to. I own my last purchase free and clear, plus I have purchased a new Mercedes. I still hold my full-time job, but it won't be long before I contemplate an early retirement. My formula is really six words, "Borrow from Peter to pay Paul."

FHA and VA foreclosures are seldom great bargains. They have been appraised and usually corrective work has been performed. The prices asked are what appraisers believe to be fair value. You don't want to pay fair value, you want buy below-market in order to make a reasonable profit.

Foreclosing lenders in many areas are faced with a multitude of problems including high vacancy factors, rent collection problems, neglected maintenance, and even vandalism. In many cases, foreclosure has resulted in administrative nightmares. Even though lenders understand money, they seldom have people with both the real property skills and authority needed to turn their problem properties around. As I have said, lender problems create unique opportunities for investors who know what needs to be done and who have faith in their ability to do. it. Lenders under pressure to unload inventories of property are open to creative offers.

Moratoriums

Some of the most creative offers I have seen involve the use of moratoriums. A moratorium is a cessation. A moratorium on payments means a buyer need not make loan payments for the period of the moratorium. A moratorium on payments could include a moratorium on interest so the amount due does not increase during the moratorium period. You can see that the effect of a moratorium is a significant reduction in price. Lenders in some cases, have accepted moratoriums when they were reluctant to cut the price. When they cut the price, they immediately show a book loss on their loan. A moratorium, on the other hand is simply a delay in recovering the investment.

My name is Thomas T., and I am a real estate investor. I particularly like turnaround property. A little over a year ago, I learned from a loan officer

I had previously done business with of a 200-unit, six-year-old apartment complex in Texas. The units had a 60 percent vacancy factor and were poorly maintained. The former corporate owner had lost all of its property and neglected maintenance for some time prior to foreclosure. The units needed cosmetic work, but several units had serious problems because of vandalism and the management was next to nonexistent.

After careful evaluation of the property and the area, I offered the lender $3 million for the complex with 10 percent down. This came to $15,000 for each of the two-bedroom, two-bath apartments. My offer, which was accompanied by a cashier's check for $300,000 (full down-payment), required the lender to carry the balance on an 8.5 percent loan, all due and payable 7 years from date of closing with payments based on a 30-year amortization. I included an unusual provision in my offer: I asked for a 2-year moratorium on payments and interest. The offer was accepted after my agreeing to increase the interest rate to 9 percent, and to be personally liable for specified repairs. I then relocated by leasing a home in Texas in order to work with this property.

The moratorium gave me an immediate positive cash flow that I used to rehabilitate the property and to do extensive landscape work. It is over one year since I made the purchase and I now have over an 85 percent occupancy rate. My net spendable for my second year should be in excess of $500,000, which will not only mean the return of my cash investment, but a profit as well. The value of the property has also been significantly increased.

When my payments begin, I will still have a significant spendable cash income, much of which will be tax sheltered. I will likely refinance the property when the balloon payment becomes due. I intend to milk cash out of the property because I anticipate the property will support a new loan of at least $5 million.

Incidentally, I have just purchased a second apartment complex in Texas with similar terms (a 2-year moratorium on both payments and interest). I intend to move to the area and start work on the new project.

Hazardous Material

If a property has been foreclosed by a lender, the one thing a lender would not want to hear about is hazardous material or waste on the property. For legal liability, they would prefer total ignorance.

An offer to purchase property that refers to the property's hazardous material or waste problem in the offer or cover letter would likely upset the lender because the lender now has notice of a problem. Having notice, the lender now would likely have a duty to disclose the problem to other potential buyers.

My name is Charles C. I am a mechanical engineer and work for a large engineering firm. Several colleagues and myself have made money buying and selling foreclosure property. We recently made a rather unusual investment.

A local lender recently foreclosed on a nearby 12,500-square-foot, light industrial building on a 1 1/2 acre site. The firm that owned the building went bankrupt. An officer of a bank from whom we had previously purchased a property asked me if we were interested in it. One of my investment partners knew the building and thought it would be easy to rent if we could keep the rental competitive. While it wasn't the type of investment we had been making, we got the keys and made an inspection of the premises.

Inspection revealed there was asbestos in the floor and ceiling tile. Asbestos wallboard was used extensively around the heating plant and in a former welding area. The boiler had asbestos cement insulation and the exposed heating pipes were wrapped with asbestos. There had been poor attempt to encapsulate much of the asbestos with a spray-on coating. We also discovered there was an underground fuel tank on the premises. Inquiry of former employees revealed it was used for diesel fuel since its installation in the late 1970s.

We did not feel the fuel tank would be a problem because it was relatively new. We did, however, realize that there was a serious asbestos problem indicating an opportunity.

We contacted a firm with extensive experience in asbestos removal. Because of the open nature of the asbestos, removal costs were estimated at slightly under $50,000, which included the disposal of the material in an approved dump site.

The bank was asking $750,000, which included the amount of their loan plus accumulated interest. The bank officer had given the impression the bank would be receptive to offers. The $750,000 was probably a little high, but was still within a reasonable price range.

We never intended to offer a reasonable price. After we realized the asbestos problems, we decided to take a relatively unreasonable approach. As we had hoped to locate a tenant before we put in any offer, we decided to put in an immediate offer at a price where we could give a tenant a bargain rent if necessary and still be in good shape.

We had our attorney set up a corporation for us. The attorney also prepared the offer from the corporation (to reduce personal liability). Our offer was for $420,000 with no downpayment. Our offer provided that we would remove the asbestos from the structure within six months of closing and prior to any tenant occupancy. The lender was to carry back a first mortgage in the amount of $420,000 at 8.5 percent interest. The lender was also to pay the first $50,000 toward the removal of asbestos and other hazardous substances presently located in the structure or soil.

Our offer included a hold harmless clause whereby we agreed that we would not hold the seller liable for any asbestos or other hazardous waste removal beyond the $50,000 agreed liability. We sent the offer by messenger to the president of the bank.

An agitated loan officer called me. She wanted to know about the hazardous material on the property. I explained where we had discovered asbestos and also that there was a possible problem with the underground fuel tank on the premises. I also pointed out that we had not taken soil samples so we did not have direct knowledge of other chemicals that may have been discharged on the property by the previous owners. Three days later, we were notified that our offer had been accepted.

The net effect is that we obtained 100 percent financing from a very worried lender. In addition, they agreed to give us the $50,000 needed to remove the asbestos. We leased the property to a very strong tenant on a triple net 15-year lease at 38¢ per square foot. The lease payments, which are tied to the Consumer Price Index, give us $4,750 per month. Since the tenant pays taxes, insurance and all maintenance costs (triple net lease), we have $1,100 spendable after our loan payments of $3,645 per month.

We have a tenant who will actually buy our building for us, give us cash in our pockets each month (which will increase with inflation), and our only expenses were attorney's and filing fees totaling less than $3,000.

WHEN YOU ARE IN FORECLOSURE

If you are having financial difficulties in paying a loan, don't wait for the lender to contact you. Instead, contact the lender and explain your problem. Let the lender know that you want to meet your obligations and would like to work with him to arrange a plan to accomplish this. Keep in mind the one thing most lenders want least is your property. They are likely loaded with foreclosures and will prefer to avoid foreclosing whenever possible.

Solutions to consider are:

1. Moratorium on payments for a stated period of time.

2. Partial moratorium with a reduced payment for a stated period. (Keep in mind that this as well as the prior solution would result in negative amortization, which means you will owe more after the amortization period than you did before).

3. Moratorium on both principal and interest payments for a stated period. (Some lenders have agreed when they have large numbers of foreclosures and/or the resale market is slow.)

4. Interest only payments for a set period of time. The reduction in payment will vary based on the age of the loan. Older loans would have significant reductions.

5. Restructuring a loan for lower payments. Extending the loan for a longer period or reducing the interest rate.

If you are going to be foreclosed, go to the lender prior to foreclosure and ask for a lease on the property (if they are the successful bidder, plus an option to buy the property back). This arrangement will enable the lender to avoid major renovation that would raise the sale price and also avoid management problems. After foreclosure, when you are in possession under a lease, give the lender an offer to buy with a small downpayment. Lenders who say they must have cash often accept leveraged offers.

OTHER DISTRESSED PROPERTY SITUATIONS

IRS Sales

Some foreclosure-type buyers prefer IRS sales to foreclosure sales because there are usually fewer bidders. One reason for this is the sales are not as well publicized as other foreclosures. Usually, it is just one publication and a posting on the property.

IRS tax liens are general liens against real estate. They do not have the priority of property tax liens. Therefore, when property is sold by the IRS for unpaid income taxes, the purchaser takes the property subject to all priority liens, so a careful title check is imperative. Realize that taxpayers have a period of 180 days to redeem their property after an IRS sale.

Tax Sales

Tax sales offer some exceptional opportunities. While some property sold for taxes has no value other than serving to hold the world together, some properties are lost for taxes that represent only a small proportion of the value of the properties. In some cases, owners have died and their estates or heirs have no knowledge of the ownership. Tax collectors are not detectives. It is not their job to determine if an owner is dead and, if so, who is the heir or heirs. In some cases of marital problems, both spouses have at times gone their separate ways each leaving the property to the other.

Tax sale purchases differ from normal foreclosure sales. Real estate taxes and special assessments for property improvements are priority liens. Foreclosure of these liens wipes out junior liens, which would even include any mortgages recorded prior to the taxes even becoming a lien. While buyers at a mortgage foreclosure must worry about priority liens, this is not the case with tax sales. In almost every instance, taxes would be the priority lien.

Some investors contact owners who are delinquent in taxes and offer them cash, notes, or a combination of the two for their equity prior to the tax sale. To buy property from an owner prior to the tax sale, you should realize that you will be taking the property with all liens fully intact, including the lien for unpaid taxes. It is therefore essential that you obtain a property profile from a title insurance company so you can determine if the owner has any equity and, if so, how much.

Most investors, however, wait for the tax sale. When you go to your first sale, you will likely find that what you considered the good properties (single-family homes in desirable areas) are not being sold. What has happened is that the owners redeemed them by paying the back taxes. I have been to sales where two-thirds of the properties advertised were redeemed prior to sale. Delinquent taxpayers are assessed interest on their unpaid taxes. In some states, the interest rates are relatively low. The result is that some sophisticated property owners will leave their taxes unpaid, but will redeem their property by paying the delinquent taxes and interest prior to any tax sale. What they are really doing is effectively borrowing from the tax collector at a below-market rate of interest. When interest rates are high, you will find an increase in the number of tax delinquencies. In larger counties, thousands of properties may be listed for tax sale. No bidder can possibly check out every property. Generally, bidders have only checked out a few properties. Even with several hundred bidders, there will be properties up for bid that none of the bidders have actually seen.

For raw land and for lots, some bidders will make their bids from subdivision maps and plat books that show the parcel size and access. If you are interested in raw land and lots, you should also check both zoning maps and government geological survey maps. The geological maps will show the contour of the land and could indicate a flood problem or land so steep it is suitable only for mountain goats. Though use of these maps will reduce your risk in bidding on land, maps can be a poor substitute for actually physically checking the land. There could be neighboring use or change that has reduced the value or rendered the land practically worthless.

If there are agents' or owners' For Sale signs for similar property in an area, call the advertisers and find out what they are asking. You should look for a pattern as to prices in an area. Keep in mind that what others are asking for their properties does not determine value. Selling prices are far more valuable in this regard. If there is a local real estate broker with whom you have done business, contact the broker and ask for computer comparables in the area. *Do not* call attention to the particular property you are interested in.

Don't be a crapshooter like some tax sale bidders. They bid without knowledge. They feel at a few thousand dollars, they can't go wrong. You can go wrong at any price if you can't resell the property for more than you paid.

Buying at tax sales is frustrating work since proper research takes a great deal of time, and much of the research will be wasted when properties are redeemed prior to sale. To be successful at tax sales and reduce your property inspection and research efforts, pick particular areas and work them. Try to check properties of many different owners rather than a single owner of many properties. In this manner, there is a greater likelihood of the number of those properties being available at the time of sale.

For single-family homes, drive by and check the exteriors of the homes. If a particular house is vacant, consider walking around the property and looking in the windows. While it is technically trespassing, you are unlikely to be prosecuted for doing this.

You should also knock on neighborhood doors to inquire about the vacant property. *Do not* mention that the property is being sold for taxes. Instead, ask why it is vacant. Is it for sale? What is the condition of the property? Do they know of any problem with the property?

Some states allow a redemption period after the sale. The owner must pay the sale costs plus a statutory interest. In some cases, the interest is sufficient to make the tax purchase a good investment even if the owner redeems the property. In some states the redemption period is as long as one year. This would preclude a buyer from reselling the property and would also discourage any major expenditure of time and/or money. For some desirable properties, there can be heated bidding that can result in sale prices approaching or even exceeding market value. Again, just because you buy property at a tax sale, this does not guarantee you a bargain.

Chapter 9

ANALYZING PROPERTY

> Every man who invests in well selected real estate in a growing
> section of a prosperous community adopts the surest method
> of becoming independent, for real estate is the basis of wealth.
> —Theodore Roosevelt

Don't count on a broker to tell you what you should buy. The broker generally represents the owner, who wants a sale at the best price and terms possible. Therefore, brokers are likely to be more interested in a sale than in what is right for you. Since you are the one putting up the money or accepting financial obligations, purchase decisions must be yours, based on your understanding of the property, the area, and the economy.

At times you will find a property that appears to be an excellent investment opportunity but find yourself uncomfortable with the idea of buying it. Though not always right, I have turned down properties for reasons I couldn't really explain at the time only to see a purchaser burned by the investment. I have learned to trust my instincts.

An exception to the above is the first-time investor, who often is so nervous that he will always be uneasy with a purchase. First-timers must overcome this fear of the water and dive in with the rest of us. You can't learn to swim if you are unwilling to get wet.

Risk is directly related to profit potential. The lowest risk investments generally offer the lowest return. If you are to accept a higher risk, the risk must be offset by greater possible rewards. The degree of risk you are willing to accept must be based on your personal needs, goals, and guts. It takes guts to invest, but guts does not mean willingness to gamble. Guts refers to your self-esteem, your belief in your ability to evaluate a property and in your ability to work to make the investment successful.

LOCATION

The first thing to consider for any purchase is location. When weighing several alternatives for long-term investment, you must use all available information in making your decisions. Chamber of Commerce information is very valuable in this regard. They will have information on planned future developments of private and public nature and will likely have studies as to future growth as well.

People generally make money in dealing in areas where they understand values as well as trends in the marketplace. Investors usually suffer large losses because they have gone outside their area of expertise. Because values vary so much by locality, don't assume anything or base a decision on opinions provided by anyone who will realize a financial gain from your purchase.

If you are contemplating purchasing property in an area you are unfamiliar with as to values, I strongly recommend you spend the money for an appraisal. You might check with local lenders as to appraisers they recommend. You want an appraiser who is *certified* by your state and, if possible, has an SREA or MAI professional designation.

Property tends to go through three distinct stages: integration, equilibrium and disintegration. During integration the area is being developed. Early users often determine the character of future development. After being developed, an area generally goes through an equilibrium stage in which the character and use of the area remain relatively unchanged. Finally, the area will start to disintegrate or go downhill. It will become less desirable. Occasionally, an area is rescued and is revitalized from this stage.

These three stages of development hold true for individual properties as well as areas. They illustrate the principle of change, which means that use and values do not remain constant; change must always be expected. To find what stage a property is in, check the area. What is happening? You should consider what has happened to an area in the last year, the last 5 years and the last 10 years. These changes will give you an excellent indication of what will happen to the area in the future. The study of trends and changes is invaluable in deciding when and what to purchase, as well as when to sell.

Positive signs would be low vacancy factors, evidence of remodeling or expansion of existing structures, or the replacement of existing buildings with new structures. In areas where commercial tenants are doing well, there will be few changes in businesses or ownerships. On the other hand, a high turnover in a location, as well as frequent changes in ownership, normally indicates marginal or loss operations. When people in an area are not doing well economically, maintenance often gets deferred. Because of rent collection problems, owners tend to reduce expenditures to a minimum.

Other negative signs are a decrease in retail volume and a decrease in the percentage of owner-occupied housing. An increasing crime rate is often accompanied by higher fire insurance rates for an area. The following are also unfavorable indicators of declining values:

- Conversions of large homes to apartments generally is a negative indicator.

- Abandoned buildings or unrepaired, fire-gutted buildings usually indicate very severe problems for an area.

- Graffiti, especially gang symbols, are a sign of decline in an area.

Such factors as income, age, family size, ethnic background, and even religion can affect spending habits of the residents, which in turn have a bearing on commercial values. New factories, golf courses, schools, and so forth will tend to raise values in nearby areas.

In most urban centers the greatest residential growth tends to be in just a few areas. Within general areas, specific pockets likely to have greater growth potential and/or greater desirability. These are the areas of preference for investing simply because the application of the law of supply and demand causes values to increase with increased demand. A forward-looking investor will, therefore, realize that what appears to be a bargain investment at present could be a poor long-term choice. Appreciation in value and income might be far less than an investment that does not *pencil out* as well in the present but will likely be positively influenced by demand increases.

Consider the following general rules in making area decisions:

1. Better homes tend to be built outward from a community in the same direction, especially if toward higher ground.

2. Commercial property tends to grow outward along major transportation routes.

3. Small service industries tend to gather around major industries.

4. One early major development in an area will affect the character of later developments.

5. Desirable recreational facilities (such as parks and golf courses) will increase the desirability for housing.

6. The close presence of colleges and universities will increase the desirability of an area for housing. Medical facilities also have a positive effect on values.

Blight is contagious. In what direction are blighted areas growing? Because of natural or artificial barriers, blight is often channeled in specific directions. You should consider the fact that the existence of present or former chemical dumps in an area adversely affects value. Also, the presence of an atomic energy plant or even a large chemical plant can reduce values and might affect them more radically in the future.

As to residential property, you should consider the location in relationship to jobs, public transportation, freeways, schools, shopping, and recreational facilities. Commercial property is also affected by transportation, traffic count, population within the purchasing area of the property as well as its purchasing power and purchasing habits. Industrial property is concerned with location in relationship to a labor supply as well as transportation and availability of utilities.

PROGRESSION AND REGRESSION

Generally, it is best to buy the least expensive property in a good area. The value of the other property will actually pull the value of your property up. This is known as the principle of progression.

The opposite is the principle of regression. It is not a wise investment to have the most valuable property in an area. The surrounding lower values will tend to pull the value of your property down. We can understand these principals if we consider a builder who builds a $250,000 home in an area of $100,000 homes. The lower values in the area will make the property difficult to sell at that price. If the house had been built in an area of $500,000 homes, it would probably be readily salable even at a higher price.

Zoning

After evaluating the area, consider the zoning of the specific property. Will it allow the present or contemplated use? Is the zoning in the area consistent with the zoning of this particular parcel? Consider area zoning as well as individual property rezoning because zoning patterns can affect future zoning changes. Many people have more than doubled the value of their properties by simply applying for and receiving zoning changes. The feasibility of rezoning to a more productive use makes a property a much more attractive investment.

Look for evidence of down-zoning, a change in zoning to more restrictive uses, such as a change from commercial to residential zoning. A number of instances of down-zoning in an area might indicate that other property might also be down-zoned. If an undeveloped property is down-zoned to a more restrictive use, it tends to lower the value of the parcel. It is also possible for zoning to be changed to make property more productive. For example, the value of a single-family home zoned for residential use could materially increase if it is rezoned for offices.

Just because a vacant property is zoned for a particular number of units does not mean that the maximum number of units under a zoning classification can be built on the parcel. When minimum square footages of each unit, parking requirements, height and side yard limits are all considered, it might be physically impossible to build the number of units allowed by the zoning.

Frequently, properties have nonconforming uses. The current use could have preceded the zoning. In these cases the use is allowed to continue but should it cease for some reason, the use cannot be started again. Generally, you can expect a property with a nonconforming use to have a lower value than if the use was consistent with the zoning.

Some property has been used for years in violation of the zoning. Just because someone else got away with a zoning violation in the past does not mean that you will be able to do so in the future. For example, in the past many people remodeled to create a separate apartment for relatives, such as an in-law unit. Later owners may have rented the extra unit in violation of the zoning. If a unit has been remodeled for a change in use, such as an apartment split into more units or a large house broken up into apartments, you should be concerned with the zoning as well as with whether or not the work was done with a building permit. Many people have "bootlegged" units. If units contrary to either the building codes or zoning are discovered, the result could be an order to tear out the work.

Covenants, Conditions and Restrictions

Besides zoning, consider covenants, conditions, and restrictions (also known as restrictive covenants). These CC&Rs are private restrictions on the use of a property placed on it by a subdivider or by agreement of all the property owners subject to them. The restrictions may apply to use, size, height, building setbacks, architectural styles, and even such things as colors. Even though zoning may allow a use, if the use violates the CC&Rs, it would be possible for any other person subject to the same CC&Rs to obtain an injunction prohibiting the intended use. When CC&Rs and zoning disagree, the more restrictive use governs. Since the CC&Rs are recorded, they are available. A title company can obtain a copy for you.

Political Climate

Property developed in an area where the supply of new property is being restricted will show exceptional appreciation in value. It is simply the principle of supply and demand in action. On the other hand, undeveloped property in such an area would likely be a poor investment. Restrictions on development would keep the value down until or unless you received approval for development.

Growth control might be based on the "I'm aboard! Now let's raise the drawbridge" syndrome, or a basic lack of resources, such as water, or the inability of the community to supply needed services. The local building inspector will be able to tell you if there are any current or planned limitations on the number of building permits issued.

Similarly, the presence or likelihood of restrictive rent control legislation will serve to dampen future appreciation of rental structures and lower the value of apartment sites.

Rent control protects tenants from the market forces of supply and demand at the expense of the property owners. While a property in a rent control area might offer a reasonable return on the investment, future growth in income and appreciation in value will be severely restricted.

Generally, a property in a nonrent control area with lesser return would be a better investment than a property at the same price with greater return but subject to rent control. There are various degrees of rent control.

In some communities increases in rent are based on the Consumer Price Index. In other areas, owners are limited to increases in their costs. Similarly, some communities allow rents to be reset when units become vacant. Other communities require the landlord to keep the same rent base. The more severe the rent control, the further you should stay away from the property as an investment. Consider the likelihood of rent control in making a purchase. The more renters in an area, the greater the possibility of rent control.

PHYSICAL ASPECTS

Sewer, Water, Electricity, Natural Gas and Cable

If you are buying undeveloped land, you will want to have information as to the availability of sewers, water, electricity, natural gas, and even TV cable. Some utilities can be relatively close to a property, but the cost to bring them out to the property can be considerable if the property is prematurely developed.

If municipal sewers are not available but septic systems are allowed, you will want to know if the property can pass a percolation test. If it cannot, a building permit will not be issued. Many people have invested their savings in land that cannot be developed because of poor percolation. Percolation is a problem where the water table is either close to the surface or where there is a great deal of clay in the soil.

Recently, a young man purchased three lake front lots at a very good price. The lots were served by sewer and water and were at the end of a street which sloped to the lake. The buyer did almost everything right; he cleared the lots of brush so the view was opened, added sand fill where needed and generally made the lots very attractive. He intended to build his own home on one lot and to sell the others. When he applied for his building permit, he discovered that he had to install a sewage lift station costing $18,000.

Check with the building department prior to purchase to avoid unpleasant surprises. Just because a natural gas line is in place does not mean it is available for use. In some areas of the country, utility companies are not taking on new customers because they are afraid they might not be able to supply their needs.

In many areas the availability of cable television is a significant factor in determining the value of residential property. This is especially true if satellite dishes are not allowed by zoning or restrictive covenants and rooftop antennas will only bring in a very limited station selection.

Compaction

Some land has a compaction problem, which means that the land cannot properly support structures. Usually this land has been reclaimed by drainage or filled land. In some cases, expensive pilings must be driven to support a structure. Excessive construction costs will reduce value. If you feel that a parcel of land may not be able to support a structure, hire a civil engineer to check the property.

Topography and Drainage

If you are buying undeveloped land, walk the boundaries of the land. If it is a large piece, you should also walk through the parcel so you fully understand its topography. Frequently problems such as drainage will be discovered by such a walk. A little time spent can save you from a mistake. Drainage is an important factor on raw land

I recently volunteered to help find a new location for a workshop for retarded citizens. I found a location that appeared excellent and the price seemed extremely low. While the fact was not visible from the ground, I discovered by checking a topographic map that the property was in the center of a natural drainage area. Further checking with local residents revealed that the roads in the vicinity of the parcel and most of the parcel itself had been under as much as two feet of water on several occasions in the past 20 years.

Many communities will deny a building permit for a property in an area prone to floods.

Roads

Roads that show on maps as nice straight liens can in reality be nothing more than a pair of tire ruts in the earth. What appears to be a public road to a property could very well be a private road over which you would not have rights. You can check with the county department of roads about a specific road.

Undeveloped property on a major road, or on what looks like it could become a major route, can show dramatic appreciation. Roads that lie on section lines (government survey lines located every mile) often develop as major roads. Generally, land fronting on a section line road sells at a premium to investors.

About 10 years ago I was offered 8 acres of land for $30,000. The seller didn't think the road the parcel was on would ever be a major traffic artery or that the land would be desirable to others. The road developed as a major artery and the parcel next to the one I was offered recently sold for $50,000 per acre. This would have been more than a 1200 percent profit if I had acted. At the time the parcel was offered to me, the state highway department had extensive plans for widening the road and diverting other traffic to it. I had not bothered to check with them. I have learned that you can't win them all, but it's hard to lose a good one.

A phone call to the county or state highway department should be a must for you whenever you are interested in any highway frontage property.

Vehicular and Pedestrian Traffic

For commercial property, the traffic count, the hours of peak vehicle traffic, traffic speed and foot traffic all affect value. If traffic is primarily during relatively short periods in the morning and late afternoon, then the property is probably on a route to a major employment area. Most of these drivers are in a hurry to and from work. Property on such a route probably will not be as valuable for commercial purposes as a location with the same traffic count spread over a longer period of the business day.

Traffic moving on a street at 50 miles per hour is much more difficult to stop than that moving at 25 miles per hour. Slower traffic is more desirable for retail businesses. Foot traffic is of course important for retail locations with window displays. An ideal location for foot traffic is between two major stores.

Parking is extremely important today for commercial, industrial and even residential properties. A 12,000-square-foot commercial building is for sale. It's in a congested area with poor access and has only 10 parking spaces. I own a much older building of the same size and use in the same general area. The street my building is on has half the traffic count of the other building. In addition, the building I owns is quite plain, while the building up for sale is very deluxe. Nevertheless, my building gets almost twice the rent per square foot as the building that is for sale. The difference is that the my building has more than 50 parking spaces in a large paved lot readily accessible from two streets.

Property Shape

Even the shape of a parcel can affect its value. A triangular lot will generally sell for less than a rectangular parcel since the rectangular parcel can be developed for greater utilization of the lot at a lower price.

People today like ranch homes that spread across the face of the lot and show all the world how large the owner's home is. Therefore, wide residential lots are generally more valuable than narrow deep lots having the same total square footage.

FINANCIAL HISTORY

In evaluating investments, keep in mind the expenses and income of the past are merely history. While history will help you in predicting future income and expenses, these figures should not be the basis of your investment. Your investment should be based on your estimate of the income and expenses that you will have with the property.

Income

The rent schedules owners provide cannot always be believed. An owner may fail to inform you that one tenant has a reduced rent for some management duties. One owner neglected to tell me that 3 of his 12 tenants had given him notice when he notified the tenants of the new higher rent schedule. He just told me that this was his *current* rent schedule and gave information on how long each tenant had been there. From the facts given, it looked good. While the facts were all true, the intent was to deceive.

An owner might rent a unit for $800 per month when the market would justify only $650 per month. The owner might have given the tenant several months' free rent to sign a one-year lease. If this were the case, the tenant can be expected to leave at the end of the lease. The best way to verify rents is to talk with the tenants. You may find that things are not always as indicated in the leases.

Bob K. purchased an almost new, furnished apartment building. The rents appeared to be above what the market would indicate, but Bob felt that this was because it was the only new building in the area. He discovered that each of the tenants had rented during a promotion whereby they were given a document that gave them the right to buy the furniture in the apartment for only $100 if they stayed for 18 months. What Bob had in a few months was a number of vacant unfurnished units and a lawsuit against a former owner who "forgot" to mention the options.

When you request rental figures or operational costs from an agent or owner, always ask that the figures be verified in writing by the owner's accountant. You will find the attractive verbal figures given are seldom the same as those put down in writing. Check rentals with the tenants themselves. You want to verify rents, find out how long the present rental rate has been in effect, and whether any concessions were given to rent the unit. Some prospective buyers want to see the owner's tax returns for the previous two or three years. These will show trends in income as well as trends in expenses. It is excellent information for helping with projections of income and expenses. However, some sellers have been known to prepare false returns for buyers and lenders.

Even though a particular building is fully rented, realistically consider a vacancy factor. By checking with a local apartment owner's organizations or with large property management firms, you can get a good idea of the vacancy rate for the area. Tenants do move, and even when units are rented quickly, there is usually a period when rent is not collected. The period can be from a few days to several months. In addition, sooner or later you will have a tenant who moves out owing money that will never be collected. You cannot realistically expect 100 percent occupancy and 100 percent collections.

When inquiring about a property, be on the alert for terms such as *scheduled rents*. This does not mean that the rents are actually being collected. Another term frequently used is *broker's net income*. This is not a net figure because it does not consider either a vacancy factor or any collection loss. It represents the ideal, not the actual, situation.

In situations where there is not a good rental history, such as in the case of new buildings, real estate agents prepare a *pro forma statement*. This is not a statement of current income or expense but rather an estimate as to what they will be. Brokers, in preparing these statements, tend to be overly optimistic. The figures given should not be accepted without your own independent analysis. I have seldom seen a pro forma statement in which the actual income exceeded what was estimated or in which expenses were less than contemplated. If you doubt figures provided by an owner, use your own estimates instead.

In evaluating property, be skeptical of the rent schedule when the property is vacant (or a number of units are vacant). If you feel the current rents are too high, make your investment decision based on what you consider to be a realistic rent. Otherwise you will likely find that you will either have to reduce rental rates or offer sweeteners such as free rent with leases.

There are actually many instances when rents are too low. Sometimes an owner has become a friend of the tenants and hesitates to increase rents. Other times it is simply poor management. Often when property is held in a trust or estate, there is no real incentive for the administrator to increase rents. The administrator is more concerned with avoiding problems. Sometimes out-of-the-area owners are unaware of the rental potential of their properties. I know one commercial tenant who scared the out-of-state landlord into giving an extremely low-rent, long-term lease with the threat of leaving, despite the fact that the property was highly rentable. In analyzing a property's income, consider the feasible income, not necessarily what is actually received. In larger buildings income from parking revenues and receipts from coin-operated laundry equipment are frequently overlooked.

Be particularly leery of projected income in sale-leaseback opportunities when the tenant has a weak credit rating. The likely reason she wants to sell and lease back the premises is that she needs the capital. Often sellers will offer to lease back property at rental terms that make the sale price appear a bargain. In these cases, all too often the seller ends up defaulting on a lease. The buyer then discovers she cannot rent the premises for the rental the seller agreed to pay. What began as a positive cash flow investment might turn into a negative one. Therefore, in sale-leaseback situations, base your purchase on what your research of the area indicates is the fair rental value of the property. Also get a credit report on the seller/lessee. Be particularly leery of sale leasebacks where the building was constructed for a special purpose and would be desirable for a very limited number of possible tenants.

Sheila F. purchased a large frozen food processing plant in a small town and leased it back to the seller. After about one year, the tenant told Sheila that if she didn't agree to rewrite the lease at significantly lower rent, he would default on the lease and go bankrupt. Sheila was unable to find another tenant for the special-purpose structure and ended up agreeing to the tenant's demands. The tenant's financial weakness and the limited use for the property served to give the tenant tremendous bargaining power.

If a tenant leaves a special-purpose building, it could be vacant for a long time. Some special-purpose buildings have had vacancy periods measured in years rather than months. You must learn to look a gift horse in the mouth. Too good a bargain from a sophisticated real estate investor or through an agent who also buys and sells would indicate that something is wrong. The problem could be a major tenant leaving the property or the area, a change taking place because of highway changes, etc. While you should always look before you leap, when the sale seems incongruous to the seller and/or the agents involved, be extra careful. Check with neighbors, the city for building and fire code violations, the leases, and even the tenants. Generally, I have found that deals that appear too good to be true are exactly that.

Expenses

In evaluating an owner's claimed expenses, understand that owners who do the management and repairs themselves do not include their labor as an expense. As a buyer in evaluating a property for purchase, add the estimated value of your labor to the expenses. Management expense is the most often omitted cost, and you must consider it even if you will do it yourself. Ask yourself, "What would it cost me for these services if I could not do the work myself?" Anyone buying the property from you will likely consider it an expense. You had better do the same or you will end up overpaying for the property.

A very unethical tactic used by some sellers has been to show average expenses for the past 5 or 10 years. While on the surface it seems very reasonable, you must consider that taxes, utilities, supplies and services have all been increasing. The net effect is that the *average figures* are unrealistically low, and you will find actual expenses will be significantly higher than the average.

In evaluating operating statements make certain that the property manager's apartment is shown as a fixed expense when it is provided to the manager. I have consistently seen *creative* pro forma statements that "inadvertently" show it as income only.

When analyzing insurance costs, obtain a copy of the current policy to determine coverage and costs. Often an owner's coverage is closer to the price the owner paid than to the current value. This means coverage may be inadequate and proper coverage would increase the insurance costs far beyond the figure shown.

Coverage is very important. You should consider smoke and water damage as well as fire and lightning. Losses from vandalism and from nature should be considered. If a property has plate glass windows, you should consider coverage. Rental interruption insurance might be a consideration. It reimburses the owner for rent loss because of damage and destruction. If personal property is included with the property, it should also be covered. In this lawsuit-happy world it is essential that you carry substantial liability coverage. Flood and earthquake insurance should also be considered in areas prone to either of these. Your actual insurance costs could end up several times higher than the present owner's costs.

Tax figures provided by the owner are usually of little value in predicting your own tax obligations. Property is often reassessed when sold. The new assessment is likely to be materially higher than the figure used for the previous owner. A better estimate of taxes can be based on the recent reassessment of similar properties.

When analyzing developed property you should be very concerned about whether the owner pays utilities and whether the utility rate increases are passed on to the tenant. In the past few years actual utility costs have increased more than the Consumer Price Index. Many properties operate at losses because they were leased under long-term leases to tenants who are not obligated to cover these increases. When you check on a property, you will be given figures on utility costs. Ask to see actual utility bills, not just figures. Make your own estimate of current and anticipated utility costs based on the actual utility consumption in the past. The only thing that is meaningful in old bills is the actual cubic feet of gas, gallons of oil and kilowatts of electricity used. Be careful: some sellers might neglect to tell you that the annual figures include a period of several months when the premises were not occupied. To avoid surprises. I recommend that you estimate that utility costs will increase 150 percent to 200 percent of the annual Consumer Price Index increase.

ASSESSING PHYSICAL STRUCTURE

Paint

In checking a structure, don't let a coat of paint fool you. Cosmetic repairs can hide serious problems. In the same manner, remember that paint is cheap; don't let the need of paint negatively affect your purchase decisions.

Electrical Wiring

Many older buildings are not wired adequately for today's living. Age isn't the only potential problem. In the late 1960s and early 1970s, aluminum wiring was used in many homes and apartment buildings because it was cheaper than copper wiring. Because this wiring creates a serious fire danger (it tends to arc where joined to copper), aluminum wiring might have to be removed, which can be expensive. By removing a wall plate, you can ascertain if aluminum wiring was used in your property. If a structure has any aluminum wiring you should use this fact to obtain seller concessions.

Roofing

Check the roof, especially if it is flat. Flat roofs have a shorter life and need more frequent repairs than pitched roofs. Get on the roof. It will generally be easy to see if the roof has been patched. Discolored water spots on the ceilings indicate leaks. If the roof has a pitched area and a flat area, the likely place for leaks is where these areas join. If an owner indicates that a roof was repaired, ask who did the work, and check with the roofer about the condition of the roof. He should give you an honest assessment, since misinformation will only alienate you as far as future work is concerned.

Plumbing

Copper plumbing will generally be in good shape. Pipes likely to cause you problems are iron or galvanized pipes. Test all faucets. Poor water flow could indicate a buildup of lime deposits in the pipes. Discoloration of water could indicate some iron pipes.

Many homes built prior to the early 1960s had galvanized plumbing. While ordinarily not a major problem, when buried in a slab or run underground, the pipes tend to deteriorate. Pipes that leak under a slab generally require costly work. Again, you should be aware of this risk and use it in your purchase negotiations to make the risk acceptable.

Property Age

When you check the plumbing in a building, you can also check its age. Until very recently, all toilet tanks had the date of manufacture stamped inside the tank. Ordinarily, a tank is installed within six months of manufacture. Unless the fixtures were updated during remodeling, this date gives a fairly accurate age of a property.

Another way to determine age is to check the walls around the water heater and furnace. Building inspectors usually nail their approvals in these areas. Often the approvals say "Do Not Remove." People generally follow instructions, so these original construction approvals are often found on buildings being torn down. A more accurate way to ascertain the age of a building is to check with the tax assessor's office. You can find the first year the improvements were taxed. Don't bother asking real estate agents how old a building is since they seldom give an accurate estimate on an older structure. Very often the age he or she quotes falls far short of the actual age of the structure.

Basements

In checking a property with a basement, look for water lines on the basement walls. These lines indicate previous flooding or sewer backup problems. Also check the foundation or basement for cracks. They indicate settling but are not usually serious. You can, however, make a fuss over small cracks, which will place an owner on the defensive and help your bargaining position. Check the floor joists in the corners with a pen knife. If use of the pen knife reveals soft or rotted timbers, then you should immediately bring in a qualified contractor to determine the cost of repairs if you are seriously considering a purchase.

Foundation

You should check the foundation for earthen tunnels running up to the wood. Be particularly alert in areas where the ground level is close to the wood. If the tunnels have been removed, you will see marks that look like a line on a map indicating a road that is not quite straight. If you find indications of these lines, then the structure has or had subterranean termites, and you should insist on or arrange a termite inspection. Again, while the damage may only be slight, the presence of termites places you in an excellent bargaining position. Be sure you know the extent of the damage before you give an offer on a property.

Insulation

If a building has poor insulation, you should consider whether the costs of added insulation would result in savings. Some states offer credits or tax deductions for insulation work. As a rule of thumb, make an improvement if increased revenues or cost reductions will offset the cost of the improvement in six years or less. Of course, improvements can be depreciated for tax purposes.

Other Items to Check

You should also check furnaces and air conditioners. Don't assume that everything is working properly. If a home has pocket doors that glide into the wall, check them out. Frequently they don't work properly and repairs can be costly. In older properties you should check flooring around plumbing fixtures for rot. One sign of a problem is loose tile. If you see neighbors outside, stop and talk with them. You can usually find out if the property or the neighborhood has any problems of which you are not aware.

Bugs are not usually a problem because they can be exterminated, and they can be an ally because their presence is a bargaining point in your favor. A roach running across a floor can knock several thousand dollars off a purchase price.

If repairs are necessary, get estimates. To be realistic, increase the average estimate by 50 percent. That is what you can expect to pay. As repairs progress, it is common to discover additional work that must be done.

HAZARDOUS SUBSTANCES

The presence of asbestos, radon gas, or any other hazardous substance in structures or on land is likely to be perceived by an owner as a significant problem. This perception can provide an owner the self-justification necessary to sell or lease option property at an unusually attractive price and/or terms. While legal liability of an owner to tenants is still in the gray areas in some states, the presence of hazardous substances has practically panicked many owners in their desire to rid themselves of a potential liability situation.

Asbestos

Asbestos describes a group of fibrous minerals that can cause severe damage and death when inhaled into the lungs. Symptoms of cancer may not occur until many years after exposure.

Asbestos is found in homes and other structures in:

- Vinyl asbestos floor tile
- Duct wrapping for heating and air conditioning

- Insulation on hot water and steam pipes as well as boilers (construction from the 1920s to 1972)
- Insulating sheets near heat sources
- Some roofing shingles and siding
- Ceiling and wall insulation in some homes built or remodeled between 1945 and 1978
- Sheet rock taping compounds
- Some ceiling tile
- Troweled on walls (it has a textured, firm appearance)
- Ceiling spray applications.

Generally, if asbestos is in good condition, it should not be removed because doing so can cause more harm than good. Friable asbestos (easily crushed or pulverized by hand pressure) is very dangerous. Get an engineering study as to the presence of asbestos prior to any purchase of a large structure built prior to the early 1970s. You should decide if immediate removal is required if asbestos is present. If so, consider an offer that would take its removal into account.

Formaldehyde

Formaldehyde is a colorless gas emitted where formaldehyde was used in the manufacture of various products. These include:

- Pressed wood products
- Urea-formaldehyde foam insulation (used during the 1970s and early 1980s)
- Some textiles

Formaldehyde presence can cause eye and throat irritation. While formaldehyde use in homes was generally before 1982, some commercial structures built since then utilized formaldehyde products.

Formaldehyde foam was used extensively by remodeling contractors and mobile home manufacturers who filled wall cavities with the foam through small openings. You can usually determine if formaldehyde foam insulation was used by removing a light switch plate. Removal can be costly because of the time consuming job of ripping out interior sheet rock. It is my understanding that because the relatively short life of formaldehyde emissions, few structures are likely to have dangerous levels of emission today. While removal is likely unnecessary, you can use the presence of urea-formaldehyde foam insulation in a property as a bargaining chip for better price and/or terms negotiations.

Lead

Excessive accumulation of lead in blood and body tissue can cause damage to the brain, kidneys, and central and peripheral nervous systems. At least two-thirds of homes built before 1940 and one-third of homes between 1940 and 1960 used lead-based paint. Since 1978, government requirements have significantly reduced the allowable lead in paint products.

The simplest way to deal with lead paint is to cover it with a durable covering. Removal methods are dangerous as they result in lead-rich dust. Again, the likely presence of lead-based paint, pointed out to an owner, gives the owner additional motivation to rid herself of the property.

Many homes built prior to 1988 had plumbing joints that used lead-based solder. Lead levels in water supplies are greatest during the first five years after construction. Mineral deposits generally form a coating over the plumbing and prevent later lead deposits from dissolving.

Radon

Radon is a radioactive gas that occurs in nature. Odorless, tasteless, and invisible, it originates from the breakdown of radioactive substances. Outdoors, radon dissipates into the air and is harmless. Dangerous levels of radon can be found in many structures. The known health effect of radon is an increased risk of lung cancer. Risk depends upon the level and length of exposure.

Above-average radon ratings can be used as a factor in obtaining seller concessions. However, for high radon readings you should realize corrective action is required such as vapor barriers over the soil, sealing concrete slabs and wells, repairing cracks, increasing ventilation, etc. Commercial radon detectors cost from $10 to $50. Also, a number of firms specialize in radon and other hazardous material detection.

Chemical Discharges

Any property that has or had an underground fuel tank likely has a toxic problem. You should have soil samples taken prior to purchase and know the likely clean up costs. On the positive side, the presence of a fuel tank is likely to be a strong seller-motivating force. By pointing out liability problems, an advantageous purchase is possible, even considering cleanup costs.

Urban property that has been used for many years for a variety of industrial uses could have a number of toxic problems. A major problem in checking for toxic problems is that tests might not reveal the presence of dangerous compounds unless you are specifically testing for the particular compound.

You should consider purchasing any structure as a separate corporate entity where it is likely that any hazardous material or waste is present. The purpose would be to offer personal protection if any tenant or invitee to the property successfully sues you for damages caused by the hazardous material or waste. You want to minimize your risk.

Professional Inspection

If you are not comfortable investing based on your own inspection abilities, hire a professional to inspect for you. Many competent firms and individuals do this type of work. Local real estate brokers can likely make recommendations. Costs for a single-family home inspection run from $150 to about $250 while commercial property would likely involve a per-hour rate. A professional inspection can not only save you from a serious mistake, it can increase your bargaining power and also provides peace of mind.

For a single-family dwelling, consider obtaining home warranty protection. Your purchase offer could require the seller to pay for the policy. The insurance covers appliances and major systems (generally for one year). If there are problems the policy can be very valuable.

Evaluating Tenants

Just as we evaluate a building, we can also evaluate tenants. Even though a tenant might be on a long-term lease or on only a month-to-month lease, it is possible to predict whether or not the tenant will remain. This is of particular importance in special-use structures. The tenant's financial strength is of course important. A Dunn and Bradstreet report will show the tenant's financial rating. The location of other businesses of the same type as the tenant's are also indications. If similar businesses have been moving out of the area, it is a negative indicator as to your present tenant. The nature and extent of tenant improvements and planned improvements can be strong indicators of a tenant's intent. You should consider what you would do if the present tenant left.

APPRAISALS

What a previous owner paid does not determine value. Don't worry that the price you offer is far more than the owner paid. On the other hand, don't feel you must offer at least what the owner paid. Values are based on what willing buyers will pay to willing sellers at the present time, not at any other time. Don't just ask the broker to tell you what the property is worth; if you are unsure about value, get an independent appraisal by an expert. Its cost can save you worry, heartache, and a financial mistake. Look for a professional appraiser who has either the MAI or SREA designation. But even with a fee appraisal remember, it is your money, not the appraiser's money that is at risk. The decisions are yours. A quick way to get a feel for value is to have a lender appraise the property for a loan. A lender's appraisal will generally be conservative. Or, hire a fee appraiser. Everyone who deals in real estate should have a basic understanding of the following methods of appraisal.

Market Comparison Method

This is the easiest appraisal method to learn and is used by most people when they buy property. They simply compare a property to other properties. When people say a price is too high, what they usually mean is that the price is higher than the price of a substitute property providing similar benefits of ownership. Using this method, we balance out amenities. For example, while one house has a two-car garage, a comparable house might have only a carport but also a fireplace. The homes might balance out, or you might feel that one is worth a particular dollar amount more than the other. We consider tenants, lease terms and financing in comparing properties. By checking the market, the average investor can get a very good feel for value based on comparables.

Replacement Cost Method

This method of appraisal is generally used on new structures or on service-type buildings where there are no comparables. Using the replacement cost approach to value, we determine what it would cost to build a similar structure today that provides similar benefits. We can then deduct the accrued depreciation (reduction in value caused by use and age). To this figure the value of the land is then added. The land value can be estimated by the market comparison method.

	_____	cost to build today
minus	_____	accrued depreciation
plus	_____	land value
equals	_____	value of the property

The problem with this method of appraisal is that it is frequently difficult to determine the amount of the accrued depreciation.

Income Method

This method is for income property. First, the net income is ascertained. In determining net, we deduct all expenses from the gross income. The only expenses not deducted are interest expense and payments on the principal. This net is then divided by a capitalization rate. Various methods are used to arrive at the rate, but it is really just the rate of return that an investor wants on an investment of this particular type. The greater the risk, the greater the rate of return an investor desires.

$$\text{rate} \div \text{net} = \text{value}$$

The income approach to value doesn't always work. The marketplace has increased values because of inflation. The basic economic principles of supply and demand underlie all evaluation. A market in which there are many willing buyers with few sellers means rising prices. The price you will pay today is determined by the marketplace, which reacts to what is anticipated. Current rents will rise in the future. Today's negative cash flows are expected to turn to healthy positive cash flows within a few years. If you believe that inflation is in our future, you can expect a general increase in real estate valuations. What today might seem a horrendous price could very well be tomorrow's bargain. In the same respect in areas where there are few buyers and many sellers, values have dropped significantly so that better-than-anticipated returns are possible.

Gross Multiplier

This is not a true appraisal method. It is only a way to get a ball-park figure. Assume that for a particular type of property investors are currently paying prices equal to nine times the annual gross receipts. Multiply the annual gross income times nine, and if the price asked is equal to or less than this amount, then you would want to investigate further.

Since the gross multiplier does not consider unusual expenses, it can be dangerous as an appraisal tool and is of little or no value to a serious investor. In years past, investors talked about cash-on-cash return or the actual cash returned on the cash investment. They also talked about cash throw-off, which is simply disposable cash income or net spendable income. Things have changed radically in the last few years. Only in a limited number of areas can quality properties be found that produce any disposable cash returns unless huge downpayments are made. Today, investors often get excited over a good break-even investment. In fact, negative cash flow investments that investors would have laughed at years ago are snapped up today if the depreciation and appreciation benefits offset the negative cash flow.

BEWARE THE CON MAN

Any time you mix money and people, you will find some people who will do or say whatever is necessary to get the money. Because real estate involves large dollar investments, there are many dishonest characters who are eager to figure out a way for you to part with your money. The deal that is too good to be true should be checked over with a jaundiced eye. While such a deal might come along, more likely it is not what it seems.

One con game to watch out for is the free lot scheme. Often at fairs people are asked to fill out a card for a free drawing. Every adult who entered the drawing is notified that he or she is a winner of one of the grand prizes, a lot in a particular subdivision. Each winner is given the legal description of the lot and is told that he or she has a period of time, usually 30 days, to pay the itemized transfer fees, which will vary from $500 to over $1,000, after which the winner will receive title to the lot.

Those who pay get a deed, but the lots used in these schemes are close to worthless—maybe only $100 to $200. What the free lot scheme has done is to allow a seller to get far more than the land could have been sold for by giving it away. The buyers feel they are getting something for nothing and are quickly parted from their money. While the scheme is generally illegal, variations on it are constantly cropping up. Remember that the free lunch went out with the nickel beer.

Dinner party sales are a little more sophisticated than free lot schemes. The way these work is that you win, or are given, a free vacation with the condition that you attend a dinner party. At the party (depending on the specifics of the scheme) you are worked by a combination of shills, presenters, and too-good-to-be-true presentations and offers. They all have one thing in common: they *are* too good to be true.

I am William P. Many years ago on a Sunday drive I stopped to check out a land subdivision. The salespeople had four-wheel drive vehicles to take people out to see various parcels. The salesperson touted one particular 2½-acre parcel which he said I could get for $4,995 with only $495 down. (Don't be deceived; the price is $5,000 but $4,995 sounds much better.) The salesperson stopped at the office, ostensibly to pick up a map before he returned us to our car. He suggested we come in for a cold drink because it was a hot day and it might take him awhile to find what he was after. The salesperson went into the next room and told another person we were interested in the particular $4,995 parcel (which was not true). The other person explained there was a mistake, that it was a $6,500 parcel and it couldn't be sold for $4,995. My salesperson argued loudly on my behalf and the "boss" finally agreed to let him sell it for $4,995 because he had quoted this price, but there would be no commission for him on the sale. I imagine many people fell for this sudden bargain opportunity and this salesperson who fought so hard for them and didn't get paid.

The reason so much real estate fraud involves raw land or lots is that there is so much of the land that serves no value other than to hold the earth together. These parcels can be purchased at very low cost and resold using unethical practices at obscene prices. It is a sad fact but when dealing with people who want to reach into your pockets, don't take them or what they say at face value. Check everything out.

WATCH OUT FOR YOUR EMOTIONS

Many investors fall in love with a property. When this happens, the desire to own can result in uneconomic decision making. In addition, if the seller is a skilled negotiator, she will use your emotions to her advantage while you lose all possible bargaining strength.

I like to point out to my students that my finest investment is a huge, ugly warehouse store. This building offers no pride of ownership. What it does offer is a national tenant on a triple net lease where the annual cash flow has grown to exceed the original total cash investment. This building illustrates that what is important is the bottom line, not pride of ownership. After you have made your millions, you might want to upgrade investments so you can take people around and point out what you own. However, pride of ownership normally costs money. Most buildings you can point at with pride, unless sold under distress conditions, do not make much economic sense. A danger to be avoided is the "I want to invest now" syndrome.

Many people have watched the investment game for years from the sidelines, when they finally decide to be players they want in immediately. Certainly it's a trite expression, but "act in haste, repent in leisure" does hold true. Take your time. Analyze before you jump at the first opportunity. When you have found a property that meets your needs and you have a feel for its value, you are now ready for the next step—your offer to purchase.

Don't rush to buy the deal that is too good to be true. As I have stated before, normally such a deal isn't true: there is usually something wrong. There are many sharp operators who are willing to lie, cheat, and steal to get your money. A seller may "forget" to tell you that the property is on a flood plain and that a building permit will not be issued or that an addition was built without a permit and must be ripped down because it violates building codes.

I was offered a commercial building at what appeared to be a bargain price. It was leased to a strong tenant, but the lease was about to expire. This didn't bother me because the property could easily be rented if the tenant failed to sign a new lease. The owner had left the country to live in Europe and had listed it for sale with an agent. I checked with the tenant as to his intentions and was told that he had an option to purchase the property in the lease and had recently notified the owner of his intention to exercise the option. The option was for a significantly lower price than the property was listed at. A purchase could have resulted in an expensive lawsuit as well as an actual loss.

Chapter 10

YOUR OFFER TO PURCHASE

Every man by nature has the right to possess property as his own.
This is one of the chief points of distinction
between man and the lower animals.

—Pope Leo XIII, 1891

Anyone can buy at retail. In fact, some people end up paying more than a fair price for merchandise. There are, however, people who seek and find bargain prices, but not for bargain merchandise. They buy quality at wholesale, close to wholesale, and even at below wholesale prices. Just as in retail merchandise, bargains await you in real estate, but you must know where to look and what to look for. Chapters 7 and 8 hopefully will have shown you how to locate wholesale opportunities. Again, you should realize that a purchase at market value means you have immediately lost at least 10 percent on your purchase.

All right, you have found a property you are interested in and want to make an offer. First of all you should realize that a "firm" price is seldom firm. Some bargaining is usually possible. Even when a seller refuses to reduce a price, he or she will frequently negotiate on what goes with the property, downpayment or interest rates.

SELLER'S MOTIVATION

If you are dealing directly with the owners or if the owners are present when an agent shows you the property, ask them why they are selling. Owners will normally answer truthfully. The greater the owners' motivation, the greater the likelihood of a purchase significantly below market value.

When a broker advertises a property and uses the word *asking* in the ad, the broker is really saying, "The price is soft." The same inference is given by using the words, "submit all offers," "motivated seller," or including a reason for the sale. Unfortunately, some ads don't reflect an owner's views. The broker might hint at a bargain just to bring in traffic. However, such ads are a starting point for your negotiating position. Ask the agent how long the property has been on the market and if the seller is truly motivated. If the property has been on the market for an inordinate period of time, a significant discount on the listed price is almost assured.

While real estate agents should not disclose an owner's motivation to sell without permission, from my experience at least half of the agents will do so if asked. In fact, many agents will volunteer the fact that an owner must sell and provide the reasons. When talking with the neighbors, you should also determine the seller's motivation. Knowing why an owner is selling can be worth tens of thousands of dollars to you in negotiation leverage.

With a must-sell owner it is possible to purchase property far below market value. Property purchased right will have a built-in safety net. Because you paid less than market value, such an investment reduces the possibility of the equity being eliminated by minor market fluctuations. It also allows you to price the property for a quick sale without taking a loss if a sale becomes necessary. The more information you have on the seller, the stronger may be your bargaining position. You should keep in mind that while you don't have to buy a particular property, the seller may have to sell. This can put you in the proverbial catbird seat. You are the one bargaining from a position of strength.

Unmotivated sellers are the reason you should avoid becoming emotionally attached to a property prior to purchase. Unmotivated sellers are *will-sell* sellers who are willing to part with property a their price. They are under no financial or emotional pressure to sell. Holding the property does not present a hardship, and they have no strong need to use the proceeds of the sale for any other purpose.

Avoid prolonged dealings with unmotivated sellers. This does not mean you should not make offers. Often sellers who claim to be unmotivated are in fact strongly motivated to sell. They have adopted a *not-very-interested* approach in order to hide the fact that they may indeed be desperate to sell. Therefore, don't be afraid of offering anyone a low offer. I have never been offended by anyone offering me money. The best approach is to give an offer under the assumption the seller is highly motivated to sell.

When buyers believe sellers are not strongly motivated to sell they generally begin negotiations at a higher figure than if sellers were motivated to sell. They will also set their purchase negotiation goals at a higher price than if sellers were motivated. In this way the unmotivated seller has won before negotiations have begun.

KNOWING WHAT THE SELLER PAID

Before you prepare an offer, it helps if you know what the seller has invested in the property. By knowing when the seller purchased the property, you should be able to get a fairly good idea of what the seller paid. By telling neighbors that you are interested in purchasing in the area, you can lead up to the property and find out when the present owner purchased it. Chances are neighbors who were living there at the time the property was purchased will even know what the present owner paid.

An owner is more likely to accept a price cut when it cuts only profit. If an owner asks $100,000 for a home and receives an offer of $80,000, he might accept it if he paid only $40,000. If the owner had recently purchased the property for $90,000, there is much less chance of the offer being accepted. In a buyer's market, bargains are more likely from sellers who have owned property for a number of years.

I purchased a condominium for $55,000 when the new units in the development were selling for over $80,000. However, this unit had been purchased in the first phase of a development when the price was $55,000. The same principle is true for financing. Owners are more willing to finance the buyer from their profit dollars.

HOW THE PRICE WAS SET

When dealing directly with the owners, ask them, "How did you arrive at that price?" This will often reveal very subjective thinking and that the price is by no means firm. A followup question to ask them is, "What is the lowest price you will take for the property?" The answer to this question really gives you a new asking price without having made an offer. Any negotiations would be based on discounts from this price, not the original asking price. This technique is simple, straightforward, and it works. The same technique can be used to receive discounts from contractors whose bids you intend to accept, "What's the best price you can give me for the job if we sign the contract right now?"

When dealing with agents, ask the agent how the price was arrived at. Ask for a copy of any competitive market analysis that was prepared. (This is an appraisal prepared for the owner.) Some agents may feel that the analysis is proprietary. If so, ask the agent to prepare a competitive market analysis showing all similar sales in the area in the last six months. In most areas computer printout material is readily available. Having competitive market information that the broker is going to show the seller gives the buyer clout in negotiating at the low end of comparable sales or even lower.

TIMING

There are times and situations when bargains are available in both prices and terms. In a buyer's market, where there are few buyers and many sellers, the best bargains are possible. There are always some sellers who for some reason must sell quickly. While a very low offer in a normal market might be rejected immediately, in a buyer's market the below-market offer will usually either be accepted or generate a counteroffer. When few offers are being made, an outright rejection of offers becomes unlikely.

In a seller's market, you may have to look for sellers who will carry paper (provide seller financing). In a buyer's market this is less likely to be a problem, since sellers realize that they are unlikely to get what they want. Owners who want all cash find that they have to carry paper if they want a sale. The better the financial condition of the seller, the greater the possibility that the seller will carry paper.

Besides economic conditions locally or on a national basis, a local marketplace can be effected by things like weather. One investor purchased two deluxe two-bedroom, two-bath condominiums in a winter recreational area after two years of little snow. He purchased both condos for under $125,000 each, even though similar units had previously sold in the $200,000 range. There were a great many units available, and the investor just kept on throwing out offers until he found owners desperate enough to accept. Incidentally, he resold both units after one year, making a profit of close to $200,000 on a total cash investment of about $40,000. That's a 500 percent cash on cash return.

Because there are more buyers than sellers in a seller's market, there are fewer truly desperate sellers. However, they are always out there. You just have to keep testing owners' motivation. You of course test them with purchase offers.

Don't give up when offers are rejected. A baseball player who gets a hit 3 out of 10 times at bat doesn't want to quit because of 7 failures. Instead, he rejoices in hitting .300.

HOW LOW TO GO

Problem properties usually can be purchased at attractive prices and/or terms. When a property has problems such as vacancies or health or building code violations, any offer may look good to an owner. If a property has developed a negative cash flow and must pay a significant sum each month to keep the property, what would otherwise be an unacceptable offer might be accepted. Don't be afraid to make too low an offer.

I liked an old drive-in restaurant which had been closed for many years. It was on a 100-by-500 foot highway lot near a small resort city where I own a summer home. One problem with the lot was that it would not perk test. This means that the soil could not support a septic system, so any user would have to use a holding tank for sewage and have it pumped out regularly. While a city sewer line was within half a mile, more development was necessary before it would be extended. The sewer problem was the reason the lot had not sold. If the property had had a sewer, a value of $70,000 would not have been excessive. As it was, the property had been listed for sale at $35,000 for several years without any buyers. I didn't think this price was really out of line, but I felt that a significantly lower offer might be accepted because of the problems and the length of time it had been on the market. The 800-square-foot building was of concrete block and in good repair. The windows had all been boarded up since the drive-in closed. I felt that I could rent the property for a number of uses such as construction office and yard, used car/implement dealer, or real estate office. In fact, I had a tentative tenant lined up. I came in with my offer after several weeks of consideration. I was too late. My offer of $24,000 was presented just one day after the seller had accepted an offer of $13,500. You never know what will be accepted until you test the seller with an offer.

What you offer is your decision. If you wish to make an offer, don't worry that the real estate agent will say it won't be accepted; it is your offer. Keep in mind that the primary responsibility of the real estate agent is to get the best deal possible for the seller, not for you the buyer. Also keep in mind that the real estate agent *must* present your written offer to the owner.

Again don't ask your friends what you should offer, especially if they aren't in the market. You are the one making the offer and who will also have to make the payments. Therefore, while you might want to listen to *some* others, especially your attorney and accountant, the offer must be yours.

Some buyers set their offers based on the seller's asking price. An asking price should not be the basis of an offer. Because you purchase significantly below an asking price does not mean you are getting a bargain. In fact, you might be overpaying. On the other hand, the offering price might be too low and actually be a better bargain than a discount from a price that is too high. Then it could be wise to offer full price. In fact the following example shows when to offer more than full price:

I'm Jim S. I formerly worked as a real estate agent, but I found I could make more money flipping (buying and selling) property for myself. I specialize in an area where the lots were sold years ago to investors and values have finally increased significantly. I look for lots for sale through brokers and owners, as well as write owners asking them to name a price for their lots.

I have found that many of the brokers and salespeople in the area are quite ignorant of lot values. Most of the sales to builders are made by middlemen such as myself, or by owners, so prices are often not reported to an MLS service.

I sell my lots to several dozen small or medium size volume builders. I know pretty well what my builders are looking for and how much they will pay.

Recently, I saw an agent putting up a for sale sign on a lot. I introduced myself and asked the price of the lot. I was told $5,600. I told the agent to please remove the sign, and that I would be at his office within the hour with a cashier's check for a full price offer.

The price was a bargain. While the price would have been proper a couple years earlier, the area had experienced a spectacular appreciation in value because of local economic conditions which, by the way, were counter to the national economy. Previously, I had offered full price on another lot soon after it was listed. In doing some checking, the owner felt she had priced the property too low and refused my offer. In another case I offered an owner less-than-asking price for his recently listed lot so as not to alert him that the price was too low. I lost out to another buyer who came up with a full price offer.

I decided in this case to take an unusual approach. With a cashier's check for $6,600 along with my offer for that amount, I told the salesperson at the real estate office I had a full price offer without conditions along with a cashier's check for the full purchase price. I stated I wanted acceptance by 6 p.m. that day or the offer would expire because I was considering other property (which was not untrue). I then handed a sealed envelope to the salesperson and left the office. It appeared to the agent and the owner that I had misunderstood the price and thought it was $6,600, rather than $5,600. Less than an hour later I received a call that my offer was accepted. Incidentally, it took me almost three months to get my price for the lot, $30,500.

When making an offer, keep in mind that while psychologically $99,900 will seem to you to be much lower than $100,000, it will appear much lower to the seller as well. It is well worth it to round off the price offered. Don't give offers that barely slice below $5,000 or $10,000 increments. When you sell property that is the time to come up with the $99,900 prices.

YOUR AGREEMENT

Don't make a verbal agreement or leave any part of an agreement to a verbal understanding. When it comes to a "friendly understanding," you will find that not everyone is "your friend." If it is agreed to, get it in writing and signed.

Your offer should specify what personal property is included in the sale. By spelling things out, you can avoid misunderstandings later. For example, if there is a swimming pool, does the pool cleaning equipment stay? Does a portable metal storage building stay? What about the drapes, slide-in ranges, fireplace screens and tools? Be specific. You can frequently induce sellers to include personal property such as washers, dryers and refrigerators, which they did not intend to include, by asking for them in the offer. This really serves as the equivalent of an additional cut in price.

Because personal property located in income property can be depreciated in a much shorter period of time than real property, you might want to specify in an offer for furnished units how much of the offer price applies to the real property and how much applies to the personal property. Chances are you will want to allocate the maximum amount possible to the personal property. An accountant can help you in making decisions in this area. If the seller is not giving up possession until after closing, your offer should cover the rent, if any, which the seller is to pay. The offer should also cover who is to be responsible for a casualty loss to the property, such as fire, prior to possession. For income properties, rent arrearages should be agreed upon. As a buyer you don't want to pay the seller for these arrearages because they may never be collected from the tenants. It can be a bookkeeping headache to try to collect them for the seller and then remit them. As a buyer you should just ask that all claims for past-due rentals be assigned to you as part of the consideration for the purchase price. If they are collectible, it is something extra; if not you are not penalized.

The word *obfuscate* is interesting in that the definition means to "confuse" or "make obscure." Because the word is not well known, readers tend to be confused and the meaning to many is obscure. If you use words like obfuscate in your offers to purchase or make it difficult for a seller to immediately understand your offer, it is doomed to failure. They are not going to accept it if they don't understand it. Say it simply and clearly. Obfuscation will mean failure.

If you are buying or selling and the other party wants to use his own *standard agreement*, be on the alert. Unless it is the exact form you have used in the past, have an attorney check it over carefully. With the use of computers and laser printers, some buyers and sellers produce their own forms, which don't really say what they appear to say. Be on the alert for added clauses in standard contract forms or nonstandard agreements as to who pays for what. In areas where sellers customarily pay for title insurance a clause might state:

> Buyer and seller share equally in the cost of a title insurance policy in the amount of the purchase price.

While the above sounds fair since sharing seems fair, as any child knows, the clause really sticks the buyer with several hundred dollars of what should be seller costs. Another trick is:

> Buyer shall assume seller's impound account at no cost to seller. Taxes
> will be prorated as of date of closing.

The above is outright thievery. The buyer takes over a valuable impound account (prepaid taxes) and gives nothing for the funds. In some cases this could amount to several thousand dollars.

When buying a property for rental or resale, you will normally want the right to show the property prior to closing. This can save you valuable time later. Consider the following clause for your purchase agreement:

> The purchaser shall have the right to show the property to prospective
> contractors, insurance carriers, buyers and/or renters at reasonable
> times prior to the close of this purchase agreement. For the purpose of
> this clause, four hours notice shall be deemed a reasonable notification
> time and reasonable hours shall be between 9 a.m. and 8 p.m.

Such a clause allows you to immediately begin getting bids for renovation work upon closing, if that is desired. It also means you can have the property rented or sold before you take possession.

If you are purchasing several parcels from one seller or a parcel that can conceivably be broken into several parcels, your offer should contain a release clause from any blanket encumbrance when there is seller financing. A blanket encumbrance is a lien covering more than one property, such as a single mortgage over several properties. The release clause provides for the release of separate parcels from the lien upon payment of stated amounts. Without the release clause, you could not resell one parcel without paying off the entire blanket loan.

Unless agreed otherwise, a purchaser who defaults can be held liable for damages by the seller. If the seller later completes a sale at a lower price, then the difference would be the seller's damages. I believe it is best to include a liquidated damages provision. Liquidated damages are damages agreed to in advance of any breach of contract, to be paid should the buyer default. Customarily in real estate transactions, the agreement is that the buyer forfeits the earnest money deposit as the damages. This is then the sole remedy that the seller can have against the buyer. As a buyer you might not want to forfeit the deposit if it were substantial. You can, however, specify a lesser amount as liquidated damages. You would probably want the liquidated damages agreement if the downpayment is low. You should provide in your purchase offer that:

Title shall be in the name(s) of _____ or nominee.

This allows you to sell prior to closing and for you to direct the seller to convey directly to your buyer. An advantage of this procedure is that you will save on title costs (title insurance or abstract), as well as the other costs associated with two separate closings.

Consider including a termite inspection clause in your purchase contract. The clause generally requires the seller, at his expense, to provide the purchaser a termite and structural inspection (this includes dry rot). The seller agrees to correct any damage or infestation prior to closing. Whether paid by the buyer or seller, a structural inspection is essential when buying older property. What you envisioned as a paint and sell fixer-upper could become a financial nightmare because of rotted support beams.

To protect against a seller's failing to make repairs if items are broken or become inoperative prior to the closing, you might consider the following:

Subject to all electrical, plumbing and mechanical equipment being in good and proper working order as of (*date*).

As a buyer you will want your offer to include a clause requiring the seller to maintain the garden, pool, buildings, and other improvements until closing. Otherwise neglect could result in substantial damage.

CONTINGENCY CLAUSES

You can tailor your contingencies to the special circumstances of a purchase. It is not wise, however, to include contingencies when they are not really needed. The more contingencies your offer contains, the less change you have of getting acceptance. Use contingencies only when they are really important.

If you really want a property, get your offer in without delay. If you are worried about something and want to check it out, you can make your offer *contingent upon* that item.

You can frequently tie up a property for a few days by placing a contingency on it such as:

Contingent upon the approval of ___ within ___ days of acceptance.

The approval person could be your spouse, a professional real estate counselor, a construction expert or any other appropriate person.

If you are unsure of your ability to finance a purchase, the following statement in an offer protects you from being in default should financing not be available:

Contingent upon obtaining a loan in the amount of 80 percent of the purchase price at no more than 8 1/2 percent interest by (*date*).

If you want a zoning change, you could include:

Contingent upon a zoning change to M 2 1/2 by (*date*), allowing 14 apartments to be built on the site.

This sort of contingency can be dangerous because it may give the seller ideas which could result in a higher price.

If the vacant property does not have sewer, you want to make certain that a septic system is possible. You could state:

Contingent upon passing a percolation test by (*date*).

If a property has a problem tenant or if you wish the property for your own use, you can save cost, time and emotional drain by having the present owner remove the tenant. You might state:

Contingent upon owner delivering premises
in a vacant condition at time of closing.

If your old property is highly salable and the property you are purchasing has been on the market for some time, the seller may agree to the following contingency:

This offer is contingent upon the sale
of the property at (*address*) by (*date*).

The following contingency is preprinted in many offers. It protects the buyer against easements or other problems that the buyer is unaware of:

Contingent on buyer's approval of preliminary title report.

Often, what a seller indicates a lease provides is not in fact what the lease states. You might consider:

Subject to seeing and approving existing leases by (*date*).

If you have not checked local codes and have doubts as to a building's compliance with the codes, you certainly would want the following provision in your offer:

Subject to seller warranting that the building complies with all building, health and fire codes.

In an older building where you were only able to see one or two units, what you saw might possibly be the exceptional units, not the typical units. You might therefore wish the following contingency:

Subject to the inspection and approval of all units in the building by the buyer.

Don't take it for granted that a loan can be assumed. You should subject your offer to a loan assumption if the assumption is important to you. A clause such as the following is very common:

> Subject to the seller's being able to assume an existing mortgage in the amount of $___ at ___ percent interest with payments of $___ per month with _____.

When an offer requires seller financing, you want the material terms of the financing spelled out in detail. For example:

> Subject to the seller's taking back as part of the purchase price a second mortgage in the amount of $___ and payable at $___ or more per month. Said payment to include interest at ___ percent. This mortgage shall be due and payable in full ___ years from date of closing.

You will want the "or more" to be included since it will allow prepayment without any penalty. Most sellers will not accept a long-term second mortgage. Normally, sellers want the buyers to agree to pay them off in five to seven years. Usually, because of appreciation, increased equity will allow refinancing to pay off this second mortgage. However, you should keep in mind the fact that values do not always go up. There is some risk.

If you have any doubts at all as to the income and expenses quoted, consider the following:

> Subject to the seller warranting that the attached income and expense statement is accurate and complete for the period indicated.

If the statement provided was intentionally prepared falsely, the seller will probably refuse to accept this warranty. An owner who does not want to accept a contingent offer can usually be prevailed upon to do so by the inclusion of the following:

> The seller has the right to continue to market the property. Should the seller accept another offer that is contingent upon the rights of _____, then _____ shall have ___ days from receipt of notice to waive his or her condition(s) as set forth in paragraph ___. Failure of _____ to waive said conditions in person or by the receipt of a registered letter by _____, shall terminate and void this offer and buyer's deposit shall be returned to the buyer.

The seller does not jeopardize the ability to sell the property with such a clause as the property remains on the market.

LEMONADING

Some investors use the term *lemonading*—adding a sweetener to a deal to make it more acceptable. Your lemonading could consist of agreeing to pay an attractive interest rate, agreeing to pay off a loan in a relatively short period, agreeing to step increases in interest rates or even to simply adding additional cash.

Lemonading can take place in the original offer or in subsequent negotiations. Never give all you can give with your original offer. Leave room so some concessions can be given during any negotiations. You must allow a seller to save face by gaining something in the negotiation process.

The size and form of your earnest money deposit can serve to sweeten what would otherwise appear as a sour offer. Large earnest money deposits in the form of cashier's checks made out either to a broker's trust account or to an escrow agent will make it difficult for an owner to turn down an offer. Don't give large deposits directly to the owner because you might have a situation where an owner can't deliver clear title and has spent your deposit. Cash can be effectively used by buyers; it seems to mesmerize people.

ASSUMING LOANS

Even if you can pay cash or intend to refinance, if there are advantageous private loans on the property, you should try to assume them. After the purchase you can then contact the individuals holding the loans and offer to pay off the loans at a discount. You can usually negotiate some sort of discount for early payment. If the individual needs money, then the discount can be substantial. I once obtained a 50 percent discount on a second mortgage, which actually amounted to more than a $5,000 price reduction after the purchase.

If the sellers will carry paper, let them, even if you could obtain similar conventional financing. Conventional lenders are not interested in discounting the loan for an early payment, but private individuals frequently are. After about six months, an offer of prepayment at a discount can be made. The seller might not accept at first, but it will be in the back of the seller's mind as a source of cash. There is an excellent chance that eventually the seller will make you a discount offer for prepayment.

"As Is"

If an owner is selling property "as is," be particularly careful. Look for the unexpected. Just because you buy a property "as is" does not, however, mean that you have given up all your rights. If a seller knows of a hidden defect and fails to inform the buyer or actually conceals the defect, many courts will hold the seller liable despite the fact that the purchase was "as is."

USING ATTORNEYS

Use an attorney to help you make your first offers. You can ask an attorney in advance what the fees will be. Legal fees to prepare an offer are very small when compared with the obligations you are accepting with a purchase. You will want to develop a good relationship with an attorney specializing in real estate. In many states, attorneys with special training or experience are allowed to hold themselves out as real estate specialists.

There is a danger in accepting definitions from a real estate agent. The agent is giving you his or her opinion, which may not be the opinion a court would have should a disagreement arise. Also keep in mind that generally the first duty of the agent is to the owner, not you. The agent also wants to make a commission. While most real estate agents are honest, as in any group there are some bad apples.

I know of an investor who customarily takes her attorney in with her as a partner on her deals. She finds the properties and her attorney prepares the offers and handles all legal and financing matters. The two complement each other very well.

ABSTRACTS AND TITLE INSURANCE

In many areas of the country, abstracts are used to verify title. An abstract is simply a copy of every recorded document dealing with the property. An attorney will read the abstract and give you an opinion as to the marketability of the title. Even though you use an attorney, there can still be problems with an abstract. An attorney would not know if a prior deed was forged or if a prior grantor had been declared insane or was otherwise incompetent prior to transfer of title. Similarly, a single owner might actually be married and there could be unknown spousal interests. I therefore recommend that your offer specify that title shall be verified by a standard policy of title insurance paid for by the seller. Sellers often prefer abstracts since bringing an abstract up to date can be less expensive than title insurance. The attorney who helps you might not particularly like this request, since title insurance has been making inroads into an area formerly held by lawyers alone. Title insurance means no abstract reading fees for the attorney.

You should consider purchasing an extended coverage policy of title insurance. As the buyer, you will be expected to pay this additional cost. An extended coverage policy provides additional protection for items such as incorrect survey or building on the wrong lot. Your title insurance company will explain the advantages of obtaining this additional coverage.

CONSIDER ALL FINANCIAL OBLIGATIONS

Before you complete an offer, carefully consider the financial obligations. Can you make the payments? Don't count on a quick resale for a profit. By using amortization tables, which all real estate agents and investors should have, you can compute your principal and interest payments. To this you should add an estimated amount for taxes, insurance, and maintenance, as applicable. As previously stated, if you would like your own amortization tables, contact a title insurance company. Many give them away free.

ACCEPTANCE OF OFFERS

Your offer to purchase should state how long it is good for. If no period is specified, the offer is considered to be open for a "reasonable period" of time. Even though you may allow a number of days for acceptance of your offer, you have the right to withdraw your offer any time prior to acceptance. Acceptance is generally considered to take place upon the mailing of the seller's written acceptance. Once the seller has placed the acceptance in the mail, you can no longer revoke your offer. Revocation, on the other hand, generally takes place upon receipt. Therefore, even though you have mailed your revocation of your offer, it can generally be accepted by the seller up to the time your revocation is actually received.

I do not believe in giving the seller very much time to accept an offer. If the seller is in the community, provide one day for acceptance. This forces a decision and usually avoids a situation where the seller runs around and gets the advice of numerous people. The seller's friends are likely to tell him or her what he or she wants to hear, which is, "Why, your property is worth lots more than that!" Often inexpert advice causes sellers to lose advantageous sales.

A real estate investor cannot take rejection personally. When you make what you consider to be a good offer and the owner rejects it, this isn't a rejection of you. Often the owner is just not motivated to sell or the timing isn't right. Many investors let the owner (or agent) know that if the owner has a change of mind, they will consider resubmitting an offer. Often many months later, the investor is contacted by the owner to see if there is still an interest to purchase.

Actually, relatively few offers are met with outright rejection. What usually happens is that a counteroffer is made. You should not worry if a seller refuses to give in an inch. If the purchase makes sense for you at the seller's price and terms, accept them. Some buyers walk away from advantageous deals just because the seller won't give any concessions. Buyers feel they are losing face if they give the full asking price. Ask yourself, "If the seller had asked 20 percent more and had come down to the present price, would I want to make the purchase?" If "Yes," then go ahead with it.

However, if the deal doesn't make sense, walk away from it. Don't try to reach an agreement for agreement's sake. Don't worry about a lost opportunity; there are plenty more coming up. You are never going to run out of opportunities.

AUCTION SALES

Auctions are an interesting way to buy property, but don't go to an auction unprepared. Know the property, set your top price, and stick to it. It is easy to get caught up in the emotion of an auction setting. While an auction can provide a bargain, there are times when property at an auction will sell for far more than the market would otherwise indicate. Unless the seller has arranged financing, have your financing lined up in advance. An auction setting does not allow you to condition your offer. You as the offeror are usually making an unconditional offer to purchase at a stated price. The offer is not accepted by the auctioneer until the gavel falls.

At an auction, it is not just the thickness of the wallet that determines who gets the property, it can also be a matter of psychology. Other bidders may increase the price by $500 or $1,000 when there are few bidders. A tactic that often scares off nonprofessionals is to suddenly up the ante of the game and increase the bid by a large amount such as $10,000. When professionals know there will be bidding competition, another tactic effectively used by some bidders is to be the one to open the bidding at a price significantly above the minimum price. Other bidders realize they cannot steal the property so they hesitate. Hopefully, their hesitation lasts long enough to allow the auctioneer's hammer to fall.

When you raise the ante, chances are those who are bidding will still top your bid by a low amount hoping you have bid your maximum. If the property value permits, a second major increase will often silence the other bidders. If the bidding had been allowed to increase in small increments, chances are the final price would have risen to the point where a purchase is either economically marginal or uneconomical.

A variation of this heavy-hitter approach is to stay out of the bidding in the early stages letting others bid by increasingly reduced increments. You can often get the opposition to fold by coming into the game late with a bid that significantly increases the table stakes.

Auction sales today are not just for distress properties. Developers often use auctions to clear out subdivisions. They will set minimum sale prices very low so they attract buyers even though it may be unlikely that any units actually sell at the minimum set.

Watch the crowd. Young couples and couples with children are generally bidding on property that will become their home. Single persons, often with note pads, can mean investors buying for rental or resale. When there are a group of properties, the first properties will generally be bid up by buyers who are buying for their own use. The investors will either not bid or will drop out early. (This will give you an idea of their expectations.)

Enter the bidding after about one-third to one-half of the units are sold. Even then, only bid if the sale prices are within an acceptable range to you. Some of the best prices are often when between 60 percent and 80 percent of the units are sold. Bidding for some units will defy any pattern because homebuyer bidders may want particular units. That is, prices will peak up significantly for a property even though similar property has sold previously for less.

Watch the other bidders. If there are a great many bidders remaining who appear to be looking at units for their own use, the final group of homes sold might sell for prices higher than any others. However, if most of these buyers have left, the final units could sell at bargain prices.

People often change their personality at auctions. It is similar to normally meek people becoming aggressive when they get behind the wheel of a car. They act as if giving a bid makes them a winner and they continue to bid against all logic to avoid losing. Don't let such a person lure you into remaining in the bidding game when it is no longer in your best interests.

Chapter 11

SUBDIVIDING—
SMALLER CAN BE BETTER

> No man acquires property without
> acquiring with it a little arithmetic.
> —Ralph Waldo Emerson, 1850

Whoever first said that the whole is equal to the sum of its parts didn't have the slightest idea what subdividing is all about. In real estate the value of a large parcel can be considerably less than the value of the same property cut up into smaller, more usable units. For example, a 20-acre parcel might have a market value of $3,500 per acre, or $70,000. If that 20-acre parcel were broken into four parcels of 5 acres each, they might sell for $25,000 each, or $100,000 total. If the parcel were broken into 1-acre parcels, they might well sell for $8,000 each, or $160,000 total. As parcels are cut into smaller acreage pieces, there is an increased demand since more buyers can afford to buy and use them. An increase in demand translates into an increase in price. Today we have many different types of subdivisions—recreational, conventional housing, mobile home and even industrial properties.

THE SUBDIVISION PROCESS

While the subdivision process sounds simple, it can actually be quite involved. There are local, state, and even federal regulations concerning subdivisions. Large subdivisions also require environmental impact reports, which can be costly. The average time for subdivision approval varies by state and community. In some areas it takes only a few months, while in other areas, such as Los Angeles, a three-year period to obtain all approvals is not unusual.

Although the raw land can usually be purchased with little money down, the payments must be made on the land; therefore, a developer must have sufficient cash flow to make the payments during approval and development stages.

Residential subdivisions in some areas must be fully improved. This can mean sewer, water, streets, curb, gutter, and even sidewalks, which can mean expenditures of thousands of dollars for every lot. Because of the development costs, many subdividers develop in phases, such as 50 lots at a time, in a development that contains perhaps 500 lots total. As an alternative, in many states municipal bonds are issued to pay for the improvements. Buyers of each lot then is subject to a bonded indebtedness. This puts the cost of the improvements on the buyer, not the developer.

While large subdivisions can require a great deal of time and effort, a simple split of a parcel into two parcels can usually be accomplished with little difficulty. In many states you can manufacture as many as four parcels from a single parcel with relatively few problems. Your local building department or planning commission can tell you what state and local procedures and regulations govern the subdivision process. There are people who will handle the detail work of a subdivision approval for you at a fee, but if you intend to handle more than one subdivision, you should get involved in the detail work so you fully understand what is required.

Before getting involved in any subdivision project, consider all the costs as well as the time required. As a rule of thumb, carefully estimate the time required from land acquisition to the first sale, and then double this time. After carefully estimating all development costs, add 50 percent to that figure. If the project does not look economically feasible based on these estimations, don't do it. It is seldom that initial time and cost estimates come close to the actual costs. Don't count on being lucky. Because of the many uncertainties involved in subdivision approval and land preparation, you should leave a sufficient profit margin to cover the worst contingencies.

The great cost in time and money of getting a subdivision approved opens up an entirely new field for investors with vision—wholesaling parcels with approvals for developers who want to build right now. The investor gets the proper zoning changes, has the engineering work completed, and obtains all approvals. This work can be worth much more than its cost to a developer. Keep in mind that payments must be made on the land while this approval work is taking place. Also, what is finally approved can often turn out to be much less desirable than what was originally contemplated. For instance, the density approved might be much less than what was originally requested. As an added risk, if the approvals are completed in a period of economic contraction, a far longer holding period than originally anticipated might be required.

Release Clauses

When you purchase property you are considering splitting, you should provide in your mortgage or trust deed a release clause or a provision for separate liens on the parcels. A release clause allows you to sell one parcel free and clear of the mortgage upon the payment of a specified sum of money. Without a release clause or a provision for separate liens, the only way you could sell one of the parcels would be by land contract. If someone wanted to pay cash, you could not give clear title unless you paid off the blanket lien covering all the parcels.

Making Lots

Most subdivisions are divisions of land for single-family residential use. Location is of primary importance in a residential subdivision because location will be the strongest influence on the sale price of the lots. Physical features such as trees, rocks, view and slope will also affect value. If land has a creek or spring and proper topography, there is the possibility of developing a lake. Lake developments, whether natural or constructed, offer exceptional investment opportunity for future residential development. Water-related property sells at a great premium. Some developers simply locate property and put in the lakes, after which they wholesale the parcel to a developer for final development.

My name is Richard R. I build vacation homes. I recently paid $15,000 down on a $150,000 purchase price for a 160-acre parcel containing a 40-acre lake. I spent $9,000 for engineering work and $28,000 for some land clearing and bulldozing of roads. An additional $11,000 was spent improving a beach and park area. I received clear title to the land so I could subdivide by getting the seller to agree to carry a first mortgage on another property I owned. Because the security was good, he agreed. By the time I was ready to sell the first lot I had almost $100,000 cash invested, which included subdivision approvals and fees.

I sold 45 lakefront lots having 100 feet or more of frontage at prices averaging $10,000. I offered the lots with 10 percent down and 10 percent interest on the balance, but about half of the lots were paid for in cash. I set the price low on all the lots for quick sale. A portion of the lake frontage was owned by the back-lot owners as common area (park). The 25 back lots were from 2 to 5 acres in size. These lot owners each had a dock space. I sold out in a little over one year grossing over $700,000 and having a final net profit of $400,000. When my interest collected is considered, I should be taking several hundred thousand dollars more out of the project.

As a side benefit, I have been selected the building contractor by nine of my lot purchasers.

RECREATIONAL SUBDIVISIONS

Recreational subdivisions are usually located within 100 to 250 miles of a major metropolitan area. Some unusual recreational clubs are undivided-interest subdivisions. Many have a club house and 1,000 or more camping or trailer sites.

Buyers don't get their own site, they just own an interest in the whole such as a one-ten-thousanth interest and the right to use an available site. The club sells lifetime memberships. While there are more members than sites, it is unlikely that all of the sites will be occupied at one time. While the profit potential sounds great, the sales costs can eat up even what was originally viewed as an obscene profit.

Own-Your-Own-Lot Mobile Home Parks

Lots are small, usually about 50 by 75 feet. Even with the loss of land for streets and public areas, developers may still obtain from 6 to 10 lots per acre. In many cases these lots sell for upwards of $40,000.

Some park owners have turned existing parks into condominiums. It is a way to sell the park quickly and obtain a premium price. Because of the immobile nature of today's installed mobile homes, the buyers are right there; they are the current renters. Everyone benefits in this type of sale. The park owner gets a premium price and the lot buyers, while possibly paying more each month toward rent, can now deduct the interest from their taxes, and they are protected from rent gouging. The net effect for many of the buyers will be a lower true monthly cost. A word of caution: In many areas it is difficult if not impossible to get approval for condominium conversions.

Breaking up Resorts

Older resorts are generally poor investments for operators who will often sell far below reproduction costs with favorable terms. In recent years a number of investors have been actively buying lake resorts and breaking them up. While a large resort operating at a loss might not be desirable, individual vacation cabins appeal to a large market.

Some investors who break up resorts have had a continuing business for many years.

I'm Anderson. I've been breaking up vacation property in Wisconsin and Michigan for about 20 years. My operation is simple. I give a cash offer for resorts having at least ten cottages. I look for basically sound structures with indoor plumbing but nothing fancy. My offers are cash offers subject to obtaining approvals for splitting up the property within a set time period. In this way, I am not at risk if there are any problems with a land division. I pay to have the paperwork handled by others. After I get my approvals, I upgrade cosmetically and put the units on the market. After I have my costs out, I will often sell the remaining units to local brokers at a wholesale price. I want to have cleared out on a project before I start another one. In this way my risk is readily manageable. The people who go broke in this business get greedy and let their risk get out of control.

Right now I am doing one resort about every 18 months. My son has come into the business with me and someday I hope my grandson will join us.

FARMS

Large farms can often be broken into several smaller farms or recreational land parcels with the resulting value of the pieces far exceeding the value of the whole. This is especially true for scenic land that really is marginal land for farm use. The increase in value in making small farms out of large farms is unrelated to the economics of farming, where larger is generally better. It is, instead, related to the demand for retirement or hobby farms as well as acreage. The buyers of these 20 acres and independence farms are not interested in productivity figures, they are generally in love with the idea of a rural lifestyle and beauty is of primary importance.

Trees and views are far more important than dollar yields. In fact, the least desirable farmland can often be sold for the highest prices when broken up into smaller farm units.

I'm Frank. It's been 20 years since my first farm purchase and I guess I must have purchased over 60 farms since then.

My formula now is:

1. Find farms of 120 acres or less within 40 miles of my home that have views, wooded land, or other features city people like. Water frontage and orchards are highly desirable features. (I avoid prime farm land.) I like farms where the buildings and 5 to 20 acres can be broken off into minifarms and the rest broken into 3- or 4-acreage parcels offering scenic homesites.

2. Get an option to buy for 30 days. (I don't pay more than $250 for an option.)

3. Check the county as to any problems in splitting the parcel as planned.

4. Have percolation tests made to determine if the likely home sites will support a septic system. (This is very important if the soil has a lot of clay.)

5. Approach all adjoining farms to see if the owners are interested in buying any of the crop land. I usually offer it at the going price and offer terms. In several cases I have sold the entire farm except for the buildings and from 5 to 20 acres around them to a neighbor. Keep in mind that if the land is good the neighbors will covet it.

6. If I can get an offer on the nonscenic part of the farm or if the purchase still makes sense without selling the crop land, I will exercise the option. I won't buy unless I feel I will make at least a 100 percent net profit on the purchase price.

7. My offers are generally low. I formerly offered 20 to 30 percent down and the balance in six months but now I make cash offers because I have the money available. The advantage of cash offers is it makes a low offer hard to turn down.

8. After survey decisions and minimum improvements, I put the property on the market with ads and signs. I will pay a commission to brokers who sell. In fact, I will even pay a commission to a broker who finds me a farm to buy. While others worry about paying fees, my attitude is that I don't care what I pay or what others make as long as the net profit is there for me.

The following investor in farms has taken a different but equally profitable approach:

My name is Gopal R. About 15 years ago, I was selling real estate in a small city. I listed a small orchard with a mobile home on it. My ad brought in dozens of calls and the orchard was sold in three days. My best friend, who also worked at the same office, suggested that we make our own small orchards and that is what our partnership has been doing every since. We buy orchards, generally orchards that are not economically productive because of overproduction in the particular variety of fruit or nut. We buy orchards rather than other farms because we know orchards have a particular attraction to people. When they see rows and rows of trees, it is different than looking at a plowed field. We make agricultural subdivisions by breaking the orchard into a number of parcels varying from 10 to 40 acres in size. The subdivision process for agricultural subdivisions is much simpler than for other subdivisions in our state. For the parcels that don't have a farm house, we put a new double wide, three-bedroom, two-bath mobile home on the site plus a large metal garage/workshop.

Our sales are to people my partner calls "Wannabees," people who desire to return to a simpler agricultural life. A Wannabee is more interested in joy than in profit. We do, however, provide each of our purchasers with a farm consultant for eight, one-half-day periods to help them get started.

There are a lot of "Wannabees" out there—to date we have turned 67 "Wannabees" into farmers. Most of our buyers regard us as friends. They are primarily active retirees. Owning an orchard gives purpose to their lives. "Wannabees" have provided me and my partner with a good living. In a few years, I will likely retire. I already own my own orchard. I guess I'm a "Wannabee," too.

COMMERCIAL CONDOMINIUMS

In the late 1960s and early 1970s some commercial condominiums had difficulty selling out. These earlier condominiums came at a time when the condominium concept was not widely accepted. In addition, the economy was relatively stable and major rent increases were not a serious threat to business. With office buildings and shopping centers now selling at less than reproduction costs, the time may now be ripe for commercial condominiums.

Today's business people are sophisticated in tax matters. They realize that ownership offers several tax advantages over renting. Besides the fact that interest and tax payments are deductible, ownership offers the further tax benefit of depreciation. Furthermore, past increases in commercial space rentals has made many realize the desirability of controlling their outlay for space requirements so as not to be at the mercy of any future inflationary economy. In addition, ownership is an investment that can over the long run be expected to increase in value and, as such, is a hedge against inflation.

INDUSTRIAL PARKS

Industrial parks offer exceptional profit potential. Generally they should be located close to good transportation arteries. A railroad siding is not required for many light manufacturing plants. However, large water mains and good water pressure are essential for sprinkler systems. Possible heavy electrical demands require the availability of three-phase wiring. Adequate sewage disposal is also required. In some better industrial parks in Orange County, California, lots are selling for more than 10 dollars per square foot. This is almost one-half million dollars per acre. Many industrial park sites are not sold to industrial firms. They are sold to investors. A one-acre industrial site offers intriguing possibilities as a long-term investment.

CONDOMINIUM CONVERSIONS

Perhaps the greatest opportunities for small investors are in the condominium conversion area of subdivisions. In a conversion situation you are usually simply changing from rental units to units owned by the individual occupants. One of my colleagues who has done amazingly well at condominium conversions calls them the greatest idea since sliced bread.

In the mid-1970s, housing could not be purchased in many areas for under $50,000. At the same time, apartment buildings could be purchased at perhaps $25,000 per unit. A person who purchased a 10-unit, two-bedroom building for $250,000 could get the required approvals and convert the existing building into 10 condominium units that could be readily sold for $50,000 each. If the buyer had purchased the building with $50,000 down, then the $250,000 profit would be a profit of 400 percent on the downpayment. This may seem like a huge profit, but there have been thousands of condominium conversions with profits of this magnitude and greater. Because of the demand, as more people have realized the potential for conversions, apartment prices have soared. Nevertheless, substantial profits are still being made. A great many condominium conversion units are sold to the tenants. By purchasing their units, they get the tax benefits of ownership plus stay in their neighborhood and avoid all the hassles of relocation.

Many developers call a tenant meeting in order to sell condominium conversions to their tenants. They offer current tenants first crack at purchasing their units (required in many states). Because they would likely update kitchens, floor coverings, baths, etc., as well as redecorate for other buyers, the developers are able to appeal to a bargain syndrome by offering the units to tenants at significant discounts on prices offered to the public. The developers set a time limit for acceptance and usually have a variety of financing options. Some developers raise the rents before the tenants option rights expire as a further inducement to buy.

A number of firms handle the paperwork on condo conversions for a fee for preparation of the package for local and/or state approval. A flexible mind will allow you to see conversion opportunities that others ignore. These opportunities are all around us. There are still opportunities available.

My name is John C. At age 32, I was a yacht salesman for a yacht broker. I was paying child support and my principal asset was a three-year-old Corvette not yet paid for.

I learned that the 400-plus slip marina where I worked was going on the market by the elderly owner/operator. Inquiries revealed that he wanted $10,000,000 for the marina. (The price was based on a professional appraisal.)

I went to my bank and arranged to refinance my car. I then went to a real estate attorney, to whom I had previously sold a boat, and had him draft an option agreement.

The option provided a 10-day right for me to buy the marina for $10,000,000. I was giving $10,000 for this option; virtually my entire net worth.

A provision of the option was that I could extend it for two separate three-month periods upon payment of $50,000 for each extension. These payments would not apply to the purchase price. (My reasoning was that I wanted the option to be as attractive as possible.)

We included a paragraph in the option stating, "The owner (Optionor) will cooperate with the optionee in any requests to local or state governmental agencies as to use, changes and/or permits/approvals, providing said requests will not reduce the marinas docking, storage or parking facilities."

I didn't want to show the owner what I planned to do. In fact, the only person I revealed my plan to was my attorney, who suggested that he contact the owner and meet with him and his attorney to present the offer.

My attorney called me and told me my offer had been accepted. While there was some objection to the $10,000 option fee, my attorney overcame this problem with the fact that it was only for 10 days and was really a binder. My attorney diverted the owner somewhat by asking for access to records and the cooperation of the seller's accountant during the 10-day period.

I had told my attorney that once I had the option to buy, I would contact several large developers I knew through boat sales. What I would propose would be a partnership. They would put up the balance of the option money, and we would then turn the marina into a planned unit development where each owner would own his or her own dock space and the recreational facilities (restaurant, bar, parking, etc.) would be owned in common. This idea wasn't completely original with me. I had read about this having been done successfully elsewhere.

Because of the lack of dock space in our area, I felt most of the tenants would have to buy their space or have a boat without a dock. Besides, with rising rentals a purchase would make sense to most of the owners.

My attorney had indicated to me that my idea had a great deal of merit. Undoubtedly, the docks could be sold separately for a significant profit. He brought the accepted offer to me and then offered to not only put up the balance of the money needed for the option, but to return my $10,000 investment and handle the subdivision approvals. He also indicated that in our state, a cooperative would be a better way to go because he felt it could be handled in less time and time was important. The arrangement we negotiated was that we would both be partners in the venture with each having a 50/50 share after all expenses including option costs and reasonable attorney fees (not to exceed $100,000) were reimbursed to my partner. My partner would advance all required cash and would receive 10 percent interest on all cash advanced.

Well, the net result was we got our approvals and over two-thirds of the boat owners agreed to buy in. They each were to receive a share of stock in an owner corporation and a lease on their unit (dock). While prices varied by the unit, we sold each share for an average sale price of over $50,000.

We had the $10,000,000 in a trust account before the second option period expired. My share of the net was more than $5,000,000 in a period less than eight months. My investment, $10,000, was for only three days.

One unusual condominium conversion involved a parking garage near Beacon Hill in Boston. The area's desirability had risen and attracted many younger professionals (gentrification). New purchasers had expensive cars, but many of the older homes did not offer garages or parking space. Developers purchased a commercial garage and turned it into a condominium selling spaces for around $12,000 each. The developers made one error. They did not research the demand. They quickly sold all of their units. While a good profit resulted, they failed to maximize this profit. Reportedly, within a year, units were being resold in the $100,000 range.

Condotels

Some motels and hotels have begun converting to condominiums. They call themselves condotels. The management will rent the unit as a regular motel or hotel unit when the owner is not there, and the owner shares the gross receipts with the management. These units have been primarily in resort areas. I don't expect this concept to be highly successful for several years, but it is a concept to watch.

CURRENT TRENDS IN CONDOMINIUM CONVERSIONS

Some investors specialize in buying an apartment, getting the condominium approvals, and selling it. In some cases they can use options and get the approvals during the option period. The investors can sell the buildings readily with the conversion approvals. In this manner large profits are possible; the only investment is the price paid for the option.

If you are interested in any type of condominium conversion, I recommend you contact your state real estate department, which normally handles state approvals. You should fully understand the procedures required for conversion. You might find that there are different requirements for cooperatives than condominiums. In some cases additional expenses such as garages may be required, or the local requirements may totally preclude an economical conversion. If you are uncertain as to whether or not approval for conversion will be granted, try to tie the property up with an option while you seek approval.

Fully analyze the market for converted units. Consider whether or not they will be saleable to the present tenants and what the individual units will sell for. Then, if the profit potential justifies the risks, go ahead. For any condominium or condominium conversion consider covenants, conditions, and restrictions (CC&Rs). An attorney specializing in real estate can help you in this area. CC&Rs that meet the needs of other condominium projects might not be applicable to your project. CC&Rs are rules binding on each owner concerning, for example, the use of the premises and the number and type of pets allowed, etc.

Stock Cooperatives

In some states, a stock cooperative can avoid many of the approvals required for a condominium. A condominium is an actual subdivision with one property broken up into small units with individual owners. A stock cooperative is not truly a subdivision in that the cooperative corporation takes title to the entire building. Each stockholder has rights to occupy a unit but doesn't really own it. There is likely to be more buyer resistance to a cooperative than to a condominium. A cooperative has dangers connected with singular ownership. Since there is only one mortgage, if several owners fail to pay their share, the mortgage covering the entire building might be foreclosed.

Time Shares

Time shares are interval ownership subdivisions. The owners normally buy the use of a resort area condominium unit for one week or more per year. The buyer is thus assured of a place to vacation at a guaranteed cost. While time share development can be profitable, buying a time share is a poor investment. Very few have appreciated in value, and resale of time share units is extremely difficult. Often the time share management will buy a block of units in a project developed by others. The management sets prices on the units so that the gross profit is at least 300 percent. For example, if a unit is purchased for $100,000, the management will try to sell 50 weeks at prices that average $8,100 each. Naturally, some weeks are more desirable and will sell for more than the average, while undesirable periods will sell for far less than the average. Usually the operators leave two weeks free for general refurbishing of the units. The owners of a week can use it, or the management will rent it for them. Some operators have time share units in many locations and also handle vacation trades. While the markup of the units may sound high, you should consider that the time share developers must make the payments until the units are sold, that some weeks are very undesirable and may take a long time to sell, and that these sales involve heavy promotional and sales expenses including 50 sales commissions for each unit. Many time share promoters have gone bankrupt.

A number of developers are offering quarterly time shares in order to avoid the high sale costs of weekly time share sales. For example, each purchaser buys a three-month period. The period is one month in the prime season, one month in a less desirable season and the third month in the least desirable season. A vacation area might offer packages of:

1. January, May, September

2. February, June, October

3. March, July, November

4. April, August, December

In this way, there are only four sales commissions to pay. These longer periods appeal to more affluent buyers who have as much use as many owners get from their vacation homes.

One group of 36, two-bedroom units with tennis courts and pools sold out in three months at $39,500 per one-quarter share. This translated to $158,000 for units that would otherwise sell in the $90,0000 range. This is a far lower markup than is found for weekly time shares. This may explain why the one-quarter share concept is gaining in popularity.

Assemblage

The opposite of subdividing is assemblage, the process of assembling several small contiguous parcels to make one large parcel. In fully developed areas, it is difficult to find any large parcels. While smaller parcels are usually relatively more valuable, large parcels can in some circumstances be worth far more than their separate parts.

My name is H. In the early 1960s, I was active in real estate as a dealer. I used options to tie up property while I sought a buyer.

I obtained an option to buy an old, vacant commercial garage building. I paid $100 for the right to buy the building for $75,000. It was located on a large, deep corner lot 150 by 300 feet in an old section of the city. Because the neighborhood was near the central city, many old homes there had recently been torn down to be replaced by new apartment buildings.

Since the building was located on a major street and there were no major markets in the area, I approached all the food chains about my location. One of the chains liked the location but stated that my lot was far too small. They told me that if I could obtain a minimum of three acres at that location they would pay $250,000. This agreement was put in writing for me. I needed the five homes adjacent to the garage to make up the three acres.

The row of small frame houses were on lots 60 by 300 feet. The recent sale price of these homes had been from $9,000 to $12,000. Two of the homes were for sale, and I was able to get 30-day options to buy them at $15,000 each, which was above the listing prices. One of the homes was owned by a broker. We verbally agreed to an option at $16,000, but when I presented the option in writing, he wanted $20,000, so I had one $20,000 option. One of the owners didn't like the idea of moving, so I found a nicer brick home a few blocks away and got an option to purchase it for $14,500. The owner of the house I wanted agreed to give me the option of trading the nicer home for his house.

Unfortunately, I had trouble with the home two houses down from the garage. The gentleman who lived there did not want to sell. He was retired and had a pension from his former employer and social security. He had a beautiful garden including a grape arbor. While his wife liked the idea of selling, he had no intention of leaving. I offered him $25,000 for his property. The answer was still no. I found a new house on a huge lot and showed it to him, offering a trade. His answer was still no.

In desperation I contacted the two sons of the homeowner and had a meeting. I laid my cards on the table. I showed them the agreement I had from the food chain and all my options. The sons told me they would get back to me. The next day we met again with their attorney present. They offered to get their father to sell, but I would pay their father $15,000 for his house plus one-half of my profit on the entire deal. I verbally agreed to this because a reduced profit is better than none. The attorney stated he would put our agreement in writing and we would meet the next day. When we met, the attorney told me he had contacted the supermarket chain and told them he represented my "partners." He had indicated that the entire parcel of over three acres was locked up now but, because of unexpectedly high acquisition costs, we could not sell it for $250,000. The attorney got the supermarket chain to agree to a $350,000 price.

I was angry that he went around me. I try to live up to my word and, while I may negotiate hard, I don't try to make a new deal once I have reached an agreement. Although I had not really understood the value of a large parcel in this area, I would not have put the squeeze on the supermarket like this. Nevertheless, we now stood to split $350,000 after our acquisition costs of $154,500. This profit of $195,500 would mean $97,750 for me.

I wish I could say everything went smoothly, but it didn't. The sons, who were sure their father would follow their advice, were mistaken. Even their attorney couldn't get the father to sell. In a way it was funny, because the two sons, smitten by greed, practically went berserk trying to get the old man to sell.

I did make a small profit because I sold my option to buy the garage and the house next to it to a developer, who eventually built an apartment building on the site.

In every deal there are many things that can go wrong. For every effort rewarded by profit, there are usually many that are unproductive. I have learned that those people who do well in any business concentrate more on probabilities than on possibilities.

Chapter 12

TRADING UP TO WEALTH

> No man but feels more of a man in the world if he has a bit of ground
> that he can call his own. However small it is on the surface, it is four
> thousand miles deep and that is a very handsome property.
>
> —Charles Dudley Warner, 1871

Exchanging goes back to earliest times. It is the oldest form of commerce. By giving up something desired less, it is possible to acquire something desired more. While some may regard barter as primitive, it has been rediscovered as an exciting real estate technique useful in our society.

TAX ADVANTAGES

One reason for the modern interest in exchanging is the Internal Revenue Code. Exchanging allows an owner to avoid taxation. While tax evasion is illegal, tax avoidance is simply good business practice. Exchanging allows a tax-free transaction of getting rid of undesirable property and acquiring desired property.

An outright sale can result in a taxable gain, but Section 1031 of the Internal Revenue Code allows a tax-free exchange between like-for-like properties. What this means is that real property that has been held for investment, trade, or business can be traded for other real property held for investment, trade or business. Real property must be traded for real property and personal property must be traded for personal property to qualify as a tax-free exchange. Nevertheless, a tax-free exchange is possible even though the character of the property exchanged is not similar. For example, vacant land can be traded for an apartment building.

Since a personal residence is not held for investment, trade, or business, it does not qualify for a tax-free exchange. It is possible to change the character of your residence so that it would qualify. If you move out of your residence and rent it, it becomes an investment property. Some exchange experts advise that a residence must be rented a minimum of one year to qualify for a 1031 exchange, but consult with a CPA or tax attorney before you consider such an exchange.

Property of dealers will not qualify for tax-free exchanges if it has been acquired or developed by the dealers for resale. It may be subject to regular income tax, even though it is traded rather than sold.

If a person would have a significant taxable gain by selling property and would be reinvesting the proceeds in another property, then they would probably want to do so with a tax-free exchange. If they had sold the property, they would have been taxed on their gain, but by using an exchange they have the total sale proceeds to reinvest. Discuss exchanges with a real estate attorney to make certain your exchange is tax-exempt and you understand fully the legal ramifications.

TYPES OF EXCHANGE

Exchanges fall into three basic categories.

Direct Exchange

Two parties agreeing to exchange properties is very rare. It is unlikely that you will find someone with a property you want and who will take a property you wish to dispose of in exchange.

Three-Party Exchange

This is the most common exchange. It involves (A) an owner who wishes to sell, but also wishes to own another property. (B) A buyer who wishes to buy A's property, and (C) an owner of property which A desires. B buys C's property to trade for A's property. C gets cash for his or her property. B gets A's property that he desired and A gets C's property.

Both of the transactions would be part of the same closing. Everyone gets what he or she wants.

Delayed Exchange

Also known as a Starker Exchange, it allows an owner to sell a property and have the proceeds held in escrow for a property not yet chosen. The seller cannot have control of the funds. The seller must identify the property to be purchased within 45 days of closing and the exchange property must be purchased within 180 days of closing.

By use of a delayed exchange, you can sell your property while you have the ready and willing buyer and then locate what you really want.

Boot

Not all exchanges are tax-free. If one person receives "boot," it is fully taxable. Boot is unlike property given to even out a trade. Although it is usually money, boot can be personal property such as an automobile or jewels. Assume you were to trade a property that you own free and clear worth $200,000 for a property also held free and clear worth $150,000. If the other party were to give you $50,000 in cash to even up the trade, this boot would be taxable. One way to avoid a tax liability would be to have the other party use the $50,000 to buy a second property, and then trade two properties for your one property.

If one party to an exchange gets debt relief because the property traded had a greater indebtedness than the new property acquired, then the amount of debt relief will be taxable as capital gains. As an example, assume you own a property on which you owe $50,000 and trade it even for a property that is free and clear of debt. The trade has resulted in your being relieved of a $50,000 debt which is treated as boot and is taxable.

> My name is Steve J. After I got out of service, I started farming in an arid area of the Antelope Valley in northern Los Angeles County. I accumulated 3,000 acres over a period of time. All of it was purchased under $100 per acre and much of it was for $5 to $15 per acre. Even with the amount of acreage I had, farming was still marginal. Around 1970, I was offered $1,000 per acre for my entire farm from a land sales firm. I approached a consultant for advice. He estimated my total tax liability in excess of $1,000,000. He then asked what I would do with the money. I told him I didn't really want to retire and my two sons wanted to be farmers, so I guess I would buy another farm.
>
> He then asked me where I really would want a farm if I could have a farm anywhere I wanted. I told him in Oregon. I would like a large cattle, crop, and apple operation like I've seen in some of the farm magazines. He sent me and my sons to Oregon on a look-and-find expedition. We found a large farm operation that had everything I could wish for. It could be purchased in the $3-million range. We set it up as a trade. The land developer built a new house on the property to my specifications and traded it to me free and clear. I also received $200,000 in cash for operating expenses (this was taxable). My net savings from the advice I received, approximately $1,000,000.

OTHER ADVANTAGES IN EXCHANGING

Taxation isn't the only reason for an exchange. People exchange to solve problems. By exchange they are able to get rid of a set of circumstances they are not happy with for a set of circumstances they desire. Exchange can solve a great number of problems.

Depreciation

Exchanging allows you to change the ratio of land to improvements, which can allow greater depreciation. For example, suppose you own a property worth $100,000 that has a structure on it worth only $20,000, you would be limited to depreciation of the improvements since the land cannot be depreciated. If you were to trade for a property also worth $100,000 but with improvements worth $90,000, you could depreciate from 90 percent of your original cost basis. Since depreciation is only a paper expense, it could shelter other income from taxation.

Geography

Some people exchange for geographical reasons. Assume a person who owns an apartment building in New York wishes to retire to Florida. Trading for an apartment building in Florida would fulfill the need without the necessity of a taxable sale.

Income Gain

Some people trade to gain income. For instance, raw land, which is a cash drain because it has expenses but no income, can be traded for apartments or commercial property offering a spendable cash flow. On the other hand, some people are willing to trade income property for raw land since they are more interested in long-term appreciation than present income, and raw land tends to have greater appreciation than income property.

Clearing Debts

Some investors become conservative and want to eliminate debt. For example, prior to retirement a person might trade a large, heavily mortgaged apartment project for a much smaller, free and clear property.

Pyramiding Property

Many other investors use exchange to pyramid their property. "Bullish" investors recommend this method strongly, especially for young investors. Smaller properties, even when purchased with low downpayments, can in a few years result in a substantial equity. By trading up, you increase the value of the property you own as well as increasing your indebtedness. Assume you traded a property worth $200,000 on which you owe $100,000 for a property worth $700,000 with a $600,000 indebtedness. While your equity in the property is the same, you are in a much better position as to appreciation. An increase in value of 50 percent in seven years with the $200,000 property would have increased your equity from $100,000 to $200,000. For the $700,000 property the same 50 percent increase in value would now give you a $450,000 equity.

Of course, trading up does lower your percentage equity in a property, and there are risks associated with this practice. A high vacancy factor or unexpected expenses could result in a large negative cash flow. A highly leveraged investment is a gamble on the future. If you could not take the loss, don't take the risk.

Consolidation of Property

Exchanging also allows consolidation of property. A number of smaller properties can be exchanged for one large property that is easier to manage. On the other hand, some owners are interested in diversifying. By obtaining several properties, they can reduce their risk, especially in the case of a large property with only one or two tenants.

Fewer Managerial Problems

Some people exchange to divest themselves of management problems. An apartment house with many problems could be exchanged for raw land that requires no real management.

Salability

A property not readily salable might be exchanged for a more salable property. In such a case the exchange is simply an intermediate step toward a desired conclusion.

Avoiding a Realized Loss

There are times when an owner exchanges in order to avoid realizing a loss. Just as there is no realized loss for a stock market investor until the stock is sold, an owner of real property does not suffer a loss until the real property is sold. Some people psychologically do not want to admit the loss. We see this in the stock market when stock owners hold stock that has gone down for many years, hoping it will increase in value enough so they can break even. Even though there are other stocks they would prefer, they still hold on. When the same thing happens in real estate, trading is a solution. A trade allows owners to get into circumstances they prefer without admitting the loss.

My name is Harold. I wanted to purchase a lot owned by a corporation. The price quoted to me by a corporate officer was far in excess of the current market value. The corporation had purchased the lot several years previously, after it had been announced that a major shopping center was to be built in the area. The shopping center was never built, and land prices, having risen on the speculation of great development, fell.

During a meeting I discovered the corporation did not want to show a significant loss by the sale. It was a fairly small corporation and the loss would upset some of the stockholders. They preferred to hold on to the lot until it was worth what they had paid. I recognized this as an ideal exchange opportunity. I was holding a number of second mortgages on property I had previously sold. These mortgages, if sold, would be worth far less than their face value. My offer was to trade several of these mortgages at face value for the lot. It was accepted. The corporation got its price, although over a period of years, and I got the lot. The trade met the needs of both parties. Since mortgages are regarded as personal property, it wasn't a 1031 tax-free exchange.

Most people can be made interested in exchanging once they understand it. People usually want cash in order to purchase something else. If they can get that something else directly, then there is really no reason for a sale.

WHAT YOU CAN EXCHANGE

You can trade just about anything—even junk land that has no value or serves no real purpose other than to help hold the world together. You can trade the land and keep the building as a lessee or even trade the building and keep the land as a lessor. In some states mineral rights are considered real property. You can trade all the mineral rights to a property or perhaps half the mineral rights. Whatever has value can be traded.

Personal property can readily be traded, but remember that personal property cannot be traded for real property on a tax-free exchange since the trade is not like-for-like. This problem comes up in trading furnished units. The furniture is considered taxable boot unless the property traded for includes furniture of the same value.

An attorney I know claims there is a way to have a tax-free exchange of real property for personal property. This attorney feels that by placing the personal property in a corporate shell and the real property in another corporate shell, they can have a like-for-like exchange of corporate stock. This method might work, but I haven't been able to find any tax rulings on it. If you own your house or other property, you can get into real estate exchanging without giving up your property by manufacturing paper. As previously stated, it is fairly easy to find a seller who will take a second mortgage on your property as the downpayment for another property. If an owner is willing to carry a great deal of paper on a sale, he is obviously not that interested in receiving the cash. The purpose of the downpayment is simply security. By taking a downpayment in the form of a second mortgage, not only does the seller retain a security interest in the property sold, but also has a security interest in your property because of the paper given as a downpayment. As values increase, it is possible to create more paper and use your increasing equity as downpayments on other property without selling your property. Of course you must realize that when you create a second mortgage, you are obligating yourself to a payment.

PROBLEMS TO WATCH FOR

Unfortunately, there are some sharp operators in exchanging; these operators hope to give something of very low value for something of great value. They are not looking for an exchange partner; they are looking for a sucker. Don't take the word of another as to what a property is worth. It is only good business to personally check out comparable values in the area. If in doubt, you should seek the aid of a professional appraiser. If taxes are a consideration in a trade, you should seek the advice of an attorney or a CPA who is knowledgeable in exchanges. Because of the specialized nature of exchanging, only a few attorneys and CPAs are really knowledgeable in this area. Most will refer you to a competent specialist.

Chapter 13

OPTIONING YOUR WAY TO SUCCESS

Endeavor vigorously to increase your property.

—Horace

An option gives you the positive right to purchase property at an agreed price and terms for a stated period of time. If you want the property, you can exercise your option and buy it. If you decide you don't wish to buy it, you don't have to. By failing to exercise the option, you only lose the price you paid for the option. An option, by giving you time, allows you to take advantage of a favorable situation even though you may lack the capital to purchase the property.

An option provides the optionee (the person getting the option) with fantastic leverage. Just a few dollars can give you rights to very expensive property. As the optionee you should endeavor to obtain an option for the longest term and the lowest consideration possible. Of course, you also want the option to provide as favorable sales terms as possible.

When you consider the bottom line—to make money in real estate—control is what is important. To control property, you need not own it. An option gives you control with the least investment.

CONSIDERATION

In order to have a valid option, the optionee (potential buyer) must actually give consideration to the optionor (owner). Consideration is anything of value. While usually money, it could be any item or right having value. It is not enough to merely state in the option that it is given for consideration; the consideration must actually change hands. While real estate professionals frequently talk in terms of an option amount related to the purchase price, such as 5 percent of the price for a six-month option, don't worry about formulas. You are dealing with people interested in selling their property. For an option you should pay the minimum amount necessary. The option price is real risk capital because, if the option is not exercised, the price will be lost.

The following is an example of obtaining options at bargain basement prices.

My name is Bradley C. Years back, I offered an owner a 40-acre parcel of land, which I had taken as part of a trade, for a 6-month option to buy an apartment building for $1.5 million. The owner accepted. This was despite the fact that the land was in another state and had a value of only about $8,000. Since then, I have obtained options on interesting parcels of land, and offer the parcels for options on a property. If my offer is accepted, I exercise my option to buy the land.

Large tracts of land without known minerals that could barely support a jack rabbit have enabled me to tie up highly desirable property. I guess it's just the natural desire to own tangible property that often results in sophisticated owners allowing me to obtain options at prices that, if offered in cash, would have been promptly rejected.

FINDING OPTION OPPORTUNITIES

You can use the telephone to locate more lease option opportunities than you can possibly take advantage of. When looking for option opportunities, begin with the classified ads of owners offering options in their house-for-rent ads. (In some papers lease options is a separate category.) Also, look for homes for rent where the owner's telephone number is out of the area. Such an owner is usually highly motivated to sell but is renting because of the need for current income. Call on single-family homes for rent and ask the owner if he or she would consider a lease option. A great many landlords are landlords by necessity, so you will likely get a positive response on 15 to 20 percent of your calls.

If you have a friend who is a real estate licensee, you might ask if you can use their old multiple listing books. While the books are for member use only, you will likely find a source for them. Call the owners of homes where listings are expiring and you will receive a fair percentage of interest in lease options. The slower the resale market, the greater interest you will encounter in your proposals.

For commercial and industrial lease options and even options to obtain a lease option, look for problem properties, properties with a high percentage of vacancies and/or long-term vacancies. Properties in need of maintenance and/or repair are also likely candidates for options. Also consider property that has been on the market for an inordinate period of time. Owners of such properties are generally willing to talk to you.

Another source of lease option property is to advertise what you are looking for under a Wanted to Rent category in the classified ads. As an example:

3 BR Needed

Prefer west side with 2 baths, double

garage and basement. Would like an

option to buy. Can pay up to $800/mo.

Call _____ at _____

Such an ad will bring a response. By advertising, you put the owner in a position of trying to sell you on his or her property. While you should immediately ask about the purchase options, don't go into lease terms on the telephone.

NEGOTIATING THE OPTION

Some unethical dealers will obtain purchase options by use of subterfuge. They will offer to buy property for cash. While their offers will be low, the all-cash nature of the offer will often result in acceptance. They normally ask for a long escrow period, such as six months. The reason given is generally either that an estate has to close or they have property being sold in another state that will not close until that date. The buyer only makes a small deposit, such as $1,000, with the explanation they won't have more money until the other event takes place. A clause in the purchase agreement provides the seller's sole remedy in event of default of the buyer is the forfeiture of the buyer's deposit.

What the buyer really has is an option to buy for what would generally be regarded as a low option price. It will be exercised only if the optionee finds a buyer for more money before the option expires.

This technique is pure deceit and cannot be condoned. Besides avoiding such tactics, be on the alert that it could be used on you. Don't tie up your property with a low earnest money deposit unless the deposit is to be increased to a stated amount within a reasonable period of time. Be alert for extremely long escrow periods. If the escrow period is longer than normal, the deposit should likewise be larger than normal.

A purchase option or lease option allows you to control property with the lowest possible cash outlay. As the optionee, you want the lowest possible option costs, the longest possible period in which to exercise the option, and, if a lease option, the greatest possible percentage of your lease payments applied to the purchase price. In addition, you will want any option price to apply toward the total price. While you may not achieve all your wishes, you must strive for them during negotiation.

In a lease with an option to purchase, of critical importance is how much of the rent shall apply to the purchase price. While an owner may balk at an option price reduction of $1,000, the owner might readily accede to a rent application to the purchase price from 30 percent to 50 percent or even 100 percent which would far exceed the $1,000 on purchase price. Keep in mind that you can often give in on a highly visible emotional figure such as sale price and can more than gain it back in the option terms.

If you negotiate an option price above the current fair market value, you will need appreciation in value to make any exercise of the option an advantageous purchase. You would likely be getting a purchase option at no additional cost if you are receiving it as part of a lease that you want. What you are in fact negotiating is the right to profit should the property undergo exceptional appreciation during the option period. However, it would not be wise to pay any significant additional fee for the mere possibility of significant appreciation unless the option period is long enough so the likelihood of such appreciation turns the betting odds in your favor.

You can offer a sweetener, such as rent paid in advance for one year as an incentive for an owner to give you an option to purchase with a lease. Before you agree to pay out rent for one year, you will want to ascertain the condition of the owner's title by obtaining a property profile. For example, you don't want to be giving an owner going-away money if he is facing imminent foreclosure.

Consider an extension to the option period if you are negotiating for an option to buy or lease. You don't want to be in the position of deciding to buy or lease when you are almost certain you have another buyer or tenant, but it isn't down in writing yet. Consider the inclusion of the following extension agreement.

> This option may be extended for (*three months*), (*up to two periods of six months each*) by delivering to _____ the sum of ($_____), ($_____ for each extension) any time prior to the expiration of this option (or extension thereafter). In the event the option is exercised, the consideration for any extension(s) shall apply in full to the purchase price.

In any option or lease option you enter into, consider the inclusion of a mandatory arbitration clause such as:

> Lessor and lessee agree that any disputes arising under this (lease) (lease option) shall be arbitrated in accordance with the applicable laws of the state of _____ as supplemented by the then current rules of the American Arbitration Association. Judgments on the arbitration award rendered may be entered in any court having jurisdiction of the parties.

You will likely also want a clause specifically giving you as lessee the right to record the lease, lease option or a memorandum of lease or lease option. This will protect you with respect to later buyers, lessees, or lenders.

Don't just go out looking to buy options; procure them selectively. If you feel a property can be turned at a profit, an option is the logical move for an investor with limited capital. The downside risk of buying an option is limited to the price paid for the option. The upside profit potential is limited only by what a buyer will pay. The lease option agreement (see Figure 13–1) has been successfully used by many real estate investors. The advantage of it is its clarity so an owner can readily understand the agreement.

It is often possible to tie up a number of properties by buying one property, and, as a condition of the offer, obtaining an option to purchase additional properties when an owner has a number of lots (or similar properties of any type). You could buy one lot with an option on 10 more if an owner has many lots for sale. Your options would require you to exercise the options at set time limits and, perhaps, in a set order). Failure to exercise an option would result in termination of the other options. This provision will make sense to an owner and will likely get you the options. For example, the option could require you to exercise the option on the second lot within 90 days of closing of the first lot, the third lot option within another 90 days, and so on.

Why ask for these options if you only need one lot? The answer is *control*. You now have control on 10 additional lots at no cost. You would exercise the options if you are able to sell additional lots. If not, your cost is only a little effort. You are likely to obtain control of a large group of properties by setting forth a reasonable period for the exercise of each option. Many builders use this procedure to ensure a lot supply at the same price. You can use it to make money on property you don't own. Again, it is control that counts.

Options on Commercial and Industrial Property

Options to buy vacant commercial or industrial property can be extremely valuable. If you can procure good tenants at long-term leases, the property becomes readily salable to investors. Good tenants not only make a property more salable, they can increase the value to the point where you as optionee might be able to buy the property without using any of your own money.

An optionee found a national tenant who wanted a 20-year lease. Based on the financial strength of the tenant and the agreed rental, the optionee was able to borrow enough on the building not only to cover its full purchase price, but actually to have cash left over. What happened was that the lease so increased the value of the property that a loan at 60 percent of the appraised value was actually more than 100 percent of what the optionee was required to pay as the purchase price.

By meeting with national franchisors, you can get to know their requirements. If you can get an option on property that satisfies their needs, a profit is likely. The franchisors normally are happy to work with anyone who can help them obtain desirable locations. Some optionees, once they obtain what they consider a good option, will try to put together a group of investors to buy the property as a limited partnership. The optionee will act as the general partner, taking a piece of the investment for his or her efforts.

With an option it is possible to list the property for sale with a real estate agent. Even after paying a commission, a good profit is possible when the option price is right. You should realize that an option is worthless once it has expired. Once you know you will not be exercising an option, you should be advertising the option or the property for sale. You can do this because you control it with your option.

My name is Juan J. I am a landscape gardener. Several years ago I leased a house on two acres of commercial land. I needed the commercial zoning to store my equipment and supplies. The owner agreed to give me a purchase option for the three-year lease.

Before the lease expired, I asked the owner about a renewal of my lease. The owner indicated he would not renew because he had other plans. I then contacted a commercial real estate broker and showed him my lease option.

The broker listed the property for sale. The owner got very agitated by the broker's for sale sign. The owner offered me $5,000 for my option. Based on what the broker had told me, I refused.

The broker sold the property and I ended up with a net of almost $200,000. The broker had used what he called a double escrow to pass title from the owner to our buyer.

What had happened was that what had been a fair-priced option became a bargain price because of changes in the area.

My advice to others, whenever you rent any property, try for a purchase option. It just might be worth a fortune and you can get it included for free.

Often owners who don't have their property officially for sale will give options at a price they consider desirable. While the price may be high at present, if the option is for a long enough period of time, such as one year, inflation as well as specific economic factors of an area could turn it into a bargain by the time an option is exercised. For instance, raw land options are usually readily obtainable. Slight changes in the economy can have great effects on land value.

I know of several investors who buy options in the area of any large new development as soon as announcements are made. While they usually set purchase prices much higher than what the property was worth before the announcement, these premium prices often rapidly become bargains. For example, when Atlantic City made gambling legal, some investors purchased options for what many considered ridiculous sale prices. The owners felt that they would be instant millionaires if the options were exercised and were eager to accept the option consideration. While the optionors became millionaires, so did the optionees. Although we don't often have a situation like Atlantic City, a new college, hospital, factory or shopping center all offer potential for option profit.

Zoning Changes Increasing Property Value

Some investors use options to tie up a property rather than buy it. They then add value by either rezoning or getting approvals for desirable uses. They then sell the package to a developer.

My name is Al J. I don't buy anything, but I cause a lot to happen. I tie up property with options, get zoning changes if necessary, arrange for engineering work and get all approvals and then sell to someone who will develop the property. I present a complete package.

I specialize in residential subdivision property. I have a number of builders I work with and I usually know the project is going to be sold as soon as approvals are in hand. One risk is a change in the economy where I get stuck with a lot of work for ready-to-build subdivisions that no one wants. I minimize this risk by providing option extensions for a total period of four years.

I also reduce my risk by avoiding communities where I have to fight for approval because of a no-growth attitude. Life is too short to have to fight public opinion. I don't want to try and force anything on anyone.

I occasionally make a mistake, and it can be costly because with engineering, option fees, legal work, etc., my costs for a 100-lot subdivision could be $300,000 or even more, and this is without any work on the land. If it is denied, the $300,000 is gone. Because of the risk, I won't touch a subdivision that I don't envision at least a $2.50 profit on every dollar I place at risk.

My tactics work for me. I get approval on 80 percent of the projects I start, and I exercise the purchase options on over 90 percent of these.

Options for Trading

You can use options you have as trading pieces. For example, if you have some interesting purchase options you are unlikely to exercise due to other demands on your resources you can use option(s) as part or all of the downpayment to buy another property. The options can be particularly attractive to someone who has the resources to exercise them and visualizes the benefits to themselves.

Tenant Options

Landlords frequently gave options to purchase to their tenants as part of the lease. The option price is usually set quite high. The landlords never expected values to climb as they have in the past decade. Often these options were for long periods of time such as five years. Tenants with leases such as these were in a position to take advantage of a bargain.

You want to make certain your lease option purchases do not prohibit subleasing. In the absence of a prohibition you can generally sublet the premises. In an appreciating market you should consider subleasing without an option when you have a long-term option, such as three years. In this way you can put the property on the market in, say, two years and your sale price would reflect this two-year appreciation. In such a situation, a lease option would be interesting even if you couldn't get enough rent to cover your lease payments. For example, assume your lease payments on a three-year lease with option to buy were $1,200 per month. If you could only sublease for $1,000 per month, you would have a negative cash flow of $200 each month. Over three years, your rental loss would be $7,200. If your purchase option was at market price, and the price was $250,000, a 10 percent annual appreciation would offer you $75,000 appreciation (without compounding the appreciation). While you normally should avoid negative cash flows, in a rapidly appreciating marketplace, you might want to consider such a situation. While 10 percent annual appreciation is more than we can expect for the next few years, eventually we will undoubtedly see that kind of inflation again.

BUYING OTHER PEOPLE'S OPTIONS

Recently, while buying furniture, I asked the owner of the store, a neighbor, if he owned the building. He said no but he had an option to buy it. Asked if he was going to exercise the option, he informed me that he could not afford to take the money out of the business to meet the downpayment requirements. When I found out the option price, I offered to buy the option for $10,000. The offer was accepted. When the owner was notified that the option was being exercised, the owner made me a cash offer to give up the option. Since the cash offer was in the neighborhood of what I expected to net by a quick sale, it was accepted.

Even though I have never heard of anyone doing it. I believe it could be possible to purchase some good options by advertising "Tenants[—]Residential, Commercial, Industrial. I will pay you cash for your option to purchase." It might even pay to knock on doors or canvass by telephone for options. You would want to concentrate on commercial tenants as options are more common in these leases. There must be thousands of good options expiring without being exercised, but it would take legwork to find them. Before you buy an existing option from a tenant, you should check with an attorney. There could be legal problems as to the transferability of the option. If transferring the option creates problems, it is possible to have an escrow in which the tenant takes title and immediately transfers it to you.

OPTIONS TO RENT

Options to rent open up an entirely different area of profit potential. For these options you should look for rentals that have been vacant for some time. Usually these will be stores, offices or industrial properties. While sale options are frequently difficult to obtain, options to rent are easy to obtain for periods of from 30 to 60 days. Owners often desperately want a tenant and are willing to tie up the property for one or two months at a very low option fee.

I recommend you try for an option for a one-year option to rental at as low a price as you can negotiate, plus options to renew for at least two five-year periods at stated rentals. The option should also allow you the right to sublet or assign the lease. After the owner has agreed to the option, ask that an option to purchase be included. In this way a purchase option can often be obtained without additional consideration.

Once you have the option to lease, get to work looking for a tenant at a higher rental than you have agreed to pay. In some cases this profit can be substantial. It can increase each year if you are paying a flat rental figure and your tenant's rental increases with the Consumer Price Index.

As previously mentioned, one very effective way to find tenants is to go through the Yellow Pages and look for categories of tenants who could use your space. Simply call each listing in each applicable category and ask if the business can use the location at a desirable rent. Although this method is time-consuming, you will not only rent property, you will also get many leads for people looking for other properties as well. While calling on the phone eight hours a day, day after day, is tedious work, it can pay off.

There are people who look for shopping centers and office buildings in trouble. They will offer to lease all the vacant space on a long-term lease at an extremely low rental, usually just enough to allow the owner to make the payments on the mortgage. If an owner is desperate, he or she will accept this type of arrangement. The lessee is not a thief, since he or she is taking a high-risk gamble. While no one else could lease this space or keep it leased, the lessee is betting that he or she will be successful in subleasing it. This type of arrangement requires a strong financial position as well as a great deal of courage and ability.

Not Exercising the Option

If you decide not to exercise an option but would exercise it if the price or terms were different, you should keep in mind that while an option price gives you the right to buy or lease at that price, you are not precluded from attempting to renegotiate the price or terms. Your chances of renegotiating would be affected by the owner's motivation to sell or lease.

Granting Options

While as a buyer you may want to buy options because of the huge profit potential they offer, you should be hesitant about giving options as an owner for any longer than a few months. Just as when buying an option you considered possible changes that would increase the value, consider the possibility of something happening of which you are not aware. You should check to see if other owners in the immediate neighborhood have been offered money for options. If they have, then the optionee knows of or hopes for something of which you are not aware.

If you as an owner are going to give an option for a long period of time such as several years, I suggest that the option be tied to the Consumer Price Index so that inflation does not lower your real price. If you have a purchase agreement to buy a property that you intend to lease-option, you can recoup part or all of your downpayment by looking for a lease-option before you have closed your purchase. If you can collect an option fee before you close your purchase, you will reduce your cash needs at closing. By charging an option fee of several thousand dollars that will apply to the purchase price, you increase the likelihood of tenants making the monthly payments on time, maintaining the property, and exercising the option.

Similarly you can charge a security deposit (in addition to any option fee) for rentals as well as lease/options. Be aware that most states have statutes that limit the allowable security deposit (generally to two months' rent). Also, in some states the lessor cannot use the security deposit, but must keep it in a trust account.

Right of First Refusal

If you lease, you should of course try for a purchase option, which can be frosting on the cake in the form of another profit potential. However, if you are the landlord, resist giving a tenant a purchase option. You can, however, safely give a right of first refusal. Under a right of first refusal, the tenant does not have the right to buy if you don't want to sell. However, if you want to sell to a buyer, before you can complete the sale, you must go to the tenant and offer the property to the tenant at the same price and terms you are willing to accept from the other buyer. You are not really giving up very much when you give a right of first refusal.

Options, if used properly, can result in great profit. They avoid the downpayment and risk of a purchase while offering profit potential by leasing or sale. Again ownership isn't necessary to reap the profit; only control is. Additional uses of options are included in Chapter 14, entitled "Special Situations."

Figure 13–1   Lease Option Agreement

RESIDENTIAL LEASE WITH OPTION TO PURCHASE

RECEIVED FROM _____

_____, hereinafter referred to as Tenant,

the sum of $ _____ (_____

_____ DOLLARS),

evidenced by _____, as a deposit which, upon acceptance of this Lease, the Owner

of the premises, hereinafter referred to as Owner, shall apply said deposit as follows:

	DEPOSIT RECEIVED	BALANCE OWING PRIOR TO OCCUPANCY
Non-refundable option consideration	$ _____	$ _____
Rent for the period from _____ to _____	$ _____	$ _____
Security deposit	$ _____	$ _____
Other	$ _____	$ _____
TOTAL	$ _____	$ _____

In the event that this agreement is not accepted by the Owner or his authorized agent, **within** _____ **days,** the total deposit received shall be refunded.

Tenant hereby offers to lease from the Owner the premises situated in the City of _____, County of _____

State of _____, described as _____

_____

and consisting of _____

upon the following TERMS and CONDITIONS:

1. **TERM:** The term hereof shall commence on _____, 19____, and continue for a period of _____ months thereafter.
2. **RENT:** Rent shall be $_____, per month, payable in advance, upon the _____ day of each calendar month to Owner or his authorized agent, at the following address: _____
   or at such other places as may be designated by Owner from time to time. In the event rent is not paid **within five (5) days** after due date, Tenant agrees to pay a late charge of $_____ plus interest at _____% per annum on the delinquent amount. Tenant further agrees to pay $_____ for each dishonored bank check.
3. **UTILITIES:** Tenant shall be responsible for the payment of all utilities and services, except: _____ which shall be paid by Owner.
4. **USE:** The premises shall be used as a residence with no more than _____ adults and _____ children, and for no other purpose, without the written prior consent of the Owner.
5. **PETS:** No pets shall be brought on the premises without the prior consent of the Owner.
6. **ORDINANCES AND STATUTES:** Tenant shall comply with all statutes, ordinances and requirements of all municipal, state and federal authorities now in force, or which may hereafter be in force, pertaining to the use of the premises.
7. **ASSIGNMENT AND SUBLETTING:** Tenant shall not assign this agreement or sublet any portion of the premises without prior written consent of the Owner which may not be unreasonably withheld.
8. **MAINTENANCE, REPAIRS, OR ALTERATIONS:** Tenant acknowledges that the premises are in good order and repair, unless otherwise indicated herein. Owner may at any time give Tenant a written inventory of furniture and furnishings on the premises and Tenant shall be deemed to have possession of all said furniture and furnishings in good condition and repair, unless he objects thereto in writing **within five (5) days after receipt** of such inventory. Tenant shall, at his own expense, and at all times, maintain the premises in a clean and sanitary manner including all equipment, appliances, furniture and furnishings therein and shall surrender the same, at termination hereof, in as good condition as received, normal wear and tear excepted. Tenant shall be responsible for damages caused by his negligence and that of his family or invitees and guests. Tenant shall not paint, paper or otherwise decorate or make alterations to the premises without the prior written consent of the Owner. Tenant shall irrigate and maintain any surrounding grounds, including lawns and shrubbery, and keep the same clear of rubbish or weeds, if such grounds are a part of the premises and are exclusively for the use of the Tenant.
9. **ENTRY AND INSPECTION:** Tenant shall permit Owner or Owner's agents to enter the premises at reasonable times and upon reasonable notice for the purpose of making necessary or convenient repairs, or to show the premises to prospective tenants, purchasers, or mortgagees.
10. **INDEMNIFICATION:** Owner shall not be liable for any damage or injury to Tenant, or any other person, or to any property, occurring on the premises or any part thereof, or in common areas thereof, unless such damage is the proximate result of the negligence or unlawful act of Owner, his agents, or his employees. Tenant agrees to hold Owner harmless from any claims for damages, no matter how caused, except for injury or damages for which Owner is legally responsible.
11. **PHYSICAL POSSESSION:** If Owner is unable to deliver possession of the premises at the commencement hereof, Owner shall not be liable for any damage caused thereby, nor shall this agreement be void or voidable, but Tenant shall not be liable for any rent until possession is delivered. Tenant may terminate this agreement if possession is not delivered **within** _____ **days** of the commencement of the term hereof.
12. **DEFAULT:** If Tenant shall fail to pay rent when due, or perform any term hereof, after not less than **three (3) days written notice** of such default given in the manner required by law, the Owner, at his option, may terminate all rights of Tenant hereunder, unless Tenant, within said time, shall cure such default. If Tenant abandons or vacates the property, while in default of the payment of rent, Owner may consider any property left on the premises to be abandoned and may dispose of the same in any manner allowed by law. In the event Owner reasonably believes that such abandoned property has no value, it may be discarded. All property on the premises is hereby subject to a lien in favor of Owner for the payment of all sums due hereunder, to the maximum extent allowed by law.
    In the event of a default by Tenant, Owner may elect to (a) continue the lease in effect and enforce all his rights and remedies hereunder, including the right to recover the rent as it becomes due, or (b) at any time, terminate all of Tenant's rights hereunder and recover from Tenant all damages he may incur by reason of the breach of the lease, including the cost of recovering the premises, and including the worth at the time of such termination, or at the time of an award if suit be instituted to enforce this provision, of the amount by which the unpaid rent for the balance of the term exceeds the amount of such rental loss which the Tenant proves could be reasonably avoided.
13. **SECURITY:** The security deposit set forth above, if any, shall secure the performance of Tenant's obligations hereunder. Owner may, but shall not be obligated to, apply all portions of said deposit on account of Tenant's obligations hereunder. Any balance remaining upon termination shall be returned to Tenant.
14. **DEPOSIT REFUNDS:** The balance of all deposits shall be refunded within two weeks from date possession is delivered to Owner or his Authorized Agent, together with a statement showing any charges made against such deposits by Owner.
15. **ATTORNEY'S FEES:** In the event that Owner is required to employ an attorney to enforce the terms and conditions of this agreement or to recover possession of the premises from Tenant, Tenant shall pay to Owner a reasonable attorney's fee whether or not a legal action is filed or a judgement is obtained.
16. **WAIVERS:** No failure of Owner to enforce any term hereof shall be deemed a waiver, nor shall any acceptance of a partial payment of rent be deemed a waiver of Owner's right to the full amount thereof.

Figure 13–1   Lease Option Agreement (continued)

17.   NOTICES: Any notice which either party may or is required to give, may be given by mailing the same, postage prepaid, to Tenant at the premises or to Owner at the address shown below or at such other places as may be designated by the parties from time to time.

18.   HEIRS, ASSIGNS, SUCCESSORS: This lease is binding upon and inures to the benefit of the heirs, assigns and successors in interest to the parties.

19.   TIME: Time is of the essence of this agreement.

20.   HOLDING OVER: Any holding over after expiration hereof, with the consent of Owner, shall be construed as a month-to-month tenancy in accordance with the terms hereof, as applicable. No such holding over or extension of this lease shall extend the time for the exercise of the option unless agreed upon in writing by Owner

21.   PEST CONTROL INSPECTION: The main building and all attached structures to be inspected by a licensed structural pest control operator prior to delivery of physical possession. Owner to pay for (1) Elimination of infestation and / or infection of wood-destroying pests or organisms, (2) For repair of damage caused by such infestation and / or infection or by excessive moisture, (3) For correction of conditions which caused said damage and (4) For repair of plumbing and other leaks affecting wood members, including repair of leaking stall showers, in accordance with said structural pest control operator's report.

Owner shall not be responsible for any work recommended to correct conditions usually deemed likely to lead to infestation or infection of wood destroying pests or organisms, but where no evidence of active infestation is found with respect to such conditions.

If the inspecting structural pest control operator shall recommend further inspection of inaccessible areas, Tenant may require that said areas be inspected. If any infestation or infection shall be discovered by such inspection, the additional required work shall be paid by Owner. If no such infestation or infection is discovered, the additional cost of inspecting such inaccessible areas shall be paid by Tenant.

As soon as the same are available, copies of the report, and any certification or other proof of completion of the work shall be delivered to the agents of Tenant and Owner who are authorized to receive the same on behalf of their principals.

Funds for work to be done at Owner's expense shall be held in escrow and disbursed by escrow holder to a licensed structural pest control operator upon receipt of Notice of Work Completed, certifying that the property is free of infestation or infection.

22.   OPTION: So long as Tenant is not in substantial default in the performance of any term of this lease, Tenant shall have the option to purchase the real property described herein for a PURCHASE PRICE OF $_____ (_____ DOLLARS), upon the following TERMS and CONDITIONS:

_____
_____
_____
_____
_____
_____
_____
_____
_____
_____
_____
_____
_____
_____
_____
_____
_____
_____
_____
_____

23.   DISCLAIMER: The parties acknowledge that speculation of availability of financing, purchase costs, and lender's prepayment penalties is impossible. Therefore, the parties agree that these items shall not be conditions of performance of this agreement and the parties agree they have not relied upon any other representations or warranties by brokers, sellers, or other parties.

24.   FIXTURES: All improvements, fixtures, attached floor coverings, draperies including hardware, shades, blinds, window and door screens, storm sash, combination doors, awnings, outdoor plants potted or otherwise, trees, and items permanently attached to the real property shall be included, free of liens, unless specifically excluded.

25.   PERSONAL PROPERTY: The following personal property, on the premises when inspected by Tenant, shall be included in the purchase price and shall be transferred by a Warranty Bill of Sale at close of escrow.

26.   ENCUMBRANCES: In addition to any encumbrances referred to above, Tenant shall take title to the property subject to: (1) Real Estate Taxes not yet due and (2) Covenants, conditions, restrictions, reservations, rights, rights of way and easements of record, if any, which do not materially affect the value or intended use of the property. The amount of any bond or assessment which is a lien shall be ☐ paid, ☐ assumed by _____.

27.   EXAMINATION OF TITLE: Fifteen (15) days from date of exercise of this option are allowed the Tenant to examine the title to the property and to report in writing any valid objections thereto. Any exceptions to the title which would be disclosed by examination of the records shall be deemed to have been accepted unless reported in writing **within said fifteen (15) days.** If Tenant objects to any exceptions to the title, Owner shall use all due diligence to remove such exceptions at his own expense **within sixty (60) days thereafter.** But if such exceptions cannot be removed **within the sixty (60) days allowed,** all rights and obligations hereunder may, at the election of the Tenant, terminate and end, unless he elects to purchase the property subject to such exceptions.

28.   EVIDENCE OF TITLE: Evidence of Title shall be in the form of ☐ a policy of _____ title insurance, ☐ other: _____ to be paid for by _____.

29.   CLOSING COSTS: Escrow fees, if any, and other closing costs shall be paid in accordance with local custom, except as otherwise provided herein.

30.   CLOSE OF ESCROW: Within _____ days from exercise of the option, or upon removal of any exceptions to the title by the Owner, as provided above, whichever is later, both parties shall deposit with an authorized escrow holder, to be selected by the Tenant, all funds and instruments necessary to complete the sale in accordance with the terms and conditions hereof. The representations and warranties herein shall not be terminated by conveyance of the property.

Figure 13–1 Lease Option Agreement (continued)

31. **PRORATIONS:** Rents taxes, premiums on insurance acceptable to Tenant, interest and other expenses of the property to be prorated as of recordation of deed. Security deposits, advance rentals or considerations involving future lease credits shall be credited to Tenant.

32. **EXPIRATION OF OPTION:** This option may be exercised at any time after _____, 19____, and shall expire at midnight _____, 19____, unless exercised prior thereto. Upon expiration Owner shall be released from all obligations hereunder and all of Tenants' rights hereunder, legal or equitable, shall cease.

33. **EXERCISE OF OPTION:** The option shall be exercised by mailing or delivering written notice to the Owner prior to the expiration of this option and by an additional payment, on account of the purchase price, in the amount of:

$_____ (_____ DOLLARS) for account of Owner to the authorized escrow holder referred to above, prior to the expiration of this option.

Notice, if mailed, shall be by certified mail, postage prepaid, to the Owner at the address set forth below, and shall be deemed to have been given upon the day following the day shown on the postmark of the envelope in which such notice is mailed.

In the event the option is exercised, the consideration paid for the option and _____ percent from the rent paid hereunder prior to the exercise of the option shall be credited upon the purchase price.

The undersigned Tenant hereby acknowledges receipt of a copy hereof.

_____ Tenant's Broker   Dated: _____ Time: _____

By: _____ Agent   _____ Tenant

Broker's Initials: _____ Dated: _____   _____ Tenant

_____ Address   _____ Address

_____ Phone   _____ Phone

ACCEPTANCE

The undersigned Owner accepts the foregoing offer.

BROKERAGE FEE: Upon execution hereof the Owner agrees to pay to _____

_____, The Agent in this transaction, _____% of the option consideration for securing said option plus the sum of $_____ (_____ DOLLARS) for leasing services rendered and authorizes Agent to deduct said sum from the deposit received from Tenant. In the event the option is exercised, the Owner agrees to pay Agent the additional sum of $_____ (_____ DOLLARS). This agreement shall not limit the rights of Agent provided for in any listing or other agreement which may be in effect between Owner and Agent. In the event legal action is instituted to collect this fee, or any portion thereof, the Owner agrees to pay the Agent a reasonable attorney's fee and all costs in connection with such action.

The undersigned Owner hereby acknowledges receipt of a copy hereof.

Dated: _____ Time: _____

_____ Owner's Broker   _____ Owner

By: _____ Agent   _____ Owner

FORM 106(a) (5-90)   COPYRIGHT . 1983, BY PROFESSIONAL PUBLISHING CORP. 122 PAUL DR. SAN RAFAEL, CA 94903 (415) 472-1964   **PROFESSIONAL PUBLISHING**

Chapter 14

SPECIAL SITUATIONS

> You make money in real estate doing
> what other people say can't be done.
>
> —Frank Curry, 1980

IMAGINATION AND DETERMINATION PAY OFF

William Zeckendorf, a legendary New York investor and developer, made millions of dollars because he was able to see opportunities where others only saw problems. A national periodical headed an article about Bill Zeckendorf with, "He Turns Lemons into Lemonade." By looking for opportunities in problems you can also find ways to sweeten the lemon.

In 1948 a very successful attorney accompanied a friend to a boat show and fell in love with one of the larger yachts on display. It has been said that the difference between a man and a boy is only in the price of his toys. Well, the attorney purchased his toy that day. The next day was not as pleasant when he discovered that all the public moorings in the area had long waiting lists. About the only way to get a public mooring was to buy a boat already tied up at a mooring, which wouldn't help him as he had already purchased a boat. A number of the private yacht clubs had moorings available but required club membership. In those days, memberships were 100 percent Gentile; a Jewish attorney could forget about even applying. One of his friends in the real estate business told him that he could help temporarily. The friend had listed for sale a coal yard on the river not too far from the ocean. The yard had a dock and since it was closed, the real estate agent thought he could arrange with the owners for temporary docking privileges.

The attorney went to look at the dock. Although located in a run-down commercial and industrial area, the yard had five acres and over 600 feet on the river. The existing dock was for large ships, so it was more than ample for his yacht. The attorney knew that this was only temporary; he wanted a place to keep his boat permanently. He offered $50,000 cash for the old coal yard. The offer, while low, was accepted. This acceptance set in motion an amazing series of negotiations.

The attorney thought that if he had so much trouble getting a place to keep a boat, other people also would need mooring space. Before the sale of the coal yard was completed, he had an architect draw up preliminary plans for a private marina.

With the preliminary sketches he contacted the major oil companies to see if they would be interested in handling the fuel sales at his marina. This was at a time when oil companies were producing more than they could sell. There was fierce competition for retail sales. Oil companies built new service stations not so much for profit as for distribution. As could be expected, a number of companies were very interested, since large boats use tremendous quantities of fuel. The attorney not only wanted the oil companies to build their own facilities, he also wanted a percentage of the gross as rent coupled with a minimum rent. In addition, he insisted on $50,000 being paid in advance rent when the facility opened. Several of the oil companies backed off at this demand, but one agreed to it and was given the oil and gas franchises.

Next, the attorney approached a firm that ran other mooring facilities. This firm agreed to construct the yacht slips and a boat ramp and to split all mooring fees 50-50 with the attorney. The company also would set up boat hoists to handle winter storage. The attorney was also to receive a percentage of this business as well as a percentage of any repair business. This agreement was for 20 years, after which all improvements became the property of the attorney.

Then the attorney looked into finding an excellent club manager. He hired away the manager of one of the exclusive clubs with a generous contract. The manager was given the job of selling 300 full memberships for $1,500 each, which included the right to rent a boat slip. These memberships were all sold within three months (all memberships without racial or religious restrictions). Social memberships were sold for $500 each. These memberships allowed the members to use launching facilities as well as to rent temporary dock space on a daily basis. After the memberships were sold, the manager's job was to handle special social functions and to oversee the entire operation.

A magnificent club house was constructed, using the membership money collected. A restaurant operator put in the restaurant and bar equipment and agreed to pay a minimum rental plus a percentage of the gross.

In less than one year from the date he had first seen this rundown coal yard, the attorney had transformed it into a quality yacht club. What is amazing is that not only did he build it without leaving any of his own money in it, but the attorney now owned the entire property free and clear of all liens.

PROBLEM PROPERTIES HAVE POTENTIAL

One of the most interesting problem properties I know of was a house of ill repute built in the late 1930s. The building, of log construction, was in a northern resort area set far back from the highway on a large parcel of land, making it quite isolated. Downstairs was one large room that originally served as a bar and dance area. It also had bathroom facilities. Upstairs were 12 extremely tiny rooms off a central hall. Each room had a sink and a window. There were also bathroom facilities on the floor. The building had a succession of owners. Several restaurants had gone broke on the premises, and the building had been vacant for several years. The house was finally listed with an imaginative broker. She wrote several hundred letters to psychologists in nearby cities and also advertised in a psychology magazine. She sold the building to a psychologist who was engaged in various types of encounter groups. The property was ideally suited for groups such as this or for training purposes.

Many small communities have serious unemployment problems. Some of these communities have set up industrial development corporations that have sold low-interest bonds to raise funds to attract industry. Many communities will build buildings for employers and rent them at very low rentals. Others even make loans to firms that will come into the community. Unfortunately, in the desire for employers, many communities have built structures for firms with financial problems with the result that many of these development groups have vacant buildings. These situations offer great potential for problem solvers. Options can often be obtained on these completed structures at extremely low rentals if the use will provide an agreed number of jobs. If you can find firms that would benefit by moving to the area, you can make a profit by the rental differential and solve a community need.

If you own a lot suitable for low-income housing or can tie up such property, contact your local Department of Housing and Urban Development (HUD) office about low-income housing programs. HUD has a number of programs where you can obtain below-market financing for low-income housing. Generally, allowable rents will provide a positive cash flow. Depending on the program, you may be free to raise rents when the loan is refinanced. Your HUD office can also give you information on urban renewal programs.

You local redevelopment agency might have redevelopment money in the form of both grants and loans for developments in designated areas. While these areas generally are not areas likely to experience great value appreciation, they can offer money that will likely mean an immediate positive cash flow. When real estate has a problem, problem solving can offer financial rewards.

MOBILE HOME UNITS

A couple in California lived in a 10-by-50-foot mobile home. They decided they wanted a double-wide unit but discovered that they could only get about $1,500 by selling their unit and, although they could get several thousand dollars on a trade-in, they could actually buy the double-wide they wanted for almost the same amount if they had no trade-in. This couple purchased their double-wide unit but kept their old mobile home, moving it to a fairly rough family park where space rentals at the time were only a $50 a month. They rented their old coach for $130 a month furnished. In fact, they had a great many calls on the rental ad. The couple did some figuring and realized that they were clearing $90 a month on their old coach, or $1,080 each year. In a year and a half this would give them as much as they would have received by selling the unit. They visited several mobile home dealers and said they were interested in buying, for up to $2,000, 10-foot and 12-foot-wide units that had been taken in on trade. The couple wanted the dealers to finance the units at 10 percent down on four-year loans. Several of the dealers were interested, since very few buyers wanted old single-wide units.

The couple then made deals with several older mobile home parks having vacancies. While better parks wouldn't take in an old single-wide, many of the smaller parks with vacancies would do so. In one park they rented 10 spaces for $25 each per month and were able to get a five-year lease at that rent. In a little over one year both were able to quit their jobs to handle their mobile home rentals full time.

This couple saw a need and a means to fulfill it. Unlike many people who just talk, they acted. Now they own well over 100 rental units and, while not prestige property, it is highly profitable.

FACTORIES

Because of manufacturing inefficiencies, many multistory factories have become obsolete. They have often been sold at very low prices and excellent terms because their use has been limited. Some people with imagination have turned these structures into productive buildings. Some have been leased to crafts people who each rent space. This draws many tourists as well as local shoppers to the buildings. Others have been converted to large nightclubs, restaurants, skating rinks and even legitimate theaters. Others have been converted to apartments. Conversion costs are high, but may still be far below the cost of building new units.

My name is Seymour T. I was a cap maker until lower-priced caps by foreign manufacturers came on the market and made it impossible for me to operate my business at a profit. I gave my employees severance pay and sold the equipment, supplies and remaining inventory of my business at an auction.

Going out of business left me with an old seven-story, brick, steel and concrete building 80 feet wide and 120 feet deep, with truck doors on both streets, which gave ample access for delivery shipments to the inside of the building. The building, which extended between two streets, was located about six blocks from the city's mercantile center. The area itself needed rejuvenation. I didn't have any takers when I tried leasing the building at bargain rent. One big problem was that there was absolutely no parking area. My employees had mostly used public transportation although there were commercial garages in the immediate vicinity.

I listed the building for sale without success. It sat vacant for two years. My son came up with a one-word idea: *lofts*. He suggested we turn the building into loft apartments. Based on the pillars we could have eight apartments to the floor. Each loft could be approximately 20 feet wide and about 1,000 square feet of floor space, face a street, and utilize the almost floor-to-ceiling factory windows. The building was also equipped with a centrally located automatic freight elevator (about 10 years old), stairways, and front and rear steel fire escapes and a balcony that ran the width of the building of each floor on both streets for fire escape access. There was a full, dry basement and 16-foot-high ceilings. The building had excellent fire suppression (sprinkler) system.

My first thought was that the loft idea was crazy. Some research by my son and visits to a former hosiery factory that was converted to lofts in Milwaukee, and a two-square block "Cobbler Square" complex in Chicago (the former home of Dr. Scholl's foot products) convinced me that my son's idea was not so crazy after all.

An architect agreed to do some preliminary work. He had an engineer check out the building, and I received some rough estimates of costs (actual costs turned out to be about 50 percent higher than those initial estimates).

My son prepared a feasibility study based on various costs to convert the structure to lofts and estimates of selling prices based on the information of several knowledgeable brokers. (Incidentally, from these conversations, we chose a broker to work with the architect to make certain we would have a really salable product.) Even if our costs doubled and the sale price estimates were 20 percent too high, the feasibility study indicated the loft conversion would still make sense.

The architect recommended a real estate attorney who had extensive experience in subdivision approvals and local zoning changes. Approvals took over one year. A big problem was that there wasn't enough room on the first floor for parking space for each unit. We considered ramping into the basement, but this idea was ruled out by the engineer. Our solution was to have local parking garages agree to lease space on long-term basis to our tenants. We also obtained statements from the city traffic engineer and parking structure operators that street parking was not a problem in our area on weekends or between 4 p.m. and 8 a.m. on weekdays, which was when most residents would require parking.

I was ready to give up on the project several times, but what kept be going was that I had so much time and money invested in a building that would otherwise be practically worthless.

After approvals, we sandblasted the building, partitioned the units, and put in zone-controlled heating to each of them. We roughed in kitchen plumbing, but except for a model unit, we didn't put in any cabinetry or appliances. However, we did complete a bath for each unit. We built a 500-square-foot open second level in our model unit.

We refurbished the elevator, installed keyed electronic door controls, built storage rooms and a laundry room in the basement, and turned the first floor into a parking area. The units were priced bare (walls painted white), with additional prices provided for finishing the kitchen and building a full or half second level, etc.

All units were sold out within five months. I estimated my investment in each unit at about $40,000 which we sold for base prices at $69,500 and going up to $84,500, depending upon floor, view, and inclusion of parking. My net cash was $1.5 million for a building I couldn't sell at any price.

LAND

When an owner is holding land for appreciation, an attractive lease could be possible where the owner gets little more than his taxes.

My name is Chris B. I own a swap meet. I have 400 seller spaces that rent for $25 each per day. (I have a waiting list for spaces.) This gives me $20,000 in rental receipts every weekend. I charge visitors 50 cents to enter. My 50 cent fees more than pays my lease, as well as operational and promotional expenses. I also lease the concession stands on a percentage basis. While I currently give free parking, I am considering a charge for this. Parking takes up the greater part of my 40-acre site.

I am considering going public and opening up swap meets across the country. My wife asks, "Why? Our net is well over $1 million per year?"

It is possible to make money from land while it is being held for appreciation. Some states pay small amounts per acre if the land is declared a game preserve. Many states also give a property tax break if land is turned into forest. Some owners have planted fir trees, getting the trees at nominal costs from state reforestation programs. These owners also take whatever tax benefits are available. Before developing their land, they harvest their crop of Christmas trees.

BUSINESSES

Many businesses are sold with real estate. Often the value of the real estate is the major value of the business. Don't buy a business for the real estate unless you can cash out of the business quickly. Don't try to run it. Running someone else's business is an invitation to disaster.

The following is an example of turning a lemon into lemonade that William Zeckendorf would have been proud of.

My name is Ira R. and I formerly owned a small shoe store in a city of approximately 50,000 people. My lease was not going to be renewed, and I was desperately searching for a new location. A small hotel nearby had a large corner restaurant that would be an ideal location for a shoe store. I checked with the owner of the hotel who told me that while he was not interested in renting the restaurant space to me, he would sell me the whole hotel for $100,000 without any downpayment. The owner operated a small bar in the hotel (like the restaurant it also had outside exits) and this would be included.

I had a builder friend check over the hotel. The roof was in good shape and the heating plant was adequate, but the 24 rooms in the three-story hotel were in miserable condition. The hotel portion of the building wasn't even paying the utility bills and the clerk's salary. The restaurant was losing $400 to $500 a month. The only positive income came from the bar. I readily saw why the owner was offering me this opportunity to purchase the hotel. After checking with the city building and planning departments to make certain the hotel was up to code and I could make some desired changes, I took the owner up on the purchase offer. I held an auction of the restaurant equipment and supplies, which netted $6,300. I closed the restaurant off from the hotel, converted the kitchen to a storeroom and office, and made minor changes for my shoe store.

I offered to sell the bar (license) and fixtures to a bartender who worked for the former owner. We agreed on a price of $20,000 cash which he obtained by refinancing his home. He agreed to a long-term lease beginning at $450 a month. We closed the bar off from the hotel.

One of the hotel's permanent residents was a rather energetic woman in her mid-60s who was on social security. I asked her to be my manager. The hotel was to be for permanent guests only. We visited several hotels in a nearby city which catered to permanent guests to find out about hotel operations and house rules.

Hiring a painter and handyman with the money from the sale of the bar, we began refurbishing the 24 rooms. We installed coin operated washer/dryer units on the first floor in what had been the hotel clerk's office. We also put in a cold drink machine.

We offered the refurbished rooms at $85 per month for a single without bath to $150 for a double occupancy with bath. Cooking was not allowed, but we did install a small refrigerator in each room. My manager took to her job with great zeal (she received her room rent free plus $150 per month). In a matter of weeks, we had a room rental waiting list. I had not realized the demand for single room occupancy was so great. Not only did I now have a shoe store where I paid no rent, I had disposable income as well.

About a year after my successful hotel purchase, I learned about a 44-room motel which had just come on the market. It was a former chain motel and had a large restaurant, and a manager's large two-bedroom suite. The motel was no longer on a major traffic artery because of a new freeway and was in a rather run-down condition. The motel was listed for sale at $750,000 which appeared to be a bargain price. There was a $360,000 mortgage against the motel which could not be assumed. I decided against the purchase when I realized how difficult new financing would be.

About a month after I looked at the motel, I learned from a talkative real estate agent at a rotary meeting that the motel was in foreclosure.

I contacted the county to ascertain if I would be allowed to change from a motel operation to a permanent residency operation. I then contacted the lender and indicated that if they would allow a loan assumption, I would give the owner an offer, otherwise they would likely find themselves managing a motel that was losing money.

After several days I was informed they would agree to the loan assumption providing the eight and one-half percent interest rate was raised to nine percent and I made the loan current. (The owner was about $20,000 in arrears.)

I offered the owner $430,000 for the property. I was to assume the first mortgage and give a second mortgage at nine percent interest to the owner for the balance of the purchase price. The broker agreed to share in this second mortgage for her commission. My offer was accepted. I now took over the motel with the only cash that for the loan arrearage and a second mortgage of approximately $50,000 (based on credits for paying the loan arrearage).

I hired a retired army sergeant and his wife as managers giving them the large two-bedroom apartment plus $400 a month as salary. We immediately began refurbishing units, painting the exterior and planting flowers. My manager supervised all the work. Some permanent residents were obtained from the hotel waiting list, and we began advertising.

The restaurant was advertised for lease. I found a good operator and leased it at $500 per month, which was an extremely low rent; I wanted to insure the operator's success. (The restaurant had been a big money loser for the prior owner who hired a manager to run it.)

Well, within four months of purchase, we reached 100 percent occupancy on a monthly basis.

I have long since sold my shoe store and my first hotel. I now own seven former motels over a two state area consisting of over 300 units, all of which are rented on a monthly basis. I purchased every one of them without a cash downpayment using the same purchase techniques. I found very few instances where lenders failed to realize that it was to their advantage to let me assume the loan. Most of the purchases were made through a motel broker who knows what I am looking for and keeps his eyes and ears open. Even then I turn down most deals either because there is too much debt or the area will not likely support my SRO (single room occupancy) conversions. (In several cases, I could not get approval to change the operation to permanent residency because of zoning restrictions.)

Right now, we are operating at over a 90 percent occupancy with significant positive cash flows from every property.

My secret—I offer clean nicely furnished rooms with private baths in well maintained buildings at a reasonable monthly rate. I include no housekeeping services, other than common areas. My tenants are mostly either single working people or pensioners. All tenants understand our reasonable rules which we strictly enforce. One key element I feel is my managers. I take care in hiring good people and I expect a lot from them, but I treat them with respect.

We have a computerized property management program and computer terminals and modems at each unit. At a glance, I can discover problem areas and make plans for corrections. I visit each of my properties every month and usually spend a full day with each manager.

Right now, lenders as well as the Resolution Trust Corporation are holding hundreds of large hotels and motels in their foreclosure inventory. Many of these properties would be ideally suited for SRO. One of my former students is negotiating to buy a large central city hotel from a lender at a price of less than $5,000 per room. While the hotel needs some work and is operating at a significant loss, his analysis for SRO use shows a cash-on-cash return ratio (downpayment to cash spendable) of over 40 percent.

STUDENT HOUSING

The conversion of apartments to student housing can be lucrative. It is not unusual for a unit that formerly rented for $350 a month to bring in $150 from each of four students. You should remember that student housing is often only rented 9 to 10 months per year. This type of rental usually means extremely high maintenance costs.

I know a very young investor who, while a freshman at college, found that the rooming house he lived in was for sale. The owner, a businessman, had purchased it a year earlier. What looked good on paper had turned out to be a nightmare for him. Besides rent collection problems he had constant maintenance and health orders from the city and generally a lot of grief. This student offered the owner $2,000 for his equity, which was accepted. He obtained the $2,000 from his parents by telling them the rooming house would pay for the rest of his education.

The young student evicted several troublemakers and commenced to clean up the place. He now owns 18 rooming houses in a university city. They are rented to students only. He has a full-time maintenance man and a student manager at each house. His full-time job is watching over his investments. This is not bad for starting with a borrowed $2,000.

RENT-CONTROLLED COOPERATIVES

There is interesting speculation in rent-controlled cooperative apartments. While you can buy the units (converted from rental apartments to cooperatives or condominiums), in many communities you cannot always get the tenants out. Under some rent control ordinances, they can remain in the units until they voluntarily move out or die. Because the rents bear little relationship to the sale value if occupancy could be given, the tenant's age and health affect the price. While a little on the ghoulish side, some investors buy these units betting on the early demise of owners.

A preferable approach is to offer the tenant a large share in the sale profit to vacate. While many elderly owners don't like the idea of moving, if you are able to contact any of their children and tell them of your offer, the children will often be allies in persuading a tenant to vacate so you can sell his unit.

Some syndicators have discovered these rent-controlled units and have set up limited partnerships for investment. The fact that units can be purchased for 40 percent to 60 percent of market value, if possession can be given, intrigues many investors.

MEETING SPECIAL GROUP NEEDS

Several apartment buildings in the Sunbelt have in recent years gone "clothing optional." These are apartment units with private interior courts, usually with a pool. Dedicated nudists have filled up the units at premium rents. In the Los Angeles area these units command rents from 25 percent to 50 percent higher than otherwise comparable units.

CREATIVE CONVERSION OF OLDER PROPERTIES

For many years consumers have had the idea that new means better. While new may be good, for many people old is better. Old office buildings with iron railings and open iron elevator cages were torn down in the 1950s and 1960s to make room for new glass towers. Today many old buildings have regained their former luster and command premium rentals. Attorneys, accountants and other professionals like the solid image these structures provide. A building should have a basically sound structure and classic lines if you are considering restoration. Old school houses and train depots can at times be purchased at very low prices. They offer exceptional possibilities for shops, restaurants, and even apartments.

Some years ago I purchased a huge old home from the state. The state had acquired the home when it foreclosed on a state veteran's loan. I paid

$7,500 with $500 down and the balance at $75 per month, including interest at 5 percent. The home had been built in a small town by a doctor over 75 years earlier. The property had some lake frontage on lake known for its poor fishing. At the time I purchased the house I didn't exactly know who would want it, but felt I could do something with it. The oak woodwork and paneling were fantastic. The home had a huge sun room along one side. All the rooms were large. The only real problem was that it had 16 rooms, three stories and a basement but only one bath. I spent about $500 cleaning the building out. I made some plaster repairs and mowed the huge lawn. I placed an ad in the *Chicago Tribune* (Chicago was about 250 miles away), advertising it as ideal for an artist, describing the large sun room as a studio. I sold the property for $16,000 to a sculptor who loved having so much space.

THE VALUE OF OLD FURNITURE

Incidentally, in cleaning out the basement and attic of that huge old home, described above, I received an indoctrination into the world of antiques. I mentioned to a friend that the attic and basement of the place were loaded with old junk. My friend was an antique buff and drove up to look at the property with me. My friend agreed to clean out the attic and basement, throwing out the real junk and selling what was salable. In exchange I agreed to let him have several old bureaus. Over the next few months she gave me a number of checks totaling over $1,000. After this experience, I started looking differently at the "junk" left in old buildings.

I have purchased a number of older furnished homes and apartments over the years. In several cases the resale of the furniture has gone a long way toward returning the downpayment. Those old 1912 Sears oak chests are now regarded as valuable antiques. In the basement of one apartment building I found six old oak iceboxes, which I sold for $200 each. A close friend purchased a lake cottage that had been part of a resort. On the same lot as his cottage was an old four-car garage full of old wicker porch furniture. The sale of these pieces gave him back more than double his downpayment.

TREE AND TIMBER VALUE

If you should find a property with a fine old black walnut tree on it, this would be like finding gold. One tree, depending on size and configuration, could be worth over $10,000. I heard of one country home that was sold with nine such trees on the front lawn. The purchaser harvested his lawn and received more than the price of the entire property from the sale of the trees.

One of my fishing companions purchased a heavily wooded lot of several acres for $5,000. In building his home and driveway he had to clear away a number of trees well over 100 years old. Rather than pay for their removal, he called in a logger who not only cleared the site but also paid him almost $3,000.

Not all timber is valuable but much of it is. People with smaller parcels of land often fail to consider the fact that there may be value in the timber.

MOVING BUILDINGS

Redevelopment and highway construction often create situations in which good structures are available at very low prices. However, they must be moved. In planning to buy such a building, you must first consider local regulations. Can the structure be put on a lot in the area? Besides the zoning, the covenants, conditions, and restrictions could prohibit it. In addition to the initial cost of the building, you should consider moving costs, cost of a lot, foundation expense, water and sewage costs, electrical hookups, driveways and walks and even insurance for the move. There will be additional electrical expenses for a basement, and some new duct work could be required. Building codes could require a new hot water heater or a new furnace. Apparently, despite all these costs, moving a structure can be a valuable investment. A few investors specialize in buying buildings that must be moved, so it must offer a profit potential. Some larger buildings are actually cut into pieces to be moved.

GIFTS CAN BE PROFITABLE

A few years ago a nationally known entertainer donated 80 acres for a community medical center. The land given was located quite a distance from any populated area. In fact, at the time, it looked as if a worse location could not have been found. With the entertainer helping with the fundraising, the medical center was completed. Land prices in the area rose sharply as new developments were started. People who purchased land when the center was first announced made tremendous profits. A person who also profited was the entertainer himself. The land given was only a small part of a much larger parcel he owned. The rest of his property has since increased in value from 20 to 50 times what it was worth before he made his charitable gift.

Being in close proximity to a major hospital, college or similar institution will of course help property values. While I don't know in this case if the results of the gift were considered at the time the gift was made, you can see that it might pay to give away some land for a particular purpose if that purpose will aid the area and if you retain the surrounding land. In addition, a charitable gift, of course, means a tax deduction.

The uses and development of real estate are limited only by your imagination. These examples are not given to show you what to do so much as to show you that you should be flexible in understanding and solving real estate problems. And remember that finding solutions to problems is meaningless unless you act upon them.

Chapter 15

MANAGING YOUR PROPERTY

The instinct of ownership is fundamental in man's nature.

—William James

UNDERSTANDING PROPERTY MANAGEMENT

Bernard Baruch gave a four-word plan for riches: "Buy low, sell high." It sounds simple, but what do you do with the property between the time you acquire it and the time you dispose of it? What you do will be an important factor in what the property will bring at a sale.

Property management includes a very broad area of planning and decision making. It involves goal setting, improvements, changes in use, tenant selection, rent collections, policies and procedures, and a great deal more. Property management requires skills in management, bookkeeping, and interpersonal relationships.

Good real estate management will maximize the net return. A higher net means a greater value. An income property should be analyzed in terms of what use and type of tenant will provide the greatest return, and a plan should be devised to achieve that goal. Costs reported by the former owner should be analyzed for need and accuracy. Realistic operational and improvement costs should be estimated.

While there are some excellent management firms, professional management will not provide you with an education in property management. There is no substitute for personal involvement. The management experience you gain will be invaluable in making future investment decisions.

BEFORE YOU BUY

Before you purchase you will want to see all current leases. At the time of closing you will want to make sure all lease deposits are turned over to you. Lease deposits can actually help you purchase a property.

I once handled the sale of a 40-unit apartment building for which the downpayment was to be $50,000. All the tenants had $200 security deposits, which were turned over by the seller at the time of closing. (In some states the owner need not keep security deposits in trust accounts and can use the money as his or her own funds.) The net effect of receiving this $8,000 was that the buyer had to come up with only $42,000 at the time of closing.

Rents are prorated as of the day of closing but are usually paid in advance. Therefore, unless the rents are all due on the date of closing, the buyer is entitled to that portion of the rent that applies to the period beyond the day of closing. For example, assume the rent is $500 and is paid on the first of the month. If the closing is on the fifteenth, then the seller would have collected rent for 15 days after the sale. The seller must pay the buyer for these 15 days. In this case the payment would be $250. Prorations are normally based on a 30-day month.

Before the sale is completed, you should have considered your insurance needs. While existing policies might be assumed with the approval of the insurer, they may not be adequate for your needs. You will probably desire an extended coverage policy that covers replacement of real and personal property without deductions for depreciation. You will want a high liability coverage, as well as coverage for vandalism, accidents, and so forth. You may also want plate glass coverage. Rental interruption coverage will reimburse you for lost rents because of a casualty loss. If you are taking over maintenance employees with the property, you should consider the necessity of workers compensation coverage as well as unemployment compensation. I suggest you review the property fully with your insurance broker prior to closing the transaction.

At closing, the former owner should turn over a complete set of keys to you. You can require this to be done in your purchase offer. Nothing is more annoying than having tenants move out and take the only keys with them. Keep a key file with a complete duplicate set of keys for all of your properties.

SETTING RENTS

As soon as the property is yours, you should immediately notify all tenants that you are the new owner and that all future rents are to be paid to you. Often units have below-market rentals. Tenants usually know when they have been getting a good deal. They will in these cases be expecting a rent increase.

Before you raise rents, try to make some sort of repair or improvement in order to show the tenants that you care about the property and will keep it up. It improves the landlord-tenant relationship if the tenants feel they are getting something for their increased rent.

You should not be influenced by what similar property is renting for in evaluating rental rates. Similar rented property does not compete with vacant property. The only competition will be similar vacant property. When there is a high vacancy factor, your units must be competitive to other similar properties in condition, amenities, and price. However, when there is a low vacancy factor, you don't have to be competitive. An above-market rental might be in your best interest considering the overall effect on the net income.

A vacant unit will give you an opportunity to reassess your rents. You should consider the law of supply and demand. If there are few vacancies in an area, a higher rental might be feasible. You should also analyze the rental market. In analyzing competing units, you should consider the following:

- Size of unit
- Condition of unit
- Appearance of building
- Security of building
- Parking or garage
- Utilities furnished
- Neighborhood
- Transportation
- Elevator or walkup
- Pets allowed

The higher you raise the rent, the greater will be your vacancy factor. Some tenants will move simply because they cannot afford to remain, while others will bear the cost of moving if they feel they can find similarly desirable property at a lower cost. If other tenants are available, don't worry that a particular tenant will move.

In your evaluation of rentals, ask yourself what effect a 5, 10, 15, or even 20 percent increase in rents will have on the long-term vacancy factor. Your goal as an owner will be to achieve the highest rent and lowest vacancy factor combination to maximize your net.

A higher vacancy factor not only means rental loss it also means increased maintenance costs because it is seldom that a vacated unit can be rerented without additional work. An increase in vacancies can more than offset a rent increase and result in a net loss. For example, suppose you had 10 units, each renting for $400 per month, or a total monthly rental income of $4,000. If you raised the rents 10 percent, you would now have a $4,400 per month gross.

Assume this increase resulted in a 10 percent vacancy factor. You would now have only a $3,960 gross, or a decline in total gross of 1 percent without even considering increased maintenance costs. Therefore, you must carefully evaluate the effect of a rent increase on your vacancy factor.

Rents should be consistent. If you rent one unit at a higher rate, you must raise the other units also, although you may have to wait until leases expire to do so. People don't mind paying a fair rental unless they find your other tenants are paying less than they are. An alternative to a rent increase is a charge for services previously provided. For example, charges for cable TV, water, trash removal, or even parking spaces are equivalent to a rent increase but are regarded slightly more favorably.

In periods of high vacancies, commercial tenants have negotiated long-term, fixed-rate rentals with motivated owners. At times such a rental can be significantly increased prior to the expiration of the lease. To do so you must have a competitor for the premises when the lease expires, and the current tenant must want to remain on the premises.

My names is Jeffrey S. I am an attorney. About 10 years ago, I purchased a large commercial building that had a long-term net lease with a national industrial tenant. The only problem was the terms of the net lease were so favorable to the tenant that I was looking forward to years of a break-even cash flow. The unattractive lease was the reason I was able to buy the building at an attractive price with only a $25,000 downpayment.

After several years of exchanging checks each month, I decided to seek a rent increase. I discovered, from checking rents in the area, that I should be charging close to $5,000 a month on a net lease (with a net lease, tenant pays taxes, insurance and all maintenance). This was about four times what I was now receiving.

I knew someone in the same business as my tenant and asked if they would be interested in renting my property when the lease expired. They were very interested because they regarded the building ideally suited for their use which included light manufacturing, storage of highly flammable material and a showroom for wholesale sales. My friend was willing to sign a lease right then even though occupancy couldn't be given for more than five years. Not only did my friend agree to a rental he agreed to the inclusion of the CPI, so when the lease started it would be at a significantly higher price. It turned out that my property had a number of important factors going for it. The building had a very heavy duty sprinkler system and met fire codes. It had loading docks and some of the only zoning for miles around that met the needs of the tenant. The 30-foot ceiling allowed for fork lift storage. In addition, large commercial users of the product were located close by. A discussion with my tenant's local manager revealed that this was the highest grossing regional operation that my tenant had.

I told my friend at the beginning of discussions that if we reached an agreement, I would give my tenant 30 days to agree to the same terms as stated beginning in 60 days. If my tenant agreed in writing to the lease terms, the lease agreement with my friend would be automatically terminated. My friend realized he would only get the premises if the current tenant failed to agree to pay a market rent for the five years plus left on the original lease. My friend and I signed an 18-year lease starting with the date the current lease expired. We included a paragraph that allowed for the lease to be nullified by the current tenant agreeing to the new lease. I contacted the main office of my tenant and talked to a Vice President in charge of real estate. I basically explained to him what he had to decide and indicated I would forward the terms in writing.

The vice president called back about two hours later and stated he would fly right out to meet with me. After a three-hour meeting, we had a new lease memorandum giving me market rent. The net effect was that I had a significant positive cash flow and the value of my building greatly increased in just 24 hours.

Giving away rent is giving away profit. Even though I generally don't believe in giving free rent to fill vacancies, giving free rent at times has advantages. It can be used to induce tenants to sign leases at above-market rent. Since rental income is used by appraisers to evaluate property for loan purposes, you want the scheduled rents to be as high as possible if a sale or new loan is likely. In addition, in the event of the enactment of rent control, your rentals will be on a higher base than owners of similar properties who reduced rents to fill vacancies.

Another advantage of free rent is that once a tenant is in on a higher rent, they will be more likely to remain when the lease expires. On the other hand, starting tenants with a low rent and later raising the rent when leases expire will result in a greater number of tenants deciding to vacate the premises.

FILLING VACANCIES

Over half of apartment rentals come from the cheapest method possible: a sign. Indicate on the for-rent sign if the unit is furnished or unfurnished. You should also consider newspaper classified ads to fill vacancies. If an ad doesn't bring much response, change it. Advertise the high points. Negative points such as no pets can be explained later. An ad is merely a teaser to excite interest and result in an inquiry. It is not a rental agreement.

If you do not reside in your units, you will want to designate one tenant to show the units and ask for deposits. You don't want someone actually renting; all you want is a deposit that gives you the right to accept or reject. I have learned from past mistakes that a prospective tenant may not be what he or she appears to be. Have the applicant for a rental fill out a questionnaire. Also make a copy of the applicant's driver's license to make certain he or she is who they claim to be. This also gives you a former address. Then you will want to verify the applicant's employment and rental history.

One rule you should have about tenant selection is that you should avoid renting to a friend. If you have a close friend as a tenant, there is a great danger that your personal relationship will suffer. How, for example, would you go about evicting a close friend?

Consider County Welfare and Federal Section 8 rentals where rents of low-income families are subsidized. Be certain that any county arrangement for tenants protects you as to tenant damage. If you rent to people on government aid, don't assume you have no management duties.

Generally, units that rent for lower amounts require more management effort than more expensive units. Units with lower rentals tend to be older and more crowded. They require more maintenance and greater renovation between tenants. Rent collection problems seem to increase inversely to the amount of rent charged.

Allowing pets will reduce your vacancy factor. However, you do need rules for pets as well as a higher security deposit because of possible damage to the premises. Keep in mind that you cannot charge a greater security deposit because a tenant has a seeing eye dog or some other support animal. You should also realize that maximum security deposits are set by state law, usually at no more than two months' rent.

If you have a commercial or industrial vacancy you have been unable to fill, offer leasing agents full commission for a tenant. In fact, you would be smart to offer the agent an additional incentive such as a Rolex watch to find a tenant for a large space when there is a high vacancy factor. Vacant space means lost rent that can never be recovered. Six months of additional vacancy at $3,000 per month means $18,000 that is gone forever.

When you have a number of rentals to fill, you cannot take a lot of time for people to make up their minds I recommend what many would consider a hard sell. When you get a call on a rental give only bare information such as, "Yes, that is a lovely three-bedroom, first-floor unit in a newer building. The rent is $400 per month and a $400 property damage bond is required. It is available on a one-year lease. I can arrange to show it to you this afternoon at 2 p.m. Is that time convenient?" If there are any restrictions such as pets, mention them at this time. The caller's response will either be that 2 p.m. is fine or that he or she can't make it, in which case ask when he or she will be available. The caller thus sets the time to see the unit and you have an appointment. You should average close to 50 percent showings from ad inquiries using this approach.

When showing the unit, point out any features that are not obvious. It isn't necessary to tell someone, "This is the kitchen." You should repeat the rental terms and state, "If you would like to apply for this rental, I will be happy to take your deposit. The customary deposit is $50. Is that all right with you?" This straightforward approach works well. At the same time, have the prospective tenant fill out a credit information card. Indicate that you will contact the prospective tenant within 48 hours. Usually you should be able to complete employment and credit checks in a few hours. Then contact the prospective tenant and ask that he or she bring in the balance of the first month's rent and the property damage bond, usually at least a week before occupancy. (Some owners charge a nonrefundable fee for checking credit and references. This is possible when it is a landlord's market with more prospective tenants than units available.)

MAINTAINING THE RENTAL UNIT

In periods when demand for housing exceeds the available supply, it is possible to rent a vacated unit without doing any work. Nevertheless, at the very least you should see that a unit is properly cleaned before it is rented. Tile floors should be stripped and waxed and rugs steam cleaned. Although all tenants are not neat and clean, they deserve to start out with a spotless unit. When a unit is vacant, it is a good time for minor upgrading such as new light fixtures or carpets. If the walls need it, they can be painted or wallpapered. Use wallpaper only in baths and in dining areas—and then a vinyl type paper that can be wiped clean. Use only a few standard colors for paint, so you can touch up walls rather than repainting between tenants. Use light colors (off-white) that make a unit appear both cleaner and larger. Some owners will provide the tenant with the paint, but I have found from sad experience that many people are completely inept. Therefore, it is generally best not to allow tenants to paint their own units.

Instead of cleaning or replacing drapes, consider new vinyl vertical blinds. The cost is relatively inexpensive even for made-to-measure blinds, and there is almost no maintenance cost.

When you upgrade a vacant unit consider the following where needed:

1. New light fixtures in kitchen and bath

2. A large mirrored medicine chest with a built-in light fixture

3. A quality vinyl wallpaper on at least one wall in the bath

4. A 40-inch wainscotting of a washable wallpaper topped with a molding strip in the dining area

5. Several rows of ceramic tile behind the stove, applied with a special mastic

The unit should be clean and free of vermin, and all appliances and utilities should sparkle and work properly. While the unit must meet the minimum standards of providing protection from the elements, it does not need to be of a quality you would like for yourself. Don't substitute your tastes for the taste of others. By doing so, you can end up spending far more for upgrading than can ever be returned in increased rents. Remember that to many people your unit will be offering an improvement in their quality of life.

In planning, economics must be considered. I know of owners who have spent more money on improvements than could possibly be recouped in increased revenues. When considering improvements, consider the principle of contribution. Ask yourself how much the improvements will contribute to the net income. I suggest a ratio of four or five to one in planning. If you do not believe the improvement costs will be paid for within four or five years by an increased net income, don't make them. I feel you can use your money better for other purposes.

A normally shrewd investor purchased a small office building. All the tenants had several years left on their leases. After purchasing the building, the investor did extensive landscaping of an interior court. He also repaved the walks with red brick and installed a very large fountain as well as several benches and tables. His costs for this work amounted to more than $20,000. At first glance these improvements appeared unnecessary, but these were his reasons for the improvements:

1. *Tenant satisfaction.* A happy tenant is likely to remain, thus reducing the vacancy factor. When leases expire, the owner will be competing with many newer buildings. He does not want to lose his tenants. Increased net can be in the form of a reduced vacancy factor as well as higher rents.

2. *Property appreciation.* When the property is eventually sold, the improvements will help sell the building and should increase the sale price.

3. *Tax benefits.* Part of the work was repair, which can be written off completely as an expense in the year of the repair. The work that was an improvement can be depreciated over the life of the improvement. The

federal and the state governments, therefore, will pick up the tab for more than 40 percent of the expenses because of the owner's tax bracket.

In deciding if a unit should be furnished, analyze the market for furnished units. Generally, furnished units rent at premium rentals. However, tenancy for furnished units is usually shorter. Unless there is very strong demand, furnished units will have a much higher vacancy factor than unfurnished units.

Some owners of larger apartment complexes make arrangements for a furniture package with a furniture store. They then tell prospective tenants that for a stated amount (rent plus furniture payment) they will have a furnished unit and own the furniture after three years. What they actually do is to arrange 100 percent financing of the furniture package. The tenant makes two payments, one for rent and one for furniture. This allows the owner to state on his sign "furnished and unfurnished."

HANDLING TENANT PROBLEMS

Often property is sold at an advantages price and terms because an owner has had problems with tenants. Visit such tenants personally and listen to their problems. I believe in complete honesty; tell the tenant either that corrections will be made and when, or if not, why not. Procrastination only causes further problems. If the tenants say they will move, write out a statement as to when they will move and ask them to sign it. If you feel a residential tenant will be a problem, you will usually prefer that he or she leave. It is normally best to allow a problem tenant to break a lease without any penalty.

While most people are really great, unlike Will Rogers, I have met people I didn't like. Some people are just unreasonable. They expect more than is reasonable of a landlord and complain about everything imaginable. You must explain to people that in apartment living they must expect to give up some of the quiet and privacy of a single-family dwelling. Nevertheless, you should usually do all you reasonably can to satisfy tenant problems. Occasionally a tenant will go on a rent strike, saying that he or she will not pay the rent until something is done. Counter by immediately starting eviction proceedings. Do not submit to extortion of this type. From experience I have found that in most cases this tenant action is simply a means to avoid paying the rent. The tenant really hopes that you will take several months to make the demanded repairs, thus giving him several months' free rent.

If a court determines that the premises are not habitable because of a breach of duty of yours (the landlord), you could find yourself with a nonpaying tenant as well as damages to pay. Don't evict for nonpayment of rent if you have failed to keep the premises habitable. The premises must be in habitable condition at the time of the rental and you as lessor have duties to maintain the premises.

For residential property you cannot generally evict a tenant for complaining of unhealthy or uninhabitable conditions. Nor can you evict a tenant for forming a tenant organization. Such evictions are considered retaliatory and can expose you to damages and civil penalties.

In managing property you will come across people who will try to take advantage of you. When a tenant cannot pay rent on time or the rent check bounces, you want to know why and when you can expect a check. You have the tenant agree on a date of payment and then send the tenant a letter showing this agreement. If the tenant does not pay as agreed, you then start eviction proceedings. I don't believe in giving a third chance.

Tenants will frequently try several ploys to gain time in paying their rent. The two most common are the wrong checks with the letter (you receive a check for a charge card while the credit company receives your check) and unsigned checks. You must also be alert for the tenant who wants to go on a 40-day month. The tenant will be 10 days late with the first check and then send a check every 40 days, thus falling farther and farther behind in his or her rent. In three years the tenant will be one year behind. Some owners won't evict since they continue to get checks on a regular basis, and the tenant will promise to make it up. The owner hopes this is true and is afraid that the tenant, if evicted, will never pay.

There are all kinds of deadbeats. One gentleman gave a small deposit on a quality unit and told the owner he would send a money order for three months' rent plus the security deposit before he moved into the city. While he was told the owner only required the deposit plus one month's rent, he said that he traveled a great deal and didn't like to bother with a check each month but always liked to pay several months in advance. The owner didn't get the money order, but the gentleman showed up for the keys. He acted surprised that the owner hadn't received the money order and asked his wife if she had a receipt for it, which she found after some digging in her purse. The stub from the money order was for three months' rent plus security and key deposits, less the deposit they had previously made. The husband said that they had cash and showed a large wad of bills. He explained, however, that this was for the movers who were due in a matter of hours.

The owner gave them the keys, expecting to receive the money order in a few days. He did not receive it, so the tenants said they would put a tracer on it with the post office. For three months they looked for that lost money order. When the fourth month's rent was due, the tenants stopped by the lessor's office to tell him they would be a little late as they had sold some property back East and would be getting $50,000 in just a few days. The gentleman also wanted to know if the owner would sell him the apartment building.

Luckily, the landlord finally realized he had been taken. He ran a credit check in the city these people had moved from and discovered they were masters of not paying bills. They had pulled similar stunts with a previous landlord. Apparently they had purchased a money order and then filled in the payee as themselves. They cashed it but had the original purchase receipt to show the owner. If the owner had believed their purchase strategy, the couple would have received several more months' free rent. There are not many people such as this, but they do exist. The mistake was in not checking on them immediately.

Most tenant problems can be solved before you rent by checking up on the tenant. Don't make a rental agreement. Use a rental application that allows time for you to check the tenant. You want:

1. *Employment verification.* Verify with the employer the length of time a tenant has been employed and earnings. (Some landlords ask to see a pay stub, but this only shows gross and deductions for one particular pay period.)

   If the prospective tenant is newly employed, find out where he or she worked before and check the previous employer for length of employment and earnings.

2. *Credit Check.* If you do not have access to a credit bureau, ask the prospective tenant to obtain a copy of his or her credit report.

3. *Prior Landlords.* Check with the current and a prior landlord as to any problems with the tenant such as rent payments, treatment of the premises, violations of rules, etc. (A prior landlord is better than a current landlord because the current landlord could be so eager to be rid of the tenant that they will lie making the tenant sound perfect for you.)

You should be leery when a credit report shows that a person has had very short or sporadic work history or where you are unable to verify prior rent history.

As a rule of thumb, if you are unsure of a tenant's reliability, don't accept them as a tenant. You must keep in mind that under our Civil Rights acts, you can never turn down a prospective tenant because of race, religion, sex, marital status, sexual preferences, seeing eye dogs or assistance animals, handicaps, or even having AIDS, but you can turn down an applicant for poor credit, for lying on the application, for a poor rent payment history, violation of rules at other rentals, damaging other property and/or failing to keep their rental in a sanitary condition. Your rental rules must be applied to all rental applicants in the same manner and you cannot discriminate in your tenant qualification process.

EVICTIONS

At one time I owned and managed a great number of low-rent units. Tenant problems were quite common. I often found it was cheaper to pay a tenant to move than to evict. For instance, if a tenant had problems and it appeared that rent collections would be difficult or impossible, I would agree to give the tenant $100 or more when he or she turned over the key to me. If I had evicted, I would be faced with the legal expense, a rental loss during the eviction and possible property damage. Vindictive tenants can also leave a property in shambles. However, when they know you are going to inspect the property before paying them, the property is usually clean with the exception of normal wear and tear.

In most states you can handle evictions without an attorney. The clerk of your local county court should be able to show you what papers to use and how to fill them out. Normally, the first step is a notice to quit or pay rent (usually a three-day notice). If the tenant doesn't leave after this notice, and he or she seldom does, it is followed by an unlawful detainer action, which is the court eviction proceedings. The court will usually give the tenant from a few days to several weeks to leave. If the tenant does not leave, you can get the sheriff to move the tenant, although you will probably pay the moving expense.

Never evict a tenant in late December. Courts and the community will regard you as a Scrooge for pre-Christmas evictions. If a property owner evicts residential tenants for a condominium conversion or a change in use, I feel that the owner has a moral obligation to his or her tenants beyond the bare legal notices to vacate that are required by law. Whenever I have evicted tenants because of a change in property use, I have actively sought other units that would meet their needs as well as helped in relocation costs. Moral values are not incompatible with profit.

ON-SITE APARTMENT MANAGEMENT

An owner can delegate many of the management tasks to a tenant. Reimbursement may be in the form of reduced rent, free rent, or even free rent and a salary, depending on the duties required and the number of units involved. Consider retired couples for this job since they have the time to devote to problems. An on-site manager also gets a psychic income in that he or she gets recognition from other tenants as a person in authority. Give your on-site manager calling cards with his or her name and a title such as "Property Management Officer."

You should carefully spell out the duties of your apartment manager. If your manager is to collect rents, you should consider a fidelity bond. (It is generally preferable to have tenants mailing the rents directly to you.) Notify the on-site manager if there is any problem with rent collection. The on-site manager's job, besides taking rental deposits and handling minor maintenance, is to solve tenant problems. Tenants sometimes expect the management to solve every personality conflict that comes up. Recommend to your managers that they try to have the parties work out their differences before becoming involved. Each year you should set a realistic budget for maintenance supplies and outside services. The manager knows the budget. If your manager cannot make a repair, then you should call a particular plumber, electrician or other tradesperson with whom you do business. If the annual operation costs are below budget and the manager has not deferred maintenance to achieve this, consider giving her a cash bonus. What will happen is that managers are suddenly able to make repairs they would have otherwise called in a tradesperson for. A little bonus system can save money for you and help keep your managers happy.

MANAGING TO MAKE AND SAVE MONEY

Coin-operated washers, dryers, and vending machines actually provide a profit in many units, especially in smaller units for singles. Some owners allow the managers to take this money for a petty cash fund. This isn't sound procedure because the money will end up becoming part of the manager's compensation rather than cash to be used for materials.

Any petty cash fund should be unrelated to machine receipts and all funds should be accounted for. In a lower-income housing I formerly managed, the coin boxes for the washers and dryers were constantly being broken open. I found that for this building it was cheaper to remove the coin boxes and provide the washers and dryers free of charge.

In larger units it is best to use a vending company rather than own your own machines because of the constant repair problems caused by the heavy use and abuse the machines suffer. In these times of high utility cost you must consider ways to save. Outside lights should be on timers. Instead of 150-watt spotlights for outside lighting, consider going to 12-volt, low-wattage systems. Keep in mind that outside lighting must be adequate for security purposes. One apartment complex I visited has put in a meter for the tennis court lights. Fifty cents allows twenty minutes of lighting.

One way to cut lighting costs is to use fluorescent hall fixtures. Besides operating on lower wattage, they actually give more light. While ordinary light bulbs tend to disappear in halls, the fluorescent tubes stay because your renters don't have any use for the long tubes.

Cutting heating and cooling costs can mean the difference between a profit and a loss. I presently don't own any units where I must supply heating and cooling, but there are many buildings with central systems. When utilities were cheap, it was an economical way to build. Many such buildings have now replaced central heating and cooling units with separate units so each tenant can pay his or her own bills. If this is not feasible, an owner of such a building should avoid long-term leases without a provision for increased rents based on utility costs. With central heating and cooling, costs can be reduced in a number of ways. Locked thermostats and thermostats that change by a clock can mean significant savings. The days when landlords provided 80-degree heat and 70-degree cooling are part of the past.

Double insulation in crawl spaces or attics, weatherstripping and storm windows and doors all help. Planting a windbreak close to the building will also significantly reduce heat loss. Simple furnace modifications such as automatic flue controls will reduce the amount of heat going up the chimney.

In managing property, a dollar's savings in management costs is equivalent to another dollar in income, and every dollar in income means about 10 to 15 dollars in additional property value upon sale. Therefore, while you will want to maintain a property well in order to protect your investment, you don't want any unnecessary or wasted expenditure. You should insist that every tenant sign a lease. Even a tenant on a month-to-month tenancy should sign a lease, as the lease will clearly set forth the duties and obligations of the owner and the tenant.

Leases can reduce vacancies. The best rental periods are different in various area of the country, but suppose in your area the best rental period is from May to September. By having all one-year leases expire on either May 1, June 1, July 1, August 1, and September 1, you will have fewer problems renting units if a tenant fails to renew the lease. You don't want leases to expire at periods when few people are moving. As an example, vacancies occurring on December 1 in many northern cities might be hard to fill unless there was a great shortage of housing.

Require a property damage bond equivalent to at least one month's rent. The purpose of such a bond is to pay for repair or replacement of furniture or for damages to the unit beyond normal wear and tear.

A property damage bond is better for an owner than collecting the last month's rent in advance. Rent collected in advance is considered accrued income and must be reported by the owner in the year it is collected for income tax purposes. However, a property damage bond is not taxable as income until it is forfeited, which may never happen. You should also require at least a five-dollar key deposit. With a deposit this large, you will seldom fail to get keys returned. (For garage door openers, a 20-dollar deposit should be considered.)

RECORD KEEPING

You must keep accurate records of your income and expenses for tax purposes as well as to aid you in decision making. A simple yet effective method for keeping records for a single property is to set up a separate bank checking account for the property. Use the large checks that provide adequate room for the purpose of each check rather than the much smaller personal type checks.

Deposit all of your income from the property into the account. For each tenant use a large tenant card that shows payment period, when payment was received and check number. Keep a large 9 x 12 envelope for each property for expenses paid. On every check you write, reference a billing or clearly show purpose of the check. When a bill is paid, indicate on the bill the check number and when it was paid. Put it in the 9 x 12 envelope. If your checking account gets too large, transfer some money out to a savings account. If you need more money, transfer more into the account.

By using a separate account for the property, you will readily realize the operational status of the property. Of course as your number of properties increases, a simple system such as this will no longer be adequate. There are a great many computer programs available for property management. Choose a program based on your particular needs.

ACQUIRING MANAGEMENT SKILLS

If you obtain professional management, your costs will range between 5 percent and 10 percent of the gross. One problem with professional managers is that they have numerous properties to consider and many problems. You are only concerned with your own property. If you can acquire the management skills needed, you can do a far better management job on your own property than a management firm can possibly do. You can obtain these skills not only from experience but also from courses in property management given by a number of professional organizations.

The Institute of Real Estate Management (IREM) of the National Association of Realtors is a large national organization of professional property managers. They provide courses of training leading to the professional designations:

- CPM—Certified Property Manager

- RM—Accredited Resident Manager

While they offer excellent courses, an applicant for these designations must be a real estate licensee. For information on their programs, contact:

Institute of Real Estate Management
of the National Association of Realtors
430 North Michigan Avenue
Chicago, IL 60611

The Real Estate Management Brokers Institute (REMBI) is an affiliate of the National Association of Real Estate Brokers, which is primarily an organization of black brokers. They offer the professional designations:

- CRM—Certified Resident Manager

- CREM—Certified Real Estate Manager

They offer courses of study particularly relevant to urban property. For information, contact:

National Association of Real Estate Brokers
1629 K Street, Suite 605
Washington, DC 20006

The National Apartment Association represents owners of apartment and multiple family units. As an owner, you can benefit from the courses they offer. They offer the professional designations:

- CAM—Certified Apartment Manager

- CAMT—Certified Apartment Maintenance Technician

For information, write:

National Apartment Association
1111 14th Street, N.W., Suite 900
Washington, DC 20005

The Building Owners and Managers Institute International (BOMI) offers a number of excellent courses for investors and managers. They also offer the professional designation: RPA—Real Property Administrator.

For information, write:

Building Owners and Managers Association
1201 New York Avenue, N.W., Suite 300
Washington, DC 20005

In addition to the many associations, many community colleges offer courses on real property management, and there are many books available on property management in general as well as for managing specific types of investment property.

After you understand the day-to-day management problems, as well as management planning, you may want to give your property to a professional management firm in order to free your time for more profitable use. In choosing a management firm, talk to owners of similar property who are using professional management. This choice can be very important. I do not recommend signing a management contract unless you feel the management firm fully understands your goals and you have a feeling of trust in turning over your property to the firm.

Chapter 16

TENANT SELECTION AND LEASES

Men honor property above all else;
it has the greatest power in human life.

—Euripides

Your tenant and the lease terms will materially affect the value of your property. Whether it is a rooming house or a shopping center, you want to obtain the best tenant possible. Quality tenants mean fewer management problems, a lower collection loss, a lower vacancy factor as well as lower expenses, which make the property more desirable to purchasers and less stressful to own. Credit reports, as discussed in Chapter 15, can eliminate many marginal or problem tenants before the property is rented. Generally a poor credit report and disregard for maintenance of your property go hand in hand.

PROBLEMS WITH COMMERCIAL TENANTS

A commercial tenant going through bankruptcy or corporate reorganization can mean uncollected and even uncollectible rent. If financial problems have arisen prior to the rental, then a credit report will indicate that the tenant is unable or unwilling to pay obligations on time. While others may disagree, I feel that a vacant store is generally preferable to a tenant with serious problems. Besides the financial loss from a problem tenant, you can expect an emotional loss in the form of stress. More important, having a problem tenant occupying premises under a lease will preclude you from making the premises available to a quality tenant. *Any* tenant is *not* preferable to no tenant. When you consider the fact that over 50 percent of new businesses fail within the first year and fewer than 25 percent are still in existence after three years, you can understand the problems relating to renting to new businesses.

Failing businesses can hurt your ability to rent to qualified tenants. Several business failures in succession at one location can give a location a bad reputation, discouraging other firms from moving in.

GETTING SUCCESSFUL BUSINESSES

Successful leasing agents actively seek out tenants. They look for successful businesses within the area and analyze what advantages the property has over their present locations. They then contact the businesses. While they are often on leases, they may open up second locations.

Some of the important points that will allow you to get successful businesses and professional people to move include:

1. More space.

2. Better parking.

3. Better location for the type of business.

4. Lower rent, when a business did not require the quality location it had.

For example, a plumbing wholesaler might be a induced into moving from a main street to a side street which offered better parking and about half the rent.

In a tenant search, particularly look for businesses of the same general type as are already located close to your vacancy. Businesses like to be in an area where others in the same business are located. Several firms together generally attract more customers than if they were separate. Also, many businesses generate business for allied firms.

You should consider businesses such as franchises that are expanding geographically. If you feel a location is suitable for a franchise, call the executive offices and talk to someone in their real estate department. Follow up the call with a letter. Often franchises want desperately to expand. One limiting factor is the ability to obtain new sites. I have usually received a very positive reaction when I have contacted franchises.

ASSUMING LEASES

Tenants can be induced to relocate if you will assume their present leases.

My name is Gary A. I had 40,000 square feet of vacant space in my office building. The office vacancy factor in our area was about 27 percent. My vacancies were killing me. Because of my reduced revenue, I was having a hard time making my mortgage payments. I came up with a plan to obtain new tenants.

I contacted all of my present tenants and asked for names of firms that did a great deal of business with who might want to be located closer to them. I followed up on the leads and was able to lease about 3,000 square feet of space. One lead was interesting. The tenant needed about 8,000 square feet, but was on a lease with 4 years to go for their present 5,000 square foot location.

After some thought I negotiated a lease where I agreed to assume the tenant's current assumable lease with four years remaining. In return, they leased my space on an eight-year lease with increases based on the CPI. I then advertised the space obtained for auction. Well, the high bid was about 55 percent of what I was obligated for, but the net result of my lease loss and renting the additional space was very positive. I then advertised stating that I would assume tenants current leases. I was able to rent all my space, auction the leases I assumed and end up with a positive cash flow. In addition my new tenants are all on leases at least twice the life of their old leases so I will begin to obtain a significant return in a few years.

NAME THAT BUILDING

In order to obtain a major tenant for a commercial building, consider offering the tenant the building name. During rent negotiations, present the prospective tenant with a color rendering or a pen and ink drawing of the building with the name of the tenant on it such as "The Preston Center," "The Preston Building," "Preston," etc. Having the name on the building or center will give the tenant prestige in the community and will give its employees a sense of pride. One developer who gave a prospective tenant a pen and ink drawing of the building with the tenant's name displayed on the structure and gate posts later saw the drawing used by the tenant on the company stationary.

TENANT EQUITY

If you are a major tenant or prospective tenant in a building, ask yourself how badly the owner needs you. IBM has done this and has negotiated leases where the building owners have given them an equity position in property in order to sign their leases. They thus became limited partners in the buildings and shared in the profits. The owners of the building obtained a prime tenant on a long-term lease that enhanced the rentability of the rest of the building and thus increased the value of the building. A tenant can have a great deal of economic clout, especially in an overbuilt market. However, most tenants don't realize the power they may possess.

The idea of tenant equity can be used as an effective tool by owners as well as tenants.

My name is Clarence R. I make money giving buildings away. Well, at least one-half of buildings. What I do is look for troubled single-tenant, commercial properties and in this market, I have no trouble finding them. I then try to tie them up with a purchase option. I want terms where little or no cash will be required (more on this later).

Next I look for possible tenants. When I find a strong local tenant who needs space and can use what I have, I give an offer they can't refuse. I offer a long-term, net lease at a fair rent that will also pay any debt service. The lease must be tied to the CPI. As part of the lease agreement, I give the owner of the company a one-half interest in the building as a limited partner. The firm pays for the building with the lease payments, the owner gets equity buildup and has half the landlord's interest. It is an offer that is difficult to say no to and when explained is often accepted. Based on the lease, I can usually get new financing that provides the former owner some cash. The balance of his or her equity is paid off by a second mortgage that the seller carries. In other words, I strive for 100 percent financing.

NEGOTIATING ACCEPTABLE LEASES

After you have located a tenant, you must negotiate a lease acceptable to the tenant that also serves your best interests. Month-to-month rentals should be avoided for commercial rentals unless you want to keep the property available for some reason. This type of rental agreement can generally be terminated by either the tenant or the owner by giving one month's notice. In all fairness, I would not enter into such a rental without full disclosure to the tenant. Keep in mind that a tenant willing to take a short-term rental will generally be fairly shaky. Even for residential property, a month-to-month tenancy is not desirable. Tenants who want such a rental usually do not expect to remain long. When tenants have short stays, it means greater expenses to the owner for advertising and related rental expenses, much greater maintenance, and a higher vacancy factor. It is seldom that a property does not require some work between tenants or that new tenants are willing to pay rent from the day the premises are vacated.

Rental agreements should generally be for at least one year. As the desirability of a location increases, the length required for the lease can be increased. In inflationary periods we have experienced a change in attitudes of landlords toward leases. Landlords are unwilling to sign multiyear leases at fixed rents or even leases with fixed-step increases. They want either short leases, such as one year, or multiyear leases tied in with an inflationary index such as the CPI. During our present period of low inflation and high vacancy rates, landlords want long-term leases.

Some landlords have found that even leases tied into the CPI have failed to protect them from inflation. No one expected fuel oil prices to rise from 13 cents to a dollar a gallon in only a couple of years. Electrical rates in some areas have increased 200 percent in a short time. An answer might be rents that escalate based on actual energy cost increases for the building, as well as a percentage of the CPI increase.

Net Leases

A *triple net lease*, which is normally just called a net lease, is a lease in which the tenant pays for all maintenance and repair expenses as well as taxes and insurance. The owner is guaranteed a net amount each month.

Net leases are usually long-term and provide the owner with a fixed income from the property. However, during periods of inflation the real value of the net rental decreases ever year. The solution is, of course, to tie the net rental into either the CPI or one of the wholesale indexes, which allow the lessor to retain the same relative purchasing power originally bargained for no matter what happens to the economy.

Percentage Leasing

If you have an exceptionally good retail location, you don't have to be satisfied with a set rent. It is possible to share in a tenant's success through a percentage lease. Under a percentage lease the lessee pays the lessor an agreed percentage of his or her gross income. Generally, businesses having higher markups pay higher percentages of the gross. A percentage lease should also require a minimum rent, with inflation increases, as well as a covenant to remain in business. This protects the landlord against a tenant closing down and paying only the minimum rent. Because each business brings customers for other businesses, if one business closes down it will hurt the gross of other nearby businesses as well. The percentage lease should also set forth the period of time the lessee has to begin operation. Otherwise the lessor could receive only the minimum rent for a protracted period of time.

Some percentage leases have *graduated percentages*. As the gross increases beyond a particular amount, the percentage decreases. This encourages a firm to advertise and have sales. The net effect of graduated percentages can be greater net income for the lessor.

Many percentage leases contain *recapture clauses*. If a tenant fails to attain a particular gross, the lessor has the right to end the lease, thus protecting him or her against a poor operator. With percentage leases, you want your tenants to advertise. Leases in shopping centers frequently require the tenants to pay an additional percentage of their gross for cooperative advertising such as shopping-center-wide sales. Remember, you as the lessor want an increased gross, as this means higher rents. Percentage leases in shopping centers usually set forth the hours stores must be open. If some stores would stay closed on a Sunday afternoon, for example, it would reduce the gross of the stores that are open because every store helps to attract customers to the center. Percentage leases normally also prohibit the tenant from having a warehouse sale or other off-premise sale where the gross would not be subject to the rent percentage.

Lessors usually require tenants under percentage leases to use a specified type of cash register that keeps a running total and cannot be set back. Honesty in reporting is not usually a problem with larger tenants. There can be problems with some smaller stores. There are protection services that will check to see that all sales are properly run up on the registers. Besides the minimum, percentage leases have built-in protection against inflation. As the costs of the goods increase, the gross increases without any real increase in the number of sales.

OTHER LEASING PROVISIONS

Design Approval

In some malls the leases require design approval, allowing for desired uniformity.

Assignment or Subletting

Unless a lease prohibits assignment or subletting, it can be assigned or sublet. In a lease assignment, the new tenant assumes the lease and pays rent directly to the owner. In a sublease the new tenant is the tenant of the old tenant, not of the owner.

If you are leasing commercial property for a long period, it is likely the lessee (your tenant) will want the right to sublease the property. If the lessee subleases for more than the master lease payments, the sublessee makes a profit. While this is fine if you are the lessee, it is not so fine if you are the original lessor.

As lessor, you should consider a profit-sharing agreement such as:

Assignment and subleasing of the premises will only be made with the approval of the lessor. However, approval will not be unreasonably withheld. Should any sublease be at a rent greater than the rent under this lease, then the lessor and lessee shall share equally in this additional rental amount.

By sharing, the clause encourages the lessee to sublease at the greatest possible rent. If you wanted it all, the lessee would simply sublease at the same rent or assign the entire lease giving you just the same old rent.

Use of Premises

Commercial leases normally specify the use that must be made of the premises. You may want a restaurant in a location to help other rentals you have. You would not want the lessee to open a pornographic book store. Some uses can also increase your insurance costs. Therefore, your lease should include a provision that if the tenant's use of the premises increase insurance costs to the lessor, then the lessee shall be obligated to pay the increased costs. For example, use or sale of highly flammable material could increase an owner's fire as well as liability insurance costs.

You should also require a tenant to carry stated high-limit liability insurance coverage naming the lessor as an insured party.

Leasing Raw Land for Storage

You should be wary of leasing raw land for storage or disposal of chemicals. A few month's rent has left some owners with worthless property. There have been several cases in which tenants have been in the business of disposing of toxic waste. The tenants have stored tens of thousands of barrels of waste on a property, ostensibly temporarily, but have then walked away leaving owners with a horrendous problem. Besides specifying use, you can protect yourself by a lease clause prohibiting the storage of toxic, explosive or otherwise hazardous materials.

If you are leasing raw land to a corporation, consider having your attorney draft a clause similar to the following:

> The undersigned agree to be personally liable for any and all damages to the leased property and/or necessary corrective action resulting from the storage, accidental discharge or disposal of hazardous and/or toxic materials on the premises.

Without the personal liability of the corporate officers, the corporation could declare bankruptcy leaving you without any recourse.

Television

Today, television interference can be an important problem. Some leases prohibit use of powerful radio equipment. The installation and removal of antennas for radio or television can damage the roof. Many leases prohibit them. Often commercial and residential buildings have a master antenna for the tenants.

Noise

Leases frequently have clauses about noise to protect against residential tenants playing loud music or commercial tenants using disturbing loudspeakers. Some leases actually specify decibel levels. Residential leases frequently have clauses on playing records and making other noise after a particular time.

Weight Restrictions

Second-floor commercial and residential leases often have weight restrictions. Overloading a building can damage the structure. Some older apartment buildings ban waterbeds both because of the weight and because damage that can result from rupture. Waterbed insurance should be required of tenants who have waterbeds. It indemnifies the landlord for damage caused by leakage.

Injuries on Premises

Liability for injuries resulting from the condition of the premises is normally covered in commercial and residential leases. Many leases require the tenant to indemnify the landlord for any losses suffered because a third party is injured on the premises. Often commercial leases require tenants to carry high-limit liability insurance.

Number of Occupants

Residential leases customarily specify the number of occupants allowed. Lessors have an interest in this because a higher occupancy means higher utility costs and greater wear and tear on the premises.

Other Restrictions

Leases can also specify whether pets are allowed and, if allowed, set forth the restrictions. You cannot prohibit children unless the property is exempt from the 1988 Amendment to the Civil Rights Act of 1968. Exemptions can be obtained for:

- Property where 80 percent of the occupants are over the age of 55 and the facilities have been designed for the use of the elderly
- Property where all occupants are over the age of 62.

You cannot discriminate based on sex, marital status, or AIDS. You cannot discriminate against handicapped. You must allow seeing eye dogs and support animals.

Anticompetition Clauses

Shopping centers often prohibit tenants from opening another location within a defined radius of the center because it reduces their gross sales.

Often strong tenants will negotiate leases prohibiting other stores from selling particular items. The lessor then places the prohibition in subsequent leases.

Attorney's Fees

Leases often provide that in any lease dispute the prevailing party shall be entitled to attorney's fees. Such a clause reduces the likelihood of frivolous suits by tenants who wish to either reduce rent liability or escape lease provisions.

Guaranty of Lease

For a new business or a business with a history of financial problems, you should consider a guaranty of lease by individuals or firms who have good credit.

Security Deposit

Most states limit security deposits for residential leases. Generally, they can be for no more than two months' rent. A number of states also prohibit nonrefundable security or cleaning deposits.

For commercial leases, however, there are generally no such limitations. As lessor you should try to negotiate the largest security deposit possible. Generally, security deposits don't earn interest for the tenant unless provided by the lease.

Holdover Clauses

At times a tenant will stay after the end of a lease or after notice to vacate has been given. This can create a serious problem, especially if you have rented the premises to a new tenant. The problem can be solved with a holdover clause. What this clause does is to set a higher rental for a holdover. It forces a tenant to either renegotiate a lease prior to its expiration or to vacate as agreed. An example of a holdover clause would be a month-to-month rental at $1,000 per month if the tenant remains in possession after the $600-per-month lease expires. With an increase like this, you know the tenant will not hold over.

Fire

Leases customarily cover the rights and duties of the parties if the premises are totally or partially destroyed by fire, storm, or flood. The lease may merely be suspended until the premises are rebuilt, or the landlord may have the option of notifying the tenant that the premises will or will not be rebuilt. If the tenant's use caused the fire, the lease could provide that the rent continue.

Electrical Service

Some tenants require greater electrical service than a building can provide. A commercial lease normally requires the tenant to pay for any additional electrical installation service required.

Right of Inspection

Leases should allow the lessor the right to enter the premises for inspection purposes, to make repairs, and to show the premises to prospective buyers, lenders, contractors, etc.

Options

If an option to purchase is given, it should be either for a very short period of time or tied to a CPI so that you are not giving away the benefit of inflation. Often leases provide options to renew for set periods. You should be certain they reflect economic changes. Right now $2,000 per month might sound great, but we don't know what this amount will be worth in 10 years. Options to purchase are covered in Chapter 13.

Form

Even though a tenant is on a month-to-month rental, a lease is nevertheless important. A lease sets forth the rights and duties of the parties and will serve to prevent problems or disagreements. You can purchase many types of lease forms from stationery stores. While they will save you money in attorney's fees, it might very well be the kind of savings you cannot afford. I recommend, except for simple fixed-rent residential and commercial leases, that you have a knowledgeable real estate attorney draft your leases.

Unless a standard form includes everything you wish to cover when preparing a commercial lease, see an attorney. Avoid trying to draft your own leases or those of the cut-and-paste variety where clauses from a number of other leases are used. The dangers involved in drafting a lease are not worth the few hundred dollars it will cost to do it right.

Lease Insurance

If you have a property that has a long-term lease with a major tenant, you should consider checking on the cost and availability of a lease insurance policy. This policy insures that your tenant will pay the rent for the term of the lease. There are two advantages of obtaining lease insurance besides your own protection as landlord. They are:

1. A lease insurance policy will make it easier to borrow on the property and the lender will likely make a larger loan than if the lease was not insured. (The loan agreement would likely provide for an assignment of rents in the event of default of the borrower.)

2. The presence of lease insurance makes the property more attractive to conservative investors. It is likely to result in a significantly higher sale price.

Chapter 17
SELLING YOUR PROPERTY

Give a man the secure possession of a bleak rock, and he will turn it
into a garden, give him a nine-year lease of a garden and he will convert it into a desert. The magic of property turns sand into gold.

—Arthur Young, 1787

When should you sell real property? There are really only two primary reasons
to sell. One is when you need money for personal use and cannot obtain it
without a sale. The second is when you believe another investment will better
meet your needs.

REASONS FOR SELLING

Some of the reasons for changing property include:

1. The belief that another property offers greater appreciation potential

2. The desire for a greater spendable income

3. The desire for greater depreciation

4. The desire to reduce management problems

5. A desire to exchange a more speculative investment for a more secure
   one

6. A belief that anticipated changes will lessen the desirability of the
   property

7. The belief that a property can be sold at a price greater than the purchase
   price of similar property.

If you didn't have the property that you now own but had the equity you now
have in that property, would you invest that equity in the property in question?
If you would not buy your own property for your equity, you should consider
selling it to get an investment that you would prefer to own. When you don't
sell property, you are really saying, "It is worth at least as much to me as I could
realize from a sale." If this is the case, hold on to it.

Don't hold on to property because, "It isn't costing me anything." A break-even investment is still costing you money. To hold such an investment you are losing the opportunity value of your equity. For example, if you have $100,000 in a property that breaks even after tax considerations, the property is still costing you money. If you could invest the $100,000 in an investment with similar safety that would yield an 8 percent return, then by keeping the investment you are losing $8,000 in potential earnings. Unless other benefits will offset this $8,000 in lost income, you should consider selling.

Most real estate investors are slow to sell. While this buy-and-hold policy will likely be successful over a long term, it fails to maximize income. A prudent investor should cull out properties that are underperforming the market and where significant improvement cannot be reasonably anticipated for the future.

If you want to sell to reinvest in another property, the market conditions are not really very important. In a buyer's market with few sellers and many buyers, you will likely have to accept less than you would like to receive in order to effectuate a sale. In the same vein, you will likely be able to purchase replacement property in such a market for a lower cost than you had anticipated spending. In a rising market you might receive top dollar for a property, but if you have to pay more for the replacement property, your net situation could be similar to having sold in a buyers' market. What you should be concerned with in upgrading properties is exchange value. What can I buy for what I can realize from a sale?

Don't sell just because a purchase offer means a profit. Unless you can place the proceeds in a more desirable investment, don't sell. Prior to accepting a purchase offer or placing your property on the market, you should fully understand the tax consequences of a sale. If you will have a large gain and expect to be investing the sale proceeds in another property, you don't really want a sale; you should be considering an exchange. Exchange techniques and advantages are covered in Chapter 12 and taxes are covered in Chapter 3.

USING AGENTS

Many people avoid real estate brokers simply to avoid paying commissions. This avoidance is a classic example of cutting off one's nose to spite one's face. Don't worry about what others are making. What is important is that you make an acceptable profit. Brokers know the market, have buyer and seller contacts and can help you sell.

There are some good reasons for paying a commission to a broker rather than trying to sell your property on your own. To start with, when you advertise your own property, you will be spending a good deal of time talking to brokers who will be trying for the listing. Besides brokers, owner ads attract the jackals who are out to steal your property rather than pay a fair price. They will often try to trade near-worthless property for yours. The most important reason for selling through an agent is qualified buyers. Consider how you purchased your present home. Chances are you went to brokers because you realized that they would know what was available and could show you a number of properties. Other qualified buyers are no different from you. They seek the help of experts and don't want to waste their time running down individual owner ads.

Another important reason for selling through a broker is that it is often very difficult to handle negotiations with a buyer. Direct negotiations often become emotional. Many deals are lost because of the natural emotional reactions of the parties involved. I have purchased and sold property directly as well as through agents. In most cases I don't feel that selling directly actually saved money.

Chances are, you will find an agent you can really relate to, an agent who fully understand your needs and will make every effort to meet them. When you find such an agent, show your loyalty to that agent with your listings and trust.

Before you give a listing on your property, contact your tenant(s) and adjoining property owners. These are the logical buyers for your property. Over the years I have sold properties to tenants and I once purchased a house where I was a tenant. In addition I have sold lots, a commercial building, and a farm to adjacent property owners. Many owners are like the farmer who only wants what is his and what is next to his. A few minutes of work could conceivably save you thousands of dollars in commissions. I don't begrudge paying a sales commission, but there is no sense in paying one when a buyer is just waiting for you.

HELP IN CHOOSING AN AGENT

Real estate agents will usually try for as long a listing as possible. In most areas, exclusive listings for homes are generally for a three- to six-month period. In resort areas they could be for longer periods. Vacant industrial or commercial property could be listed for one year or even longer. Generally, the more saleable a property is, the shorter the listing. Since a listing ties you to a broker for a set period of time, you should only sign with a broker you have confidence in.

With the number of real estate licensees around, everyone seems to know people in the business. Many owners give listings out because of friendship rather than expertise. Don't mix business with friendship. It is bad business to give a listing to an office that is not active in the particular geographical area of your listing or in the particular type of property that you have for sale. In addition, real estate has attracted many retirees and part-time people. Because

238 Selling Your Property

these people do not have to be successful in real estate, they usually are not. You want your listing handled by an office staffed with successful people who really want your property to sell and are willing to work to accomplish that sale.

You might want your prospective agent to prepare a marketing plan for you as to how they intend to market your property. You might also consider asking to see the ads the office has run on a similar property that they currently have for sale. Some small real estate offices will not advertise a property adequately.

For residential property you are usually better off giving a listing to a larger office. The large firms with many salespeople and offices, as well as franchise brokers, usually specialize in residential property. However, many small offices specialize in particular geographical areas where they may actually dominate the market. In such cases they might be preferable.

Smaller offices often specialize in nonresidential property. For example, I know of a number of smaller brokers who sell only industrial property and a few who sell only mobile home parks. These specialists can usually do a far better job for nonresidential property sales than large general brokerage offices.

Some brokers just want to get listings, which they give to their MLS in the hope that someone else can sell them. This type of broker won't do enough for you; you want a broker who will use his or her best efforts to obtain a buyer. Nevertheless, you would generally want to list with a broker who belongs to a major MLS so that the property will get maximum coverage. However, MLSs are generally dominated by residential listings and don't do much for specialty property such as farms, motels, or industrial buildings. Giving these listings to large groups of salespeople who primarily sell residential property isn't really going to help you in finding a buyer.

EXCLUSIVE RIGHT-TO-SELL LISTINGS

Consider giving an exclusive right-to-sell listing to a broker whom you trust. Under an exclusive right-to-sell listing, the broker earns a commission if the property is sold during the listing by anyone, including you the owner. If you don't want to give an exclusive right-to-sell listing because you have already talked to several possible buyers, I still recommend the exclusive right-to-sell listing with an exclusion. Most brokers will agree to exclude several named buyers for a short period of time such as 10 days. Now you will have a real club for the buyers. If they are at all serious, they have 10 days to buy without obligating you to a commission. They will realize that they can make a more advantageous deal right away than they can expect to make after the 10-day period. The exclusion will often result in a quick sale. If the named individuals don't buy, chances are they were lookers only and not serious buyers. People such as this could have wasted a great deal of your time.

OPEN LISTINGS

Some real estate agents will agree to work with an open listing. Under this type of listing the licensee earns a commission only if he or she actually sells the property. If the owner sells it or any other agent sells the property, then the agent with the open listing has not earned a commission. While an open listing might sound like a good deal to you since you can sell the property yourself without paying a commission, it is actually a very bad deal for the owner. Very few brokers will advertise an open listing, since it means he or she really doesn't control the product advertised. If a salesperson has the choice of trying to sell a property on an exclusive listing where a commission is assured or an open listing where the owner is trying to sell the property without paying a commission, you can guess which property will get the greatest sales effort.

What is everyone's responsibility will turn out in practice to be no one's responsiblity. The Chinese have a saying which expresses this thought, "A pig who has two masters shall surely starve."

DETERMINING VALUE

Before putting your property on the market, consider what it is worth. What you may have paid for it does not determine its value and may bear little relation to what it will sell for. Value is of course influenced by supply and demand. Demand is meaningless unless the demand is coupled with purchasing power. If there are more buyers than sellers, prices tend to rise while, conversely, a market with more sellers than buyers tends to reduce prices.

When a supply has become limited, property may sell for far more than similar property in the past. For example, the last available lot in a desirable subdivision could conceivably sell for far more than the price received at the last comparable sale. By checking similar property available on the market, you can find asking prices. Property is usually listed for sale at the high end of the sales range or above it. Therefore, the fact that property similar to yours is listed at $100,000 does not mean that either that property or yours will sell for $100,000. What is important is actual sale prices and terms for recent sales of similar property. Terms given are important because they can affect the price paid. When your checking has given you some general ideas of value, contact one or more competent real estate brokers who are active in your area. A professional real estate agent will usually have accurate sales figures of comparable property.

If the real estate agent asks what you want for the property, do not give a figure. This can be very dangerous. If you quote a low price, some unethical agents will tell you that you really know the market and that is exactly what they think it is worth. Some agents forget that their first responsibility is to the owner and not to earning a commission. By taking a listing at a below-market price, such agents seek to enhance the likelihood of selling the property and earning a commission. Often owners sell at huge profits only to later learn that they actually sold their property at a bargain price. Other agents will try to buy the listing by quoting an unrealistically high value. They are offering more than the other agents in order to appeal to your greed. After the agent gets the listing, he or she will then start coming up with good comparables and try to prepare the owner for a much lower price.

When an agent suggests a listing price, ask why. You want the agent to defend the price suggested. If an agent cannot adequately support his or her recommendations, you should not be interested in working with him or her any further. You want to work with a professional, not an amateur.

I have mentioned the extremes for your protection. Most real estate licensees are honest and knowledgeable. As I have previously stated, you will probably develop a relationship of trust and respect with one or two agents. When such relationships develop, try to deal exclusively with those individuals.

If, after your own investigation and checking with agents, you have still not decided what price to ask, hire an independent fee appraiser. The dollars you spend will be well worth it. Besides peace of mind, a professional appraisal can save you the time wasted in trying to sell a property at an inflated price or the dollars lost if you sold the property at too low a price. (See Appraisals in Chapter 9 for recommendations about finding a professional appraiser.)

No appraiser can tell you *exactly* what a property will sell for, but a professional appraiser can usually predict the price range into which a sale will fall. For example, a lot may be worth between $45,000 and $55,000. An appraiser could determine this range by various means, most commonly by analyzing actual sale prices of similar property.

When you want to sell in a market where prices are declining, don't chase the market down. An example of an owner who chased the market is a case where an owner listed a property for sale at $795,000. A $650,000 price would have been a fair price based on an appraisal. The owner took the position that he could always lower his price if he got an offer. Well, the market declined and the owner lowered the price to $695,000. Since the value at the time was closer to $575,000, he failed to find a buyer. By the time this was being written, the owner had again lowered the price to $550,000, which is likely $75,000 more than the market would indicate is a fair price. You can see that this owner chased the falling market. While pricing above market makes sense in a rising market, it almost insures that the property will not sell in a falling market. The owner, however, did not understand this. He only saw that he had cut his price $245,000 and had not found a buyer. In a falling market, the price should have been set to appear as a bargain compared to similar properties in order to increase the likelihood of a sale.

HOW YOU WISH TO SELL A PROPERTY

You should have fully considered how you wish to sell a property before it is placed on the market. If you want cash, you should ask yourself why. Many people ask for cash but really don't need it. If you intend to invest the cash in a safe, interest-bearing account, you are probably better off leaving some of the purchase price in the real estate. You will probably get a higher rate of return, and you will have the security of the property.

Downpayment

The likelihood of default bears an inverse relationship to the amount of the downpayment. This means the larger the downpayment, the less likely the purchaser is to default. You can reduce the danger of a buyer default by getting as much of a downpayment as possible. If the buyer does not have cash accept personal property such as a snowmobile, or even jewelry. I once took a boat as a downpayment. You want the buyers to feel they have an equity that needs to be protected.

Further protection is possible by having the buyer supply you with a computer printout of their credit information. The printout can be obtained from one of the credit reporting agencies.

Wrap-Around Loans

If there is an assumable loan on your property at a favorable rate of interest, you might want to consider carrying part of the purchase price using a wrap-around loan. In this way you will obtain the benefits of the loan, not the purchaser (see Chapter 4).

Balloon Payments

Chances are you don't want to leave your money in property for 20 years after you have sold it. If this is the case, consider a balloon payment, which requires the buyer to pay you off in full at a particular time. For second mortgages 5 to 7 years is about average. Normally the buyer will have sufficient equity in the property, because of appreciation, to refinance it. If the buyer cannot refinance the property when the balloon payment is due, you can either foreclose or rewrite the loan at more advantageous terms. The latter is the course many people take in these cases. There is a lot of money to be made in real estate, and it isn't necessary to prosper by foreclosing on anyone.

Graduated Interest Rates and Payments

You can structure mortgages to encourage buyers to pay off early with a graduated interest rate and graduated payment mortgages. For the first one to two years I may agree to accept a below-market interest rate. For the third year the rate will rise to the market rate (at time of the sale). Each year thereafter the interest rate rises one percent. The buyer has a strong incentive to refinance and pay off as soon as possible. In most states when the seller carries back the loan, the state usury limits don't apply. You should, however, check with a real estate attorney in your area prior to using this method.

Lease Options

Many people have good incomes and can make significant monthly payments who nevertheless don't have any downpayment to buy a home. Many of these people have been rebuffed by real estate agents who lacked knowledge and experience to tailor a purchase to their needs. These people will often be very responsive to a lease option.

The advantage of selling with a lease option is that, if structured properly, there is a high probability the tenant will buy plus take good care of the property and possibly even make improvements. A tenant with a lease option will normally pay a higher-than-normal rent if he or she really hopes to buy. A significant portion of the payments applied to the purchase price means the tenant will build up an equity that is lost if the option is not exercised. If you are able to get a thousand dollars or more at the time of the lease option (as the option price), it practically guarantees that the tenants will do their best to exercise the option. The option price can also apply to the purchase price.

Lease options are a quick and relatively management-free way to *flip* (turn-over) property purchased with a very low or no downpayment. Other advantages of selling by using a lease option are that you retain the income tax advantages of ownership, there is less haggling over option price than purchase price, and in a slow market it is easier to find a tenant on a lease option than it is to find a buyer. For sample lease-option forms see Figure 13–1.

Sharing Appreciation

It is possible, by using an option to buy back, to share in future appreciation without using a normal sharing appreciation agreement.

My name is George P. I buy and sell homes. I look for homes with assumable loans and motivated sellers. I try to structure my purchases with little or no cash outlay. I am able to quickly resell the homes because I sell the terms (little or no downpayment), although I carefully check the credit of my buyers. I sell on land contract (sales agreement where the seller retains title as security and the buyer does not get a deed until the property is paid for).

I make my money on the price differential between what I paid for the property and what I am selling it for, as well as on an interest differential. Thus, each sale gives me a positive cash flow because my payments on the mortgage are less than the buyer is paying me.

Some years ago, I learned about equity sharing. It seemed to make sense for my sales. In some cases my no-downpayment buyers have benefited by fantastic appreciation in value. I attended several seminars on sharing appreciation, but met buyer resistance when I tried to put the techniques learned into practice. To escape buyer's resistance to sharing in profit, I came up with the idea of an option. As part of the sales agreement, the buyer gives me the right to buy back the property within five years of sale for a specified price. I have set the repurchase price at one-third more than my sale price plus the verified cost of improvements made (not repairs or maintenance). For example, if I sold a house for $120,000, I would have the option within five years of buying the home back for $160,000. The no- or low-downpayment buyer would receive $40,000 profit plus the amount of any downpayment and loan amortization as well as costs spent for improvements. Basically, what I am doing is retaining the right to any unusual appreciation. I have exercised the option to repurchase in four situations of homes I sold from 1981 to 1985. I only exercised the option in cases where the appreciation exceeded 70 percent of the property value. I have been generous in evaluating what is or what is not an improvement. In all of the cases where I have exercised my repurchase option, the former owners felt I was fair in my dealings with them. I believe this is very important.

PREPARING PROPERTY FOR SALE

Before you place your property on the market, make sure it is ready to be shown. You want your property to present as favorable an image to a prospective buyer as possible. Many potential buyers are lost by owners who don't prepare their properties for sale.

While every improvement will not improve the sale price, many will. Consider possible improvements and how they will affect the value. If an improvement cannot be expected to return at least 200 percent of the cost in added value, then don't undertake it. I also know from experience that actual costs generally exceed initial estimates.

Besides increasing profit, improvements also increase salability. A dirty property is difficult to sell; cleaning it up will increase its salability. Paint and landscaping expenses usually improve salability as well as increase value.

Repainting

When you repaint, colors are important. Don't try to copy the decorators with currently fashionable colors. Although people like to visit far-out models, they are usually more traditional in their own homes. You seldom go wrong with light interior colors such as white or cream. They tend to make rooms appear larger and convey the impression of freshness. For exteriors, light colors accented with slightly darker complementary colors usually work very well.

Wallpapering, Paneling, and Carpeting

A little textured wallpaper, perhaps on one wall in a living room or as wainscotting in a dining area, can help a sale. If a wall needs plastering, it will usually be less expensive to put up prefinished plywood paneling than to replaster. Carpets should be in medium to light colors such as beige.

Flowers, Plants, and Trees

Seeding and seasonal flowers can help a building. Blooming petunias or other flowers outside an apartment building, home, or even a commercial building can do a great deal to attract a potential buyer. You can buy many plants and even young trees at discount houses and even supermarkets. If you need help in planning your plantings, consult a nursery. Many have reasonable planning services.

Lighting Fixtures

For older residential units I have found that new lighting fixtures in the kitchen, dining area, and bath are well worth the investment. For the bath I usually combine the lighting fixture with a large, modern, mirrored medicine cabinet. Remember that as a seller you are competing with other sellers. You want your property to be more desirable than competing properties.

Furniture

If a property is being sold furnished, you must avoid overfurnishing it. Too much furniture or furniture that is too large makes rooms look crowded and small. Upgrading the furniture will improve salability. It is difficult to sell a unit furnished in "Salvation Army Modern" and get the maximum market price.

When I formerly owned a number of furnished units, I would watch the want ads. Frequently, because of divorce, death, or the high costs of moving, an entire household of quality furniture could be purchased very reasonably.

Other Features

Cleanliness is of course important. The kitchen appliances and bath fixtures must shine. I actually use a wax for this purpose. A roach or a rodent will usually ruin an otherwise favorable impression. A pest control company can quickly solve this problem. The property should be well lighted when you show it and as airy as possible. Drapes should be open and lights on. If a building has air conditioning, in summer you should turn it on at least an hour before showing the building. See Chapter 2 for additional suggestions on increasing salability of property.

The Offer

Should you receive a verbal offer to purchase property, ask that the offer be put in writing even though it may be unsatisfactory. Once a person actually gives a written offer, he usually starts to think in terms of actually owning the property. While he might have thought, up until the time of the written offer, that he would not exceed a certain price, a written offer often makes a potential buyer ripe for a counteroffer. I know that I have reevaluated my position and have accepted counteroffers at prices I originally would not have considered for an initial offer.

Counteroffers

When you receive an offer, realize that your acceptance will form a binding contract. If you give a counteroffer, you are rejecting the buyer's offer and are saying that you won't accept the offer as made but that you will agree to sell at the price and terms stated in your counteroffer. If the buyer is nervous, you are giving the buyer an opportunity to back out of the purchase. Many buyers get "buyer's remorse" and look for opportunities and reasons not to buy. Therefore, don't counteroffer if the basic offer is acceptable. If you try to wring the last penny from a property, you could lose the entire deal.

When you refuse an offer or give a counteroffer, you are competing with the buyer. You are really saying, "No! I will pay more for the property!" Not accepting an offer indicates you feel the property is worth more to you than the offer provided. If, on the other hand, you wouldn't consider buying a similar property at the price and terms offered, then you should seriously consider accepting the offer.

You should generally give a counteroffer rather than an outright rejection. Try to make the counteroffer appealing by giving in on one or more of the following areas:

1. Price

2. Downpayment

3. Interest rates

4. Other loan terms

People want to think they have driven a hard bargain. They want to obtain some advantage from the bargaining. It really helps a buyer's pride to have purchased property at better terms than were originally offered. I have seen excellent deals fail because an owner wouldn't allow a buyer to save face by giving even a token concession.

When to Seek Legal Help

If you receive an offer that you don't fully understand, see an attorney. Don't accept the buyer's or broker's explanation as to what the written offer means. While most people are straightforward, there are some who will try for an advantage any way they can get it.

An elderly woman had 10 acres of land for sale. The buyer offered $100,000 which, while less than she had been asking, was a reasonable price. The buyer offered only $5,000 down on a land contract but agreed to pay the balance of the purchase price within three years. The buyer also agreed to a 10 percent interest rate which, at the time, was a very high rate of interest for land contracts. The deal really looked good, but there was a twist. The buyer wanted release clauses on 2 1/2 -acre parcels by paying $23,750 for each release. The 2 1/2-acre parcels were laid out as shown in Figure 17–1.

Figure 17–1

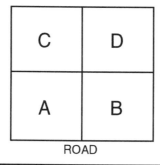

ROAD

The owner sold the land at the price and terms indicated. Immediately after the land contract was signed, the buyer tendered $47,500 for the release of parcels A and B. The buyer made no further payments after receiving deeds to these parcels. The seller was left holding parcels C and D. Parcels A and B were the highway frontage parcels and were worth about $40,000 each. The two back parcels were worth only about $10,000 each. By setting up equal release amounts, rather than releases based on the relative value of the parcels, the buyer was able to purchase $80,000 worth of real estate for a total of $52,500 ($5,000 down plus $47,500 to release parcels A and B).

I don't believe the buyer ever expected to pay for parcels C and D. I regard this particular buyer as a swindler.

Chapter 18

WHAT'S FOR ME?

Mine is better than ours.

—Benjamin Franklin
Poor Richard's Almanac, 1756

What others are investing in may not be the right property for you. Real estate investments should be tailored to each person's needs and abilities.

UNDERSTANDING YOURSELF

In determining what areas of real estate you wish to invest in, you must ask yourself: "What are my goals?", "How much money do I want to make?", and "Am I willing to endure the risks required to reach that goal?" Risk is of course related to return. Low-risk investments generally offer the likelihood of more modest returns than high-risk investments. If you are willing to endure the risks necessary to reach your goals, you are ready to become a real estate investor. If you are not, you must either modify your goals or hope that you can live comfortably in your retirement years off your pension.

I rate the order of risk in real estate investments from least to greatest as:

1. Your home

2. Duplex in which you live

3. Apartment unit in which you live

4. Single-family homes purchased for rental or resale

5. Multi-units purchased for rental and/or resale

6. Smaller commuter-type farms

7. Single-family lots

8. Commercial property

9. Larger farms requiring management

10. Industrial property

11. Raw land and lots (other than single-family residential)

Your investment plan must be based on the risk you are willing to endure as well as the negative cash flow your can live with. While buying right, careful analysis of a property, the area, and the marketplace can reduce risks, they are still present. You can also minimize risk by buying without personal liability and with a low cash investment. Risk doesn't mean you should invest as you would approach a crap table and leave success or failure to the game of chance. Risk can be managed. You can also increase or reduce risk by tenant selection, the loan terms you negotiate, the price you pay, etc.

To help you in understanding yourself I recommend a self-analysis. Start by asking yourself the following questions:

1. Why am I interested in a real estate investment? _____.

2. How much time am I willing to devote to seeking out and managing real estate investments? _____.

3. Am I willing to devote time at inconvenient hours to property or tenant requirements? _____.

4. What types of maintenance and repair work am I capable of handling myself? _____.

5. Am I willing to get my hands dirty in maintenance and repair work? _____.

6. Can I visualize the effect of paint, landscaping, remodeling, etc., on a property? _____.

7. How do I react to pressure situations and personal complaints? _____.

8. How much do I have in savings? _____.

9. Do I have an insurance policy with loan value? _____.
   If yes, how much can be borrowed on it? _____.

10. What other property do I have that can be mortgaged or used for trade purposes? _____.

11. How much capital am I willing to invest? _____.

12. Do I require a positive cash flow from my investment? _____.

13. What would happen if I lost my entire investment? _____.

14. How much actual negative cash flow am I able or willing to pay out each month? _____.

15. What, if any, change in income do I expect over the next five years?
    _____.

16. How will this affect my ability to make payments? _____.

17. Am I willing to decrease my present standard of living for future benefits?
    _____.

18. Do I like the excitement of a gamble or do I prefer greater safety?
    _____.

19. Do I like the challenge of games like chess, which require organized plans, as well as changes in tactics to meet changed conditions?
    _____.

20. Am I willing to make decisions that might adversely affect the lives of others? _____.

21. Do I like working with people? _____.

22. Is the nature of my investments, such as prestige, important to me?
    _____.

23. My last year's federal tax return shows that my highest dollars of income were taxed at a rate of _____ percent.

24. My last year's state tax return shows that my highest dollars of income were taxed at a rate of _____ percent.

25. I expect my regular income to put me in the _____ percent bracket within five years (state and federal).

26. The type of property I am most interested in for my investment is:
    _____.

27. Why? _____.

YOUR GOALS

Your goals must be compatible with the effort you are willing to put out and the risks you are willing to endure. If they are not, your goals will only be wishes that are unlikely to be fulfilled unless it's by chance.

With realistic goals based on your willingness to succeed and willingness to take risks, what would otherwise be merely a daydream can be yours by design. In setting goals you should really be setting a plan. You must have a plan to reach a goal.

The following goal form will help you in your planning as well as defining your goals.

Real Estate Investment Goals of _____

I will invest in _____ (Type of property)

I will buy property _____ (To hold for appreciation, income or resale)

I will devote a minimum of _____ hours per week to actively seek investment opportunities.

I am prepared to make an initial investment of $_____ and I can accept a monthly negative cash flow up to $_____

Particular requirements of my first investment will be: _____

_____

I will place my first offer by _____

If my offer is not accepted I will make at least _____ offers per month on suitable property.

If my first offer is accepted I will _____ (Fix for resale, lease, etc.)

I will start looking for my second investment property within _____ of _____ (Sale of first property, lease of first property, closing for first property, etc.)

I will continue the same investment pattern. One year from this date I will own _____

Three years from this date I will own _____

_____

I will have a positive cash flow from my property of at least $_____

Five years from this date I will own _____

_____

_____

I will have a positive cash flow of _____

Keep in mind that goals are not cast in stone. Changes in your needs, your experiences, and even opportunities can change your goals. When this happens, commit your new goals to writing. A written goal is much more of a plan than a mental one and is more likely to be honored by you.

Show your goals to your spouse or a close friend. Discuss the goals. When you have revealed your goals to another, it acts as an incentive for you to make them happen.

Your goals must flow naturally from your plan. If you plan is to buy one house every 5 years, your likelihood of reaching a monetary goal of $5 million in 10 years is not likely to be fulfilled.

While goals are not always fulfilled, wishes are seldom fulfilled. Goals, again, must be working plans. Without them you are likely to sit on the sidelines of life watching the investors play. With goals and a plan to implement them, you can be a player.

EPILOGUE

O.K.! I have told you what took me years to learn. It will be meaningless if you don't put it to work. As your first step, I suggest an investment plan where you devote a particular period each week to checking out properties, learning values, and analyzing your local marketplace. You should plan on at least eight hours per week dedicated to these tasks. After devoting two months to these tasks, decide how much of your savings, if any, you can commit to a purchase. Also decide how much of a negative cash flow (if any) you can live with. Set goals for your investments such as 1 year, 5 years, and 10 years.

Based on your analysis of the market and your resources and goals, now decide on the type of investment that is right for you. This decision must be yours. Your next step is to look for your first investment. Don't rush, but when you find an investment that meets your requirements and you have fully analyzed it, act by making an offer. If negotiations fail, keep on looking.

I never said getting rich was easy, but if that is your goal you can get there as many thousands of us have and we have done it in good markets and bad markets. In a poor market, it may be harder to do, but it can still be done.

I hope that you will become excited over at least some ideas expressed in this book, but some of you won't overcome inertia. It takes time and effort to break free, but it can be done. Don't become one of those people who after 40 years of earning wages, is sent off with a gold watch and a modest pension to live a frugal coupon-clipping retirement. Don't be one of those who sits all day at the seniors center and tells cronies of all the great opportunities you let pass by. The saddest words of the almost investor are, "I could have . . . ."

Index

A

Abstracts, 153
Adams, John, 101
Adjustable rate mortgage, 55-56, 64, 67
Advantages, to real estate investment, 2-5
  inflation, 2-4
  tax benefits, 2
Advertising
  for financing, 59-61
  for location leads, 93-94
Age, of property, 132
Agents. See Real estate agents
Air conditioners, assessing, 133
Alienation clauses, 50-51
Amortized and unamortized loans, 52-53, 55, 64
Analyzing property, 119-40
  appraisals, 136-38
  assessing physical structure, 131-33
  emotions and, 140
  financial history, 127-31
  fraud, 138-39
  hazardous substances, 133-36
  location, 119-22
  physical aspects, 124-27
  progression and regression, 122
Anticompetition clauses, 232
Apartments, 26-28, 37

see also Property management
  filling vacancies, 211-13
  on-site management, 218-19
Appraisals, 120, 136-38
Appreciation, 15
  sharing, 242-43
Arbitrage, 62-63
ARM, 55-56
Asbestos, 133-34
"As is" properties, 152
Assemblage, 168-70
Assessments, 21
Assignment, 230
Assuming leases, 226-27
Assuming loans, 49-50, 66, 67, 103, 152
Attorney(s)
  fees, 233
  and purchase offers, 153, 246-47
Auction sales, 155-56

B

Balloon payment, 67, 241-42
Bargains
  finding, 94-99
  bargaining with lender, 51-52
Basements, assessing, 132
Bid chilling, 109
Boot, 173

257

Bruss, Bob, ix
Bug infestation, 133
Building, for resale, 25-26
Building names, 227
Building Owners and Managers Institute
        International, 222
Businesses, sold for real estate, 199-202
Business use, of home, 42
Buyer's market, 11, 144
Buying, timing of, 10-12

C

Cable TV, 124-25
Carry back financing, 65
Cash-out buyer, 60
Certified Property Manager, 221
Certified Real Estate Manager, 222
Certified Resident Manager, 222
Charitable donations, 205-6
Chemical discharges, 135-36
Code violations, 98
Commercial property, 28-31, 37
    leases on, 231
    options on, 183-85
    parking and, 126
    successful businesses, attracting, 226
    tenant problems and, 225
Commission, 67
Commuter farm, 31
Compaction, 125
Conditions, 123
Condominiums, 21-23
    commercial, 163
    conversions, 163-70
    mobile home, 160
Condotels, 166
Con men, 138-39
Consolidation of property, 175
Contingency clauses, 149-51
Contract for deed, 55
Contractor's licenses, 26
Contrarians, 11
Conventional loans, evaluating, 49, 64
Cooperatives, 21

Cosmetic improvements, before sale,
        243-44
Cost basis, 42
Cost-push inflation, 3
Cost-to-sale price, 24
Counteroffers, 245-46
Courage, 13
Covenants, 123
Creative financing, 65-81
    basic choices, 81
    methods and techniques, 66-79
    raising cash, 79-81
    sellers financing buyers, 65-66
Credit cards, loans on, 80
Credit checks, 217
Curry, Frank, 193
Cycles, in real estate, 11

D

Deadbeats, 216
Deductible expenses, 2
    property tax, 39-43
Deed of reconveyance, 46
Default, 46
Deferring taxes (two-year rule), 40-41
Deficiency judgment, 5, 46, 49-50
Delayed exchange, 172
Demand-pull inflation, 3
Depreciation, 26, 32, 42-43
    exchanges and, 174
    of personal property, 147
Design approval, 230
Determination, 193-95
Developers, 25-26
Direct exchange, 172
Disadvantages, to real estate investment,
        8-10
Disintegration stage, 120
Distressed property, 18, 116-18
Divorce records, and property location,
        97
Down payments, 241
    mortgages as, 73-75
    single-family homes and, 16

Down-zoning, 122
Drainage, 125
Due-on-sale clauses, 50-51

E

Electricity, 124-25, 131, 233
Emerson, Ralph Waldo, 157
Emotions, and real estate, 140
Employment verification, 217
Environmental impact reports, 157
Equilibrium stage, 120
Equity, 4, 5
    loans and, 15, 48
    lots and, 36
    sharing agreements, 59
    sweat, 70
    tenant, 227-28
    trading on, 7, 62
Euripides, 225
Evictions, 96-97, 218
Exchanges, 44, 171-77
    advantages, 171-72, 173-76
    problems, 177
    types of, 172-73
    what can be exchanged, 176-77
Exclusive right-to-sell listings, 238-39
Expenses, from property, 129-31
Expired listings, 96

F

Factories, 196-98
Family loans, 80
Fannie Mae, 49
Farms, 31-32, 37
    subdividing, 161-63
FDIC, 28
Federal Deposit Insurance Corporation, 28
Federal Home Loan Mortgage Corporation, 49
Federal Housing Administration, 16
Federal National Mortgage Association, 49

FHA loans, 57
    foreclosures and, 112
FHLMC, 49
15-year loan versus 30-year loan, 54-55, 64
Fifty-five year old exemption, 41
Financial history, of property, 127-31
    expenses, 129-31
    income, 127-29
Financial partners, 84-85
Financial plan, 13
Financing, 16, 45-64
    see also Creative financing; Leverage
    conventional loans, evaluating, 64
    finding money, 59-64
    loan types and terms, 52-59
    methods of, 45-47
    primary, 47-48
    secondary, 48-52
Finder's fees, 98
Fire, 233
Fixer-uppers, 23-25
Flippers, 15
Flooding, 125, 132
FNMA, 49
Foreclosure(s), 28, 46, 101-16
    buying after sale, 110-15
    buying at sale, 106-10
    buying before sale, 102-5
    FHA and VA, 112
    personal, 115-16
    rate, 6
Foreign investors, 3-4
Formaldehyde, 134
Foundation, assessing, 132
Franchises, 184
Franklin, Benjamin, 249
Fraud, 61, 138-39
Freddie Mac, 49
Free rent, 67
Full disclosure, 67
Furnaces, assessing, 133
Furniture, value of, 204

G

General Services Administration, 30
Gentrification, 166
Gifts, 205-6
Glickman, Louis, 45
GNMA securities, 6-7
Goals, 251-53
Good-guy/bad-guy lenders, 49
Government loans, 57-58
Graduated interest, 71, 242
Graduated payments, 71, 242
Graduated percentages, 229
Gross multiplier, 138
Guaranty of lease, 233

H

Hard money loan, 54
Hazardous material, 113-15
    assessing, 133-36
Holdover clauses, 233
Home business use, 42
Home equity. *See* Equity
Horace, 179
Housing demand, 3
HUD, 195-96

I

Illiquidity, 8-9
    raw land and, 33
Imagination, 12, 193-95
Impound accounts, 148
Improvements, 23-24
Income, from property, 127-29
Income method appraisals, 137-38
Industrial property, 31, 37
    options on, 183-85
    parking and, 126
Inflation, 2-4, 5
    rentals and, 28
Initial interest rate, 56
Inspections, professional, 136
Installment sales, 43

Institute of Real Estate Management,
    221-22
Insulation, 133, 220
Insurance
    assessing costs on potential property,
        130
    lease, 234
    policies, borrowing against, 79
    title, 47, 153
Insured mortgage, 72
Integration stage, 120
Interest, 2
    deductions, 39-43
    graduated, 71, 242
Investment alternatives, 15-37
    analyzing types of, 37
    apartments, 26-28, 37
    building homes for resale, 25-26
    commercial property, 28-31, 37
    condominiums, 21-23
    farms, 31-32, 37
    fixer-uppers, 23-25
    industrial property, 31, 37
    lots, 35-36, 37
    raw land, 32-35, 37
    single-family homes, 15-26
    vacation homes, 20-21
Investment clubs, 88
IRS sales, 116

J-K

James, William, 207
Keepers, 15

L

Land
    appreciation, 198-99
    lots, 35-36, 37
    raw, 32-35, 37
    separating from building, 75-77
Land contracts, 47, 55
Landscaping, 244

Lawyers, and purchase offers, 153, 246-47
Lead, 135
Lease(s)
  borrowing based on, 70-71
  form, 234
  insurance, 234
  negotiating acceptable, 228-30
  net, 229
  options, 242
  percentage leasing, 229-30
  provisions, 230-34
  tenant selection and, 225-28
Lease option, 16, 180, 190-92
Legal advise, 153, 246-47
Lemonading, 152
Leo XIII (Pope), 141
Leverage, 4-5
  percentage return on investment, 6
Liability, 232
Lien(s), 47
  see also Foreclosures
Life tenancy, 67-70
Limited partnerships, 85-87
Lincoln, Abraham, 1
Line of credit, 80
Lippman, Walter, 65
Liquidity
  single-family homes and, 15
Listings
  exclusive right-to-sell, 238-39
  open, 239
Loan types and terms, 52-59
  adjustable rate mortgage, 55-56
  amortized and unamortized, 52-53, 64
  assuming, 49-50, 66
  15-year versus 30-year, 54-55
  government, 57-58
  hard money loan, 54
  participation, 58
  prepayment penalties, 53
  purchase money loan, 54
  rollover, 56-57
  sharing appreciation mortgage, 58-59

wrap-around, 55, 241
Locating property, 89-99
  advertising leads, 93-94
  analyzing location, 119-22
  finding bargains, 94-99
  location value, 89-90
  using real estate agents, 90-93
Loss, in real estate, 1
  see also Tax sheltering
  from sale, 44
Lots, 35-36, 37
  making, 159
Low-income housing, 195-96

M

Macaulay, T.B., 83
MAI appraisers, 120
Management. See Property management
Manufacturing mortgages, 74-75
Market comparison appraisals, 137
Mobile home units/parks, 160, 196
Money finders, 61
Moratoriums, 112-13
Mortgages, 45-46
  manufacturing, 74-75
  moving, 77
  primary financing, 47-48
  recording, 46
  release clauses in, 158
  using, 73-74
Moving buildings, 205

N

National Apartment Association, 222
Natural gas, 124-25
Negative amortization, 53
Negative cash flow, 8
Negotiation techniques, 11
  options, 181-86
Net leases, 229
Noise, 231-32
Nonconforming uses, 123
Notices of abatement, 98

O

Offer. *See* Purchase offer
Office buildings. *See* Commercial property
Older property, creative conversion of, 203-4
$125,000 exclusion, 41
Open listings, 239
Options, 29, 179-89, 234
   buying, 186-87
   commercial and industrial property, 183-85
   consideration, 179-80
   finding opportunities, 180-81
   granting, 188
   lease option agreement, 190-92
   negotiating, 181-86
   not exercising, 188
   rent, 187-89
   right of first refusal, 188-89
   tenant, 186
   trading, 185-86
   zoning changes and, 185
Overbuilding, 29

P

Paint, assessing, 131
Parking, 126
Participation loans, 58
Partnerships, 83-87
Passive losses, 43
Payments in advance, 71
Percentage leasing, 229-30
Persistence, 12
Personal approach to real estate, 249-54
   goals, 251-53
   understanding self, 249-51
Personal property loan, 80
Pets, 212
Petty cash funds, 219
Phantom income, 5
Physical aspects, assessing, 124-27
   see also Physical structure, assessing

compaction, 125
property shape, 126-27
roads, 125-26
topography and drainage, 125
traffic, 126
utilities and cable, 124-25
Physical structure, assessing, 131-33
Planned unit developments, 21
Plumbing, assessing, 131-32
Political climate, 123-24
Pope Leo XIII, 141
Prepayment penalties, 53
Price, setting, 143
Price increases, 3
Price versus terms, 72-73
Primary financing, 47-48
Principle of contribution, 23
Private mortgage insurance, 48
Probate, 97-98
Problem properties, potential of, 195-96
Profits, and real estate, 1
Progression, 122
Property
   analyzing property. *See* Analyzing property
   locating, 89-99
   shape, 126-27
Property damage bond, 220-21
Property management, 9-10, 207-23
   apartment, 27, 218-19
   exchanges and, 175
   expenses, 129-30
   evictions, 218
   farms, 32
   filling vacancies, 211-13
   maintaining units, 213-15
   pre-sale, 207-8
   record keeping, 221
   setting rents, 208-11
   skills, acquiring, 221-23
   tenant problems and, 215-18
   understanding, 207
Property profile, 117
Property tax, 2

depreciation and, 42-43
installment sales, 42
and interest deductions, 39-43
$125,000 exclusion, 41
Purchase money loan, 54
Purchase offer, 141-56, 245
abstracts and title insurance, 153
acceptance of, 154-55
agreement, 146-49
"as is," 152
assuming loans, 152
attorneys and, 153
auction sales, 155-56
contingency clauses, 149-51
financial obligations and, 154
lemonading, 152
lowest price, 144-46
seller's motivation, 141-42
seller's purchase price, 142-43
setting price, 143
timing, 143-44
Pyramiding, 7-8, 174-75

R

Radon, 135
Raw land, 32-35, 37, 157
drainage on, 125
leasing for storage, 231
retirement buying, 35
Real estate agents, 90-93, 236-37
choosing, 237-38
Real estate commission, 67
Real estate investments
advantages to, 2-5
disadvantages to, 8-10
profits and, 1
reasons for, 1-14
safety in, 5-8
taxation and. See Taxation, and real
estate
Real estate investment trusts, 87-88
Real Estate Management Brokers
Institute, 222
Real Estate Owned, 24, 110-11

Recapture clauses, 229-30
Record keeping, in property manage-
ment, 221
Recreational facilities, 121
Recreational subdivisions, 159-61
Redevelopment funds, 80
Refinancing, 62
Regression, 122
REITs, 87-88
Release clauses, 158-59
Renovating property, 23
Rent
agreements, 228
control, 124, 210
setting, 208-11
Rent-producing properties, 6, 203
assessing financial history, 127-31
REOs, 24, 111
Repairs, 133
Replacement cost appraisals, 137
Reservations, 18-19
Resolution Trust Corporation, 28
Resorts, subdividing, 160
Resourcefulness, 12
Restrictions, 123
Retirement
raw land and, 35
vacation homes and, 20-21
Right of first refusal, 188-89
Right of inspection, 234
Risk, 5-8, 9
acceptance, and success, 12
commercial property and, 28
secondary financing and, 48
Risk-profit curve, 10
Risk capital, 9
Roads, 125-26
Rogers, Will, 89
Rollover loan, 56-57, 64
Roofing, assessing, 131
Roosevelt, Theodore, 119
Rousseau, Jean-Jacques, 15
RTC, 28

S

Safety, in real estate, 5-8, 9
Sale-leaseback opportunities, 129
SAM, 58-59
Secondary financing, 48-52
Second mortgages, 47, 48
Security, 219
Security deposits, 212, 233
Seeing-eye dogs, 212
Self-confidence, 12
Self-organization, 12-13
Seller financing, 65-66
Seller's market, 11, 144
Seller's motivation, 141-42
Selling, 235-47
    agents and, 236-38
    determining value, 239-41
    exclusive right-to-sell listings, 238-39
    legal help and, 246-47
    method of, 241-43
    open listings, 239
    property preparation, 243-44
    reasons for, 235-36
    timing of, 10-12
Sewer, 124-25
Shape, of property, 126-27
Sharing appreciation mortgage, 58-59
Shelters. *See* Tax sheltering
Short-term fixed-rate loan, 56-57
Single-family homes, 15-26, 37
    building, for resale, 25-26
    condominiums, 21-23
    disadvantages of, 16
    fixer-uppers, 23-25
    liquidity of, 15
    subdivisions, 18-20, 159
    vacation, 20-21
Soft money loan, 54
Special needs, meeting, 203
SREA appraisers, 120
Standard agreements, 147
State loan, 58
Stock cooperatives, 167

Straight loan, 53, 64
Student housing, 202
Subdivisions, 18-20, 157-70
    condominiums, 163-70
    farms, 161-63
    industrial parks, 163
    process of, 157-59
    recreational, 159-61
Subletting, 230
Subordination, 77-79
Successful investing, 12-14
Sweat equity, 70
Syndicates, 87

T

Taxation, and real estate, 39-44
    assessing costs on potential property,
        130
    exchanges and, 171-72
    losses from sale, 44
    property taxes/interest deductions, 39-
        43
    tax-free exchanges, 44
    tax sheltering, 43-44
Tax Reform Act of 1986, 42-44
Tax sales, 116-18
Tax sheltering, 43-44
Teaser rate, 56
Television interference, 231
Tenant(s)
    equity, 227-28
    evaluating, 136
    options, 186
    problems, handling, 215-18
    selection and leases, 225-28
Termite inspection, 132, 149
Term loan, 53, 64
30-year loan, 54-55, 64
Three-party exchange, 172
Time shares, 167-68
Timing, 10-12, 143-44
Title insurance, 47, 153
Topography, 125
Toxic waste, 31, 113-15, 135-36

Trading. *See* Exchanges
Trading on your equity, 7, 62
Traffic, assessing, 126
Tree/timber value, 204-5
Triple net lease, 229
Trust deeds, 46-47, 48
  release clauses in, 158
Two-year rule, 40-41

U

Unsecured notes, 72
Usury laws, 48, 63
Utilities, 124-27, 233
  assessing expenses, 130-31
  cutting costs of, 219-20
  in subdivisions, 157

V

Vacancy factors, 209
Vacation homes, 20-21

VA loans, 57-58
  foreclosures and, 112
Value, determining, 239-41
Vending companies, 219
Veterans Administration, 16
Voltaire, 39

W

Warner, Charles Dudley, 171
Water, 124-25
Weight restrictions, 232
Wiring, 131
Wrap-around loan, 55, 241

Y-Z

Young, Arthur, 235
Zeckendorf, William, 75, 193
Zoning, 33, 122-23, 150
  increased property value and, 185

ABOUT THE AUTHOR

William H. Pivar, J.D. is currently the Real Estate Coordinator and Professor of Business Education at the College of the Desert in Palm Desert, CA. Here he teaches real estate, ethics, and business law. He is also the producer and director of college credit television courses in Business Law and Real Estate. Prior to this, Dr. Pivar practiced as a private, corporate, and government attorney. He has served as an expert witness on real estate ethics at several trials. Besides being an active real estate investor, Dr. Pivar is the author of more than 30 real estate books, and numerous articles. His books include *Real Estate Ethics,* Second Edition (Dearborn, 1989) and *Power Real Estate Listings,* Second Edition (Post/Dearborn, 1988).